THE**AUTOBIOGRAPHY**

THE**AUTOBIOGRAPHY**

—

RICHARD**HILL**

First published in hardback in Great Britain in 2006
by Orion Books
an imprint of the Orion Publishing Group Ltd
Orion House, 5 Upper St Martin's Lane,
London WC2H 9EA

1 3 5 7 9 10 8 6 4 2

A CIP catalogue record for this book
is available from the British Library.

ISBN-13: 978 0 75286 970 4
ISBN-10: 0 75286 970 1

Printed and bound at Mackays of Chatham plc,
Chatham, Kent

The Orion Publishing Group's policy is to use papers
that are natural, renewable and recyclable and made
from wood grown in sustainable forests. The logging and
manufacturing processes are expected to conform to the
environmental regulations of the country of origin.

www.orionbooks.co.uk

For Claire, Mum, Dad, Tim, Fenella
and all those who have kept faith
and believed in me

ACKNOWLEDGEMENTS

There are many people I would like to thank. First and foremost are Claire and my family. They have been instrumental in my development and encouraged me to 'live the dream'. Claire's patience has been unerring with all the sacrifices that are made for my rugby.

To Tony Lawrence, for his patience and hard work in pulling together my stories. I would also like to thank the team at the Orion Publishing Group for their assistance in producing this book.

Since June 2005, much of my life has been dominated by my knee injury. Many people have stuck by me and none more so than those in the medical world. Each has played an important role and I thank them all, particularly my surgeon, Fares Haddad.

The story would never would have been heard if it wasn't for the encouragement, support and advice from Nick Keller and Matt Jones of Benchmark Sport.

My enthusiasm for rugby has never diminished and for that the credit has to go to my two major clubs, Salisbury and Saracens, and the many coaches who have had such an impact on my career.

CONTENTS

1

'I CAN'T GO THROUGH THAT AGAIN'

26 June 2005. It felt as if my world had fallen apart.

I only heard his first few words, and then I shut off. It was as if I had gone into shock. 'It's blurred around your anterior cruciate ligament; it's not a clear picture, which suggests...' he began.

But I already knew full well what he was going to say. To the radiologist, it suggested the ligament was damaged. To me though, it was far more serious. It suggested my playing career was over.

The first reading of the MRI (Magnetic Resonance Imaging) scan, moments before, had seemed to offer hope. I had injured a different ligament, I was told; the medial one, as well as my left knee cartilage. 'I can live with that, I can handle that,' I thought, breathing a sigh of relief. I knew my 2005 Lions tour was over, of course, even before it had really begun, and that I faced yet another long period of rehabilitation, but at least it wasn't the cruciate ligament that I had ruptured the year before. Thank goodness it wasn't the same injury.

The radiologist, however, then asked me to come and look at the films. The shots were still on his computer and he was talking me through them. Then he dropped the bombshell. It *was* the same ligament after all. He went on talking but I wasn't listening. It was exactly the news that I didn't want and which I hadn't seen coming.

I don't even remember leaving the room. Suddenly I was back with the others, just about holding myself together. Brian O'Driscoll, the Lions captain, and Gary O'Driscoll, one of our doctors, looked up as I got back to the waiting room. I just slumped over my crutches. 'I can't believe I have done it again, I can't believe I have done it again,' I said. 'Why did it have to happen? Why me, again?'

I knew Brian and Gary wouldn't know what to say. There was nothing they could have said. In a way, I felt sorry for putting them in an impossible situation. It wasn't as if Brian was feeling much better. I had lasted almost twenty minutes of the first Test against the All Blacks, Brian had barely managed sixty seconds before dislocating his shoulder. Lying on a treatment couch next to me the evening before, he had groaned in agony for around twenty-five minutes before the doctors had managed to pop the joint back in. Now he had received terrible news – he had been ruled out of the rest of the three-Test series. He would also need an operation, followed by four or five months on the sidelines. They walked towards me, put an arm on my shoulder, then walked away again as my tears began to flow.

My mind wandered back to the game. In truth, it had been a freak incident, totally unconnected to my first injury. It wasn't the case that my left knee was in any way weak or vulnerable. The damage would have been just as severe if my right knee had been involved. I had been tracking across field as the All Blacks moved the ball right. Suddenly, they moved back infield. I was forced to check in an attempt to cover the player receiving the ball on the switch. My studs caught in the turf, with the bottom half of my left leg, from knee to ankle, caught underneath me at a 45-degree angle. Lock Ali Williams, all 120kg of him, thundered towards me. Despite my awkward position, I decided to try and go through with the tackle as powerfully as I could, by sinking my shoulder into him and hitting him hard to try and stop him in his tracks.

The full force of the collision fed back down through my knee. There was a crunching noise as I went down. It sounded almost like the ball of the joint had been compressed back into the socket. I just lay there as play continued around me. The first ten seconds were the worst. You don't know what to do with your body. I remember twisting back and forth, looking down at my leg as the pain welled up. Soon the physios arrived. 'What did you do, how does it feel?'

A day later and I could still hear the noise my knee had made as it collapsed. I hobbled outside to the front of the hospital. Christchurch was overcast, the sun trying to break through. I was on the same crutches that Lawrence Dallaglio had used a few weeks earlier after dislocating his ankle. He had already returned to England. Back home it was the middle of the night, but I had to talk to someone and phoned my partner Claire. The only words that came out of my mouth were: 'I've done it again.'

She said all the right things. She reminded me that I had come back from the same injury once and had made the Lions tour against all the odds. My career had hung in the balance but I had refused to be beaten. I could do it again. Later, though, I would learn she was as distraught by the news as I was. She had almost gone into shock and was speaking on auto-pilot.

As I rung off, a depressing thought struck me. My last game for my club, Saracens, had ended with me leaving the field with an injury. My last game for England had also been cut short, by a twisted ankle. And now this. I could not think of a more wretched way to end a career. The first knee reconstruction had been a massive battle, both mentally and physically.

'I can't go through that again,' I thought. 'I simply can't do it.'

2

HEATHROW (WITHOUT THE CROWDS)

5 July 2005. My return from New Zealand was pretty low key. It didn't exactly compare with my return after the 2003 World Cup with England. The World Cup had been the high point of my career. The 2005 Lions tour was the absolute low.

Two years before, thousands of fans had crammed into Heathrow to greet us. They had queued up for hours just to get into Terminal 4. We had been pretty hopeful of some sort of a reception but it was, after all, 4.45 in the morning when we touched down. You had to be realistic. I thought a few hundred people, mostly relatives and die-hard friends might show up. We really had no idea what impact the tournament had had back home.

Flying back with the World Cup in a Boeing 747 renamed Sweet Chariot had been pretty special. Even the William Webb Ellis trophy got allocated its own seat on flight BA16. There had been a bit of partying on the way home. The Bath boys, I think, were at the centre of it, with Mike Tindall to the fore and Lawrence Dallaglio not far behind. Tinds was meant to be challenging the record of fifty-two cans of beer, downed by Australian batsman David Boon on the same journey before the 1989 Ashes series, although I'm not sure he got very far before falling asleep. Some guys said they drank all the way to Italy before giving in. Lawrence, Matt Dawson, Ben Cohen and Jason Leonard paraded the trophy through the plane, while the fans took photos and sought autographs.

I missed most of the celebrations, though. I was sitting with Jonny Wilkinson and a handful of others on the top floor, in the bubble of the plane. We had celebrated for the past two nights and now just wanted to relax in peace and quiet. Nobody realised we were up there, apart from the odd passenger or flight attendant who wanted Jonny's signature.

When we arrived home we were ushered past the baggage collection straight to the customs area where a police officer addressed us.

'Unfortunately,' he said, 'there's a mass of people out there. For safety reasons we can't let you go through in one group. We're going to have to take you through in twos and threes. It's not for your safety, it's for theirs.'

The doors to the arrival hall were still closed but we began to hear an undercurrent of noise beyond. Somebody joked that we should send Jonny through first, as some sort of sacrificial lamb, but in the end he waited until last. The first group was made up of Neil Back, who had the Cup, Clive Woodward and Martin Johnson, and all hell broke loose. Then the next lot went through and the cheers and the singing of 'Swing Low, Sweet Chariot' and 'Jerusalem' started again. I hung back and went out in the penultimate group with Will Greenwood and Lawrence, but the cheering just went on and on. The noise was phenomenal and came at you in waves. The World Cup final in Sydney had been noisy enough, but this was in a confined space. People were crushed in, leaning forward trying to touch you, there were banners and flags being waved and hundreds of camera flashes were going off at once, dazzling you as the light bounced off the windows and glass doors. I had never,

ever experienced anything like it.

That was then, almost two years before. The only thing I was feeling this time was anxiety. I hobbled into the same Heathrow arrivals hall with Tom Shanklin, the Welsh centre who had also been ruled out of the tour. It had been a pretty lonely return – Shanks had slept pretty much the whole way, so I spent most of the flight watching films and wondering what lay ahead. This time there were no cameras and no cheering. I had a reception committee of one – Claire.

At least she recognised me. Nobody else did. I must have looked like any other holidaymaker, except for the crutches. Anonymity, though, suited me fine. At that particular moment, apart from Claire, there was only one person I really wanted to speak to and that was my surgeon. And there was only one sub-ject to discuss – the date of my second knee reconstruction. I wanted to nail it down as soon as possible. In 2003, I had got home with Buckingham Palace and No. 10 Downing Street top of my list of public engagements. This time I was heading for the operating table.

I had gone through a rollercoaster of emotions since the injury in New Zealand but by the time I reached London I was back on an even keel. It was back down to business. Claire was right. I had been here before and I could deal with it again.

Career-threatening injuries, you would think, should be dra-matic and shocking, but that hasn't been my experience exactly. On both occasions that it happened to me, within a nine-month period between October 2004 and June 2005, there was almost a comical side to events. Each time I had no idea how serious the situation was. I actually got rid of my crutches and walked around for a day or so after the first injury, before the scan showed how serious things were.

The second time, in Christchurch, I had managed to con-vince myself, initially at least, that I might get back for the third and final Test. Yes, the knee had made that horrible noise on impact, but I thought it might be some old scar tissue left over from the first time. With O'Driscoll flat on his back and hogging the buggy stretcher, I had had to limp off the pitch with the help of the medics. I told Phil Pask, the physio, that I'd walk back around the pitch but he ordered me to stay put, to avoid causing any further damage. That led to a surreal stand-off with one of the pitch stewards. I sat down on one of the advertising boards to take the weight off my leg and he rushed up and told me to get off it in case I damaged the sign. I explained to him, in no uncertain terms, why I was waiting there. He changed his tune, before politely asking me if I could at least go to the end of the board, to avoid bending it. So I did. My career was at risk but hey ho! At least his sign came through OK.

I was still hoping for the best that evening, when the squad met up for a post-match meeting to discuss our defeat in the first Test against the All Blacks. My scan was booked for the next morning and I was still telling people that the knee felt OK when Clive suddenly announced to the whole room that my Lions tour was over.

'What's he on about?' I thought. 'Let's not jump the gun here.'

Clive, though, was right. He and the medical team had obviously known a lot more about the injury than I had. I went to bed determined to prove them wrong, icing my knee and then stuffing a pile of pillows under the far end of my mattress to keep the leg up and reduce the swelling. The next morning, though, after precious little sleep, I discovered just how bad it really was.

I don't think I have ever experienced a worse day than that one in the hospital. I simply didn't know how to react. I suppose my first thoughts were totally negative. I had played 256 times for Saracens, seventy-one times for England and five times for the British and Irish Lions and suddenly it was all over. We went straight back to the hotel because the squad had to catch a flight to Wellington. I had to go back into the team room, with fifty-odd people asking me how things had gone.

'It's fucked. It's buggered. It's useless,' I said.

Anyone stupid enough to stick around for the whole conversation got the works from me. 'I don't know if I will ever play again.'

I found myself going over the incident again and again, wondering what I could have done differently. If I'd just been a bit slower across the pitch I would probably have been in the perfect position and that would have saved me. But, to this day, I have never regretted trying to complete the tackle as I wanted to. That's part of my game, part of the way I play and part of my role. The only small comfort I could find was that any other player would have sustained a similar injury if they had put their knee under the same pressure. It wasn't a case of the surgeon having done a bad job the year before. It wasn't a case of me not working hard enough during my rehab or coming back too early. It was just rank bad luck.

I reckon that within forty-eight hours of that shock I managed to get a grip on things. 'Come on,' I told myself. 'It's not necessarily the end. And anyway, even if I can't go on, I am still going to rehab this knee so that I can get on with daily life without complications. If I don't rehab it properly, I'm not going to have a full range of movement in it when I'm forty years old and that's going to mean I can't kick a football around in the park. So why not attack it properly?' And then the thoughts came back to me of the smile on my face when I started running again after the first reconstruction. With a bit of luck I could experience that elation again. It was something to look forward to.

Claire drove me home from Heathrow and we discussed the

day ahead. After snatching a quick shower, it was off to see my long-suffering surgeon, Fares Haddad, at the Princess Grace Hospital in central London. Fares didn't see the injury when it occurred; he was operating at the time. But within a few minutes, one of his registrars had passed on the news to one of the anaesthetists in theatre, who passed it on to Fares. A medical version of Chinese whispers, you could call it. By the time I got back, he had examined the match video as well as the knee scans. As I walked in, he just lifted an eyebrow, as if in exasperation.

'So you're back? Can't keep some people away,' he said.

We managed a bit of a joke because there didn't seem any point in dishing out doom and gloom. It was depressing enough just to think what lay ahead. The meeting lasted thirty minutes. It was the same procedure as before. Fares explained the options. 'Let's see what we find when we get in there,' he said. 'What I suggest, with your permission…'

The previous time, they had used part of my hamstring to replace the ligament. They couldn't use the same one this time, but they could have snipped some tendons from the other leg. The patella tendon, from just below the front of the knee, was another possibility, but Fares felt my left knee joint had taken enough punishment already. And while the patella might be robust enough to deal with everyday life, it would have been far less suited to coping with the demands of professional rugby. The emphasis from the outset this time seemed to be on using a donor – or, more bluntly, using a ligament from someone who had died. Claire and I asked a few questions, including one about the risk of infection, but he assured us the ligament would be checked, cleaned and screened. There was no talk, at that stage, of the possibility of the ligament being rejected by my body.

Later that day we headed for a meeting with my agents, Nick

Keller and Matt Jones at Benchmark Sport, and my publishers, to discuss plans for writing an autobiography. Previously, I had turned down the idea. I wasn't sure I had much to add to what had already been said by other players, following the World Cup. Nor did it appeal to me to go around slagging people off or, indeed, praising them to the skies. Also, I didn't want to be portrayed as someone I'm not. I had gradually been talked round. It would fit in with my benefit season, I was told. But now the project seemed pretty ill-timed. I should have been dashing about the pitch, making a name for myself, and instead I was on crutches, not knowing what the future held. At one stage during the meeting there was a discussion over a possible title for the book. Nobody came up with a definitive suggestion, but how many of them were thinking 'Over the Hill' or 'All Downhill from Here' might be appropriate?

3

THE PALE, SKINNY MR HILL

August 2005. I tell myself it's like any other transplant but, it still bothers me, so I try not to dwell on it too much. Put bluntly, if I ever play rugby again it will be down in large part to a dead man's knee ligament. The word 'donor' sounds a lot more comfortable but the plain truth of the matter is that my good fortune masks another person's tragedy.

I felt I had dealt with the issue and put it to one side but it forced itself back into my thinking prior to my operation. On 7 July, two days before the surgery, London had been rocked by a series of bombings on the transport system which killed fifty-two people. I couldn't help wondering whether my donor might have been one of the victims. Later, though, I learnt that the ligament could not have been surgically prepared in time. I read a newspaper interview with Fares, where he said most donors in such cases were the victims of road traffic accidents. Not that that really makes it any better.

Initially, there was talk of me seeing Fares immediately on the Tuesday morning and having the operation that evening. That idea, though, was ruled out. Fares felt my body should be given time to recover from the effects of the decreased air pressure on the flight home. He wanted to make sure there was no chance of a blood clot. So instead I went under the knife on Saturday, 9 July, the date of the Lions third Test. I had a word with the medical staff and they booked me in as the final operation in the morning so that I would be able to watch the Eden Park game. To be honest, though, I couldn't concentrate. Every few minutes I was interrupted by nurses asking questions or checking things. The result, as well as the final 3–0 series score line, didn't do much to cheer me up.

There was the cricket, though. My operation was carried out at the Wellington Hospital, just outside Lord's, which was hosting a one-day international between England and Australia the next day. It seemed too good an opportunity to miss and I enquired whether I might be allowed to take a little wander over there, if I could find someone to put me up in a corporate box. I was told to forget it. 'What about a top-floor room with a view then?' I suggested. Instead they directed me to the second floor with no view at all over the main road.

At least I knew what lay ahead this time.

Before my first operation towards the end of 2004, we had not been sure as to the full extent of the damage. That time, I had signed a consent form, effectively giving Fares permission to do whatever was necessary, once he had had a look inside the knee. He had gone over the risks and likely side effects and I had been wheeled into the operating room, still hoping that he would be able to patch up my anterior cruciate ligament without too much difficulty. It was only when I woke up that I discovered that it had been ruptured and that he had been forced to reconstruct the knee completely, replacing the ligament with tendons stripped from my hamstring. It beggars belief what can be done nowadays. Apparently Rahul, one of the other medics I've got to know well, had sat in the corner and folded the hamstring over four times and sewn it together before it was threaded through holes on the side of my knee, and fixed with bolts.

'Sorry Richard, I'm afraid it will take you between six and nine months, not six weeks, to get back,' Fares had said when I came round.

It was no great consolation to discover that Rahul had enjoyed the operation. He told me I've got good-sized hamstrings, which made it easy for him.

This time, though, I pretty much knew the score before the surgery, even if the internal damage would again prove worse than I had feared. There was no avoiding a second knee reconstruction.

When Fares got inside, he saw that I had done 'a proper job', as he put it, this time. The cruciate was torn again, and so was the medial ligament on the inner side of the knee. The posterior cruciate ligament had been stretched and the cartilage was torn, while the joint's two bone surfaces had been badly damaged after smashing together. In layman's terms – as I had correctly explained to my Lions team-mates – my knee was buggered.

The surgery seemed to have been a complete success again and I was sent home after a couple of days.

'It'll take nine months this time,' Fares said. 'Let's aim for an early April comeback.'

My run of bad luck, however, was far from over. Soon, indeed, it turned into a nightmare. Within days, I started to feel tired and off colour, with a soaring temperature. One night I hardly slept. I thought I had 'flu but Claire got hold of my mobile, without telling me, and phoned Fares. I thought he might tell me to take a few aspirin. Instead he took one look at my face – Claire says it was an unpleasant shade of grey – and admitted me to hospital. One minute I was walking along the street and the next minute I was being hooked up to a battery of machines and monitors.

At first, Fares was concerned that the problem was linked to the surgery. But my knee was relatively pain free, there was no excess swelling and it was not red or hot. It did not seem to make sense. There was a worry that my body was rejecting the new ligament, even though Fares had never heard of such a case before – the ligament is not a living organ, as used in many other transplants, so by rights there should not have been any danger of rejection. He started consulting other specialists in Britain and abroad.

By now, I was feeling seriously unwell, and sweating buckets, particularly at night. I felt lethargic and reluctant to eat. Anybody who knows me well would have known how sick I had become simply from the fact that I also stopped moaning. One of my nicknames, courtesy of my England team-mates, is 'Victor Meldrew', but I was too ill to speak at times, which did not exactly reassure Claire on her regular visits.

Initially, my big worry was that they would decide to remove the ligament in case of infection. That would have meant a three-month wait for a new ligament while the knee bone repaired itself. It would also have meant saying goodbye to the entire 2005–06 season. Goodness knows how I would have coped with that.

But there was no evidence to support the idea of ligament infection. I underwent three more keyhole operations, with my knee being flushed out, and each time the biopsies came up negative. That was the good news. The bad news was that the team of doctors and specialists now buzzing around me still could not make sense of what was going on.

How bad was it? Well, Fares said after I had recovered: 'I didn't think at any stage that you were going to die, but…'! Before the operation, he was dealing with a rugby player trying to make a comeback. Afterwards it was a case of urgently trying to recover a patient's health, no more, no less. In his words, my body was highly toxic. He had never seen anything like it before. They were having case conferences about me every few days. A senior Department of Health microbiologist was even brought in. I, meanwhile, was being checked and screened for absolutely everything. I pretty much had every viral test known to man – there were skin tests, immunity tests, tests for tropical diseases. I even got asked about my sexual history. Everything came back negative.

The dreaded routine would start every morning at 7.30 – in marched the nurses with their needles. If my temperature went up, I'd have more blood tests later on. I was close to developing a phobia of them – both the nurses and the injections. One needle was shoved straight into my knee joint and I could still feel where it had gone the next day.

Nothing seemed to go smoothly. The antibiotics, for instance, had to be changed when I reacted to them. Then, after my white blood cell count dipped dramatically, they said they were going to test my bone marrow. That meant cancer and leukaemia. Worse still, I discovered that this particular procedure would be far more painful than all the rest.

Looking back, it made me appreciate what people go through in hospital. One of the charities I'm supporting during my benefit year is the Anthony Nolan Trust, which puts together a register of bone marrow donors. I have come to meet a lot of these people, like little Max Horwood, a young lad who has been through it all. He was a guest at one of my benefit functions. I looked at him smiling away and thought: 'That's tough going, at his age.'

In the end, my luck turned. I had been pumped full of antibiotics and suddenly, for whatever reason, I began to feel better. The blood tests were still not quite right and the cause of the infection remained a mystery but they allowed me home at last, after three and a half weeks in a hospital bed.

One thing still strikes me about that period – Fares's commitment. He's a guy I trust totally, even if I wish I had seen a little less of him in recent times. At times he seemed as depressed as I was. Fares has worked with Saracens for ten years. Every time he watches a game on television he invariably spots someone whose knee he has fixed. He carries out around 200 operations a year, though not all on elite sportsmen. During both my rehabs, he has responded to my injuries as if they were personal to him. Even now, he always wants to know what the latest is. 'Text me,' he says. 'Or ring me, any time, day or night.' One of his children was born soon after I got hurt in New Zealand but he tells me that my injury had been the most significant event of that period. He's joking, of course. I think.

So I headed home, loaded down with a suitcase full of pills and medicines (one box was worth something in the region of £12,000 – that was about £200 per pill. It makes me smile to think that if someone had broken into my house they would have stolen the television or CD player and left the pills behind). To be back in Winchmore Hill gave me a huge boost. I had lost almost one month of my recovery and I felt pretty ill for another week or so, but I could now start concentrating on fighting back.

Not, of course, that anybody else really noticed what I had been going through. There had barely been a line about me in the newspapers since my exit from the Lions tour. Perhaps I had been written off after suffering the same injury for a second time. Perhaps people expected me to retire. The injury itself had been overshadowed by the furore surrounding the tackle by Tana Umaga and Keven Mealamu on Brian O'Driscoll. That controversy would rumble on for months. A lot of the rugby journalists who had followed the Lions took their holidays after the tour, I suppose, another reason for the radio silence. I'm not complaining – I prefer the quiet life to too much attention.

The media did eventually catch up with me, or so I thought. I got a phone call asking for an interview but I was still in hospital and not feeling great at that stage so I asked them to get back to me. Five minutes later and there was another call, from the BBC or Sky. All of a sudden, after no contact for weeks, I get two phone calls in five minutes. What was up?

'Just checking up on your injury,' they assured me.

'Give me a couple of days,' I replied, and turned my mobile off.

Next morning, at ten past eight, it rang again.

'I wonder if you would like to comment on Clive Woodward giving up rugby to help coach at Southampton Football Club?' the voice said.

I couldn't believe it. It was almost comical.

'How could I have been so foolish to think they might actually be concerned about me?' I thought.

If I wasn't exactly feeling myself at the time, I wasn't looking like myself either. The first occasion I went out in public was to watch Saracens play Harlequins at Harpenden Rugby Club in a pre-season friendly. I went up into the clubhouse and ran into my England team-mate Will Greenwood. He looked straight through me. 'Hi Will,' I said, and he did a double take. I had probably lost around 8–9kg since the operation, and I was probably just below 100kg, not counting my leg brace.

He turned to Claire and said with a laugh: 'Sorry, I didn't recognise the pale, skinny Mr Hill.'

And he was right. Later I saw some pictures of myself. I looked like a ghost.

Looking back, the immediate aftermath of the operation was my low point. There was – and still is – the nagging worry that we didn't get to the bottom of the infection saga and that it could return any time in the future. Yet I was determined to give my recovery my best shot. Fares never once said I should pack it in and that helped. And anyway, what else could I do? I am a rugby player. I'm not qualified to do much else.

(★ (★ (★

My rugby qualifications go back more than a quarter of a century, to the time when I began playing mini rugby at the age of five in Salisbury. The sport has dominated my life ever since. Even before then, as a rugby ball-shaped toddler almost as round as I was tall, I had displayed a taste for throwing my weight around. My mum, Penny, says I was the hardest of the three children to bring up, a hyperactive boy who was always dismantling things with a screwdriver inside the house and getting into all sorts of scrapes outside.

I was two years old when my sister Fenella was born. I took one look at her in the maternity ward cot and pushed her away, declaring: 'Don't want that!' Apparently, I was once caught riding my trike over the back of her legs. As soon as she learnt to walk, I would shove her aside and take her place in the pushchair. Fenella probably had every right to complain. After all, she was regularly dragged along to watch me play rugby; while I was only forced to go and watch her dance once (I sulked throughout). And perhaps my elder brother, Tim, and I should not have used her as a tackle bag quite as often as we did.

She was interested in ballet and horses. I preferred mud and Action Men (which, my parents keep reminding me, are still awaiting collection from their loft, along with the fort and toy soldiers). I didn't get girls.

I didn't talk much, as a young child. I could, it seems, I

just chose not to. Some things never change. I was sent to a Montessori nursery to encourage my communication skills. It didn't seem to be working until a girl walked out of the door and onto the busy street without the teachers noticing. Apparently I rushed up and told them. They were shocked – not so much that the girl had got out but that I had uttered my first words since arriving at school.

My introduction to rugby came via Tim. He was six years older but could not stop me tagging along whenever he and his friends staged a game of cricket, football or rugby. I used to get kicked about the garden but kept coming back for more. Tim, I suppose, just put up with me (except, that is, on one occasion when I deposited a gob of phlegm on the heads of two of his friends from the first-floor landing as they practised kissing at one of his parties).

Whenever Tim played for Salisbury's youth teams, I would hop about on the touchline, dressed up in my own toddler's kit. A friend of my parents, Dave Wilkins, eventually gave in and let me run around behind the others, well out of harm's way. 'One day that boy will play at Twickenham,' he said.

The headmaster of my village primary school was a New Zealander, Jim Grice, whose son played top-class rugby, so he probably approved of my developing passion. The rest of the staff were less approving whenever I introduced British Bulldog – a rather physical game of tag – or full-blown rugby to my smaller classmates at break time. Each time the game would be broken up I would be sent in to explain myself. I would go home with holes in my trousers and a big grin on my face. 'The little boy with the grubby knees,' one of my Mum's friends called me.

Perhaps rugby was in my blood. My dad, John, hadn't been that good a player – he was better at hockey – although he later helped set up mini rugby at Salisbury rugby club. Mum maintains the influence came from her side of the family, the aptly named Rucks, some of whom had emigrated to New Zealand. Mum's brother, uncle John, had loved the game, playing week in, week out, concussed or not. Tragically, he died in his mid-thirties, so I never got to know him. As for Tim, he led the way, first at Salisbury and then by going on to prop for British Polytechnics and finally Portsmouth. By the time I started to progress though the game, he was pursuing a sensible, successful career as an accountant.

When I was five I met Marcus Olsen, who remains a good friend to this day. He lived on one side of Salisbury Rugby Club and I lived on the other. We met in the middle and messed about together, kicking and passing and learning how a rugby ball bounced. We would go through the same routine when our parents went to watch matches at the club. I would always know if there was a midweek evening game – you could see the glare of the ground's floodlights from our house – and I would tug at Dad's sleeve, asking to be taken along. Our parents would watch the action from a grass mound, while we passed a ball around with our mates Dave Griffiths and Dave Coveney on an adjoining pitch. As a kid, I would pretend to be Dean Richards or Peter Winterbottom. Little did Marcus and I know that we would both play for England schoolboys and England Under-21s, as well as teaming up years later at Saracens. We were even sharing a flat when I won my first England cap.

I don't remember standing out as a youngster, although my parents argue through rose-tinted spectacles that I was way ahead of my classmates. Apparently the coaches said I had something special about me, that I could read the game. I just remember being a roly-poly kid who wanted to run with the ball. We had a good side at mini level, regularly winning local tournaments. I was lucky like that. When I went up to secondary school, there were lots of good players in my age group, which rubbed off.

Looking back, it was as close to an idyllic childhood as you could get. I was born in Dormansland in Surrey but the family headed to Salisbury soon after. We moved into a house at the end of a quiet close in the village of Stratford-sub-Castle, backing onto a water meadow, with the River Avon 100 metres away. It was meant to be a temporary arrangement but my parents still live there today. When the meadow flooded, the water came right up to our garden fence and I would set off in a makeshift fibreglass canoe. Later, that canoe provided the perfect vehicle to get to some of Salisbury's pubs. I'd paddle past the fire station, moor up outside The Boat House, have a few drinks and paddle back without worrying about being breathalysed.

Many of our holidays were spent up with my grandparents in Norfolk. They took a huge amount of pride in their house, in the little village of Cringleford just outside Norwich. The back garden had a precious, child-free croquet lawn, a little summer house, apple trees and a vegetable patch. Granddad had been the assistant chief constable of Buckinghamshire police and knew how to deal with young upstarts. He was very loving but was also very Victorian in terms of discipline, as I found out when I broke one of the croquet mallets, or when I unwisely committed the heinous crime of talking during the Queen's Speech one Christmas. Driving through Norfolk with Claire many years later, I made a detour, just to get another look at the house.

My grandparents also owned a small bungalow at Bacton, on the Norfolk coast between Cromer and Great Yarmouth, about 200 metres from the beach. We'd play cricket, throw Frisbees and walk along the mudflats, with mud squelching through our toes, or stalk pools with shrimping nets. My enthusiasm for swimming, though, was dampened when, one evening, we saw a fisherman on the promenade pull in two foot-long baby sharks. At nearby Blakeney Point we'd collect samphire, a type of seaweed, boil it up, add butter and eat it off the stalk.

Years later, Mum was walking around the old Saracens club-house at Bramley Road, peering at pictures of pre-war teams after watching me play a game, when she noticed a familiar face staring back from one of the frames. Looking down at the names inscribed below, she found 'George H.W. Wilkinson'. It was Granddad. By an extraordinary coincidence, grandfather and grandson had ended up playing for the same London club.

Sadly, my granddad had had several strokes by then and had not been able to tell us more about it. That 1938 team picture was included in the book, *Saracens, 125 Years of Rugby*. It would have been nice to swap notes. I also discovered that, as a young policeman with the Met, he had walked the beat in Winchmore Hill, a stone's throw away from the house I share with Claire.

My sporting education began in earnest at secondary school. I managed, miracle of miracles, to pass my Eleven Plus and get into Bishop Wordsworth School, a state grammar lying in the shadow of Salisbury Cathedral and with a fine reputation for rugby. My fate was sealed.

As for my educational education, well, for years my school reports would have the same ring to them. One year it would be: 'His determination in sport does not unfortunately carry over into his academic work.' The next: 'Richard must not relax his efforts in his academic work. He puts a great deal into his sport and the school, but he must also think of his own future.' And the next: 'Richard must tackle his weaknesses with the same spirit of determination he shows on the rugby field.'

I didn't, though. I was sport mad and so were my friends. In class, I was never top in any subjects and near the bottom in some. I certainly remember getting 17 per cent in a religious education exam. I had a phase of being, by all accounts, a disruptive pupil who sat at the back of the class and chatted. My parents tried to encourage me to study, but it was a losing battle. I don't remember doing a mass of homework. Offered a distraction, I would take it.

One of the more pleasant diversions was providing overnight security with my mates at the annual Salisbury Real Ale and Jazz festival. We watched over the various kegs and barrels in the marquee and, in return, were shown how to help ourselves to a few glasses of Tanglefoot. I'm not sure I would have hired us. One year we woke up to find a disturbed old lady wandering around the tent with a mallet in her hand. We ducked down in our sleeping bags and pretended to be asleep until she wandered off.

My main distractions, though, were sporting in nature. For a while, I played tennis to a reasonable standard, and I even came second in the Wiltshire Under-17s shot putt. (I came last, though, at South West level.) Rugby's grip, however, was never seriously threatened, particularly after Steve Ralph-Bowman got hold of me.

The school's celebrated rugby coach, who also trained the local team, must have done a double-take the first time he heard my name. About ten years before, he had helped develop another Richard Hill who, like me, had a father called John who worked in the insurance business in Salisbury. The Mark I version, a scrum-half, went on to play for Bath and England, as did Dave Egerton, a No. 8 from the same school side. Soon Richard Hill Mark II – playing at No. 8 after flirting with the front row as a youngster – and Marcus Olsen – at 9 – began following in their footsteps.

Ralph-Bowman was a passionate, fiery man, who demanded total commitment. He had been known to lock teams in their changing room for a short while after bad defeats. He filled some of his young charges with fear but I got on well with him most of the time. He knew his stuff. He was an RFU-accredited coach, and was involved in selection and coaching at county, regional and national level. It probably did me no harm that his son, Ben, was in my year group. And it certainly helped that the back row was one of his areas of expertise. It was the first time I had come across such a technical approach. He didn't just teach you moves, he made you understand how they worked, why certain positions or angles of running would succeed in unlocking defences while others would not.

He also made us work hard. There were the obligatory cross-country runs through the streets and down by the river and back past the cathedral. For the senior teams there was 'fitness lunch time' on Mondays, with circuits in the school hall or a jog to Harnham Steps, a long flight of stairs of different gradients. Once at the top he put you through a variety of lung-busting exercises to finish you off.

It paid off, though. We had a fixture list which included public schools like Sherborne, Marlborough College, Canford and Millfield. They didn't like losing to us. I used to fancy myself as a bit of a kicker in those days – I was a very rustic version of John Eales – and I remember kicking two penalties in a game against Millfield to seal a 6–3 'classic'.

It's hard to put an exact measure on Ralph-Bowman's importance to my career. But I think he knew much better than us how good we could become if we were pushed. When he retired, both I and Richard Hill Mark I spoke at a function marking the event.

If only there had been someone with as much influence on my academic work. Perhaps I was lulled into a false sense of security by some reasonable GCSE results. The school was obviously lulled as well. They made me deputy head boy and allowed me to study Mathematics, Geography and Business Studies at A level. By then, though, I had begun making headway in representational rugby sides and my schoolbooks gathered dust.

When our A level results came out, everyone met up to celebrate and discuss the future. I didn't want to be a killjoy so I went along. 'What did you get?' they asked me. 'I got none,' I replied. 'Spelt N-U-N.' I smiled it off but, to be truthful, I was in a state of shock. I knew the maths hadn't gone well – I had done all I could after the first fifteen minutes of the three-hour exam – but I had no inkling the other results would be so bad. It was a pretty dark day and threw my future into doubt.

As a young boy, I had wanted to be a farmer. There had been a farm just down the road and I used to help out occasionally with the pigs and hay baling. Later, I set my heart on further education. I didn't have a clue what I really wanted to do, but I vaguely thought I might become a teacher or a gym instructor. I remember my Mum coming up with a whole series of suggestions, which became more and more bizarre the more desperate she became. Physiotherapy seemed logical enough an idea, but she must have been really panicking when she suggested hairdressing.

I filled out a careers advice questionnaire at school which was sent off for computer analysis. When the list of possible careers came back, I picked one that sounded good to try and keep my parents happy. 'I think I shall become a chartered surveyor,' I announced, to satisfaction all round. Now, though, without any A levels, even that option had gone.

Still, things did not turn out all that bad in the end. If you look up my old school's website, there is a section on former Wordsworthians. William Golding, author of *Lord of the Flies*, taught there, while Ralph Fiennes, the actor, was a pupil. Well, my name is on the list as well. It talks of Saracens, England and the Lions. My exam results don't get a mention.

(* (* (*

August 2005. It would be nice to add another few lines to that school website entry, but as things stand at the moment, I can't be sure what the future holds. I'm making decisions as I go along, day by day. I'm still on a six-week course of antibiotics as I write this, and my rehab is just starting. All I've managed is walking on my toes up and down the swimming pool and pacing the length of the Saracens training ground gym, looking in the mirror to make sure my left leg mirrors the right.

People ask me when I hope to be back playing for Saracens or England. I can't think like that. England is away in the far distance, beyond my horizon. If I were honest I would say that I don't know for sure if I will ever play rugby again.

With a nine-month recovery programme ahead of me, I have to keep things simple. One of my friends from my Salisbury Rugby Club days, Don Parsons, has asked me to be the best man at his wedding this month. I've not exactly lived up to the best man's duties so far, since I had to miss the stag do, but after missing one important wedding already – my former Saracens team-mate Tony Diprose's marriage to Mo – I am determined to be present this time.

So this week's training will be to try to walk without crutches in church. That's my immediate goal.

4

ANOTHER MONTH IN SOLITARY

September 2005. I got in to a bit of a panic the other day. You'd think, having gone through this before that I should know what to expect from this sort of injury. There will be twinges and aches and sudden pains, almost on a daily basis. The knee will swell up without warning and make strange noises that I would rather not hear. The key is not to let your imagination run riot about what is going on inside the joint.

However, I had forgotten that bit of advice after I had been at Twickenham, to watch Saracens' first league match of the season against Wasps. I managed to get a first-row seat in the royal box, so I had more room than usual, and I had propped up my leg against the front wall. Everything was fine (apart from the result, a 23–11 defeat) until afterwards. Suddenly I felt a sharp pain around the main scar on my knee. I walked it off and thought nothing more about it. Next morning, though, I could barely get out of bed. I couldn't walk on the left leg at all and had to cling onto the furniture to get across the room.

I hobbled off like an old granny to see the club physio, then got in contact with Fares. I couldn't help wondering whether something had gone wrong with the ligament graft – you hear stories of fractures around the screw sites after my sort of operation. When something similar happened after my first knee surgery, I had been taken in for another operation within a week, to remove a 'floater', a bit of tissue or cartilage which had broken away (we had kept it from the press that time, since I was fighting to be fit for the Lions tour and we didn't want any fuss). It could have been something similar this time, according to Fares, but he didn't want to be operating on my knee again so soon. We just had to see if it settled down, and planned to have a scan a couple of weeks later.

To make matters worse, after the physio session I had to go straight to a corporate sevens day at Saracens. I had to put my brace back on to support the knee, which of course meant that I was bombarded with questions. People mean well – indeed, perhaps it would be rude not to ask – but it's quite tiring when you are on the receiving end. One person will say: 'So can we expect you back in a couple of weeks?' Then the next asks: 'Is it true your career's over?' Others sigh deeply when I tell them I expect to be out for nine months. Sometimes I wonder what answers they want. I'm hoping to get to all our home games this season, as well as some of the away ones, but each time you turn up you get cross-examined. It reminds you of your situation all the time.

Match and corporate days aside, being injured is a lonely business. The more long-term the injury, the more solitary you feel. I'm not very good on my own. I'm a pack animal, I suppose (no pun intended). I can be quite reserved in certain situations, meeting people for the first time. I've always been like that. Let's face it, most of my life has been spent as part of a fifteen-man group.

My day-to-day friendships are with other Saracens players. I have good mates in the England squad and particularly so back in Salisbury, but there isn't much opportunity to see them regularly. I'm not a great one for phone conversations, although I get the odd texts from Jonny (ever since the World Cup, it's almost been a competition to see which of us has spent the most time in rehabilitation). As one of the walking wounded, though, you feel like you're stuck on the fringes.

It's fine when there's a match on. You feel part of things again. Some people think it must be frustrating to watch the other guys playing, but I don't feel that. If you are not fit, you are not fit, so why get frustrated? I still get very nervous about results. I'm passionate about the club and I want them to do well. That means encouraging the guy playing in my position, even if he might keep me out when I return. You accept that. I'm always ready to help analyse match videos with the younger guys if they want. I look at it this way; I also need the results to go my way, it's my future they are playing for as well.

At other times, though, it's tough. I go down to our Hertfordshire University training ground in Hatfield but for the most part I'm having physio on my own or doing gym work-outs when the other guys are not there. I miss the banter of training. Often the players organise something social after one of their sessions, be it a meal or a quick coffee, but I'm usually not around and end up missing out.

I've never liked missing out on group events, even before my injuries. If training was from nine to eleven in the morning I would sometimes go in at seven to fit in an extra weight or fitness session so that I could finish at the same time as everybody else. I hate being in the gym when I know the other guys are off playing golf.

At the moment I'm spending some afternoons alone at home. They don't encourage you to hang around the place at Hatfield. It was different during the amateur days, when everybody socialised after training. Now the professional philosophy is 'come in, work hard, then go home and recuperate'. I'm one of the worst culprits, apparently, for hanging around for an extra chat and a mug of tea. I suppose that is one of the main reasons why I want to carry on playing. I love the feeling of being involved with a team. It's all I've ever known.

(* (* (*

As a youngster, most of my spare time seemed to be spent in a rugby shirt of one colour or another. At Bishop Wordsworth's, I would have played in the school team on Saturday (navy blue) and then played for Salisbury (green, with a single white hoop) on Sunday. Before long, I was also playing representational rugby for Wiltshire's Under-14s (green and white hoops). At school level, I had already come across Kevin Yates who, after a successful, eventful career, ended up with me at Saracens. I crossed swords with my World Cup team-mate Matt Dawson even earlier – he turned out for Marlow Under-13s against Salisbury. As I remember it, Daws and I both kicked two penalties in a 6–6 draw.

The more you progressed, the more team trials you were invited to. By Under-16 level, the system was so complex that I'm not sure anybody understood it. I would have played for my school and Salisbury. Then we would have had to play other parts of Wiltshire to get in the county side. Then we would play Dorset to form a Dorset and Wilts XV. Next came a match against Hampshire and Sussex, leading to another team, which would play other amalgamated teams before forming the South of England. Next came the South West...etc., etc., until, aeons later and if your luck held out, you would get the coveted invitation to an England trial.

No wonder I never got any schoolwork done. On big weekends I would leave school at lunch time on Friday, missing afternoon lessons, and return on Sunday night. I did take books with me on the train, but I never actually opened them. Perhaps I suffered from travel sickness.

If that was not enough, there were regional training courses, followed by the annual summer course at Trent College in Nottingham. The idea was to hand-pick the best players in the country. They would work you flat out for five or six days, then play a couple of matches to see what you had taken in.

I learnt a lot, but some of the theory was very rigid. The course was run by Don Rutherford, the RFU technical director. He had this big thing about 'pass, pass, penetrate!' Moving the ball away from contact was fine, but then you had to hit it up again rather than look for space. A lot of the thinking was built around the success of the 1990 Grand Slam-winning team. That was the way they thought we should all play.

It was there that I first experienced the monstrous bleep test. I was fifteen and had never done a fitness test in my life. In effect, it's a 20-metre shuttle run, with bleeps on a tape recorder letting you know how much time you had to get from one end to another. At first you can do it in a fast walk, but the bleeps then speed up. You go on for as long as can keep up, or for as long as you can avoid keeling over. I wasn't too bad – you were meant to get to level ten and I think I got to twelve. As for weight training, though, I hadn't done much of that so I could barely lift the bar.

My real spiritual home was Salisbury Rugby Club. Don Parsons – whose wedding I attended as best man last month – remembers our first meeting well. Don, at nineteen, the same age as my elder brother Tim and playing for the first XV, dropped a scoring pass as he crossed the try line during a game. Afterwards, 'a lippy thirteen-year-old runt of no conse-quence' came up to him and said: 'You should learn how to keep hold of the ball, mate.' I don't remember the incident, but Don assures me that the runt was rammed up against a tree and warned to mind his own business. Funny, how friendships are formed.

I made my first-team debut three years later and Don and Mark Piper, who played at hooker, looked out for me. The call had come out of the blue. Marcus and I had only just started training with the club and had played one game for the seconds. The first team No. 8 broke his leg just before a cup match against Swindon and the club approached my parents and my school teachers to ask if they were happy for me to play.

Today, a sixteen-year-old would not be allowed to take part in an adult match, but things were more lax back then. Playing at the base of the scrum while weighing in at barely 13st soaking wet, I was so petrified of being caught in possession that I discovered an extra gear and scampered over for two tries. Don and Mark – and Tim, on the odd occasions when we played together – made sure nobody got too near me, although my personal protection vanished that evening when, in the first of many rugby initiations, I was publicly stripped naked on the disco floor. It may sound mad to some people, but when I'm asked which games of rugby I remember most, my Salisbury club debut comes high up on the list.

I kept my place for the rest of that season and we went on to win the Dorset and Wilts Cup final. Travelling back on the bus, I remember the guys laughing at the fact that we had pulled it off with a pack of forwards containing six squaddies, one civilian and a schoolboy barely out of short trousers.

My Salisbury days, put simply, were great fun. We played hard on the pitch and to a good standard, then, win or lose, we had a good laugh. It wasn't just about the game at Salisbury, it was about the whole day and night. We stayed together in the clubhouse after matches until nine or ten o'clock and then headed off into town in search of a burger, a bar and a nightclub (there were never any women involved – according to

Don, we were both too unattractive and tongue-tied for that). Salisbury may have been short of resources as a club but it had a great community feel. Everybody chipped in. When the pitch was levelled and re-seeded one year, each player and his family were given a quadrant and asked to clear it of stones.

We would always have a theme after a game. When Ralph-Bowman left us to coach Bournemouth, one of the reasons given was that he would get a car at his new club. So the next time we played Bournemouth, the theme was obvious. In the bar afterwards, every Salisbury player had a toy car in his hand to greet our former coach.

Things could be chaotic at times, which only added to the memories. My first game against a first-class rugby club, for instance, came against Blackheath, one of England's most historic clubs, in the Pilkington Cup. I had turned up as a spectator. I was seventeen and it was half term so I didn't have a Saturday fixture. My parents and I had polished off a picnic of pork pies and sandwiches in the car park before heading for the bar when one of the Salisbury guys suddenly approached us to say they were a man short because of injury.

I had no kit. A pair of boots – about two sizes too small – were unearthed in the Blackheath's 'lost and found' cupboard and the ladies in the canteen boiled up an old gum shield for me in a kettle. We lost, of course – I think Blackheath were in the second division at that stage – but put on a decent show. I ended the game with blistered, bleeding toes. At one stage I stuck my head out of a maul and found myself staring straight into the face of a fierce-looking forty-year-old lock. I ducked back down as quickly as possible.

Then there was the 1992 Dorset and Wilts Cup final against Sherborne at Dorchester. We turned up without a No. 6 shirt, so Don and I both wore 8. Don was bigger and more physical than me and managed to knock one of their players out with his knee. He still swears it was an accident. The crowd, though, was furious. The trouble was they identified me as the guilty No. 8. For the rest of the game I was booed and heckled: 'Dirty bastard, you're a disgrace, call yourself a rugby player!' I found it really upsetting. Don found it hugely entertaining.

If Salisbury had got to play in the highest English divisions, I'm sure I would never have left.

I enjoyed the informality of club rugby. It was a different kettle of fish, higher up. When I was selected for the South of England Under-16s, I received a letter announcing: 'You will wear school uniform. If your school does not have uniform, then a jacket and tie will be worn.' Not long after, I got another letter, inviting me to the Salisbury Under-16 end-of-season tour dinner. 'Don't turn up drunk for this meal or you'll be sent to your room for the night…and probably get a slapping from the captain in the morning,' it said.

At least a lot of my county rugby was played among school friends. The majority of the Bishop Wordsworth team played for Dorset and Wilts. By the time the regional Under-16 matches came round in 1989, however, there were only two of us left. Peter Coryndon, who played at 7, and I were in the South and South West side. We won the divisional championship and were both invited to the final England trial, to be held at Queen Elizabeth Barracks in Strensall in Yorkshire.

The idea of playing for England crept up on me almost unnoticed. I remember Marcus had gone up for the 16 group trial the year before and had said on his return: 'Richard, you could play for England.'

'What are you talking about?' I replied. It hadn't really registered as a possibility.

Peter and I went up on the train together – it was probably the furthest north I had ever been – armed with a cheque each. Whoever got selected for the England tour of Italy would need to pay up for the England V-neck blue jumper, the England blazer badge and, of course, the infamous 'purple nasty', a lurid tracksuit that identified you as an England squad member. In the end, I got picked and Peter returned home with his cheque still in his pocket. He must have been gutted but he handled it well. Years later, during the 2003 World Cup, I met him out in Australia, where he had settled after getting married.

My first involvement with England, however, was to end in disappointment. Years later, my CV in match programmes would announce that I had completed a full house of national honours – England Under-16s, Under-18s, Colts, England Under-21s, England Students Under-21s, Students, Emerging Players, England A and England. I never got on the pitch for the 16 group, though.

The squad included Daws and Paul Burke, who later played for England Under-18s before switching allegiance to Ireland. Eben Rollitt, son of the former England international flanker Dave Rollitt, also made the trip. Rollitt was taller and bulkier than me. Perhaps as importantly, I was quiet and shy, while he was a confident public schoolboy.

We played Italy B Under-16s, followed by the national side. Only two players missed out on caps and I was one of them, along with Matt Singer, a future Saracens team-mate. I returned home in tears but Matt helped me drown my sorrows with a bottle of red wine at the back of the team bus. It was probably the first time in my life I had missed out on team selection.

My tour report from Michael Williams, however, gave me cause for hope. 'The man I feel most for,' he wrote. I was a good decision-maker and had a good sense of timing but my character had counted against me. 'We felt that perhaps Eben was harder and more forceful and more aggressive, but these are qualities that it is quite possible for you to put into your game...because body forcefulness and assertiveness are as much a function of technique as they are of personality,' Williams added, before concluding: 'I think you will find that you overtake Eben if you have a mind to... There will be progress, I have no doubt.'

It would be the first of many times that people questioned my character, but I think, over time, I've proved them wrong. There are all sorts of reasons why other players didn't quite make it to the highest level. Some, like my brother Tim, put careers ahead of sport. Some stopped progressing or got injured. Others found themselves continually overshadowed by close rivals and never quite broke through.

Then there were those who took different routes altogether. Few rugby union fans will have heard of Steve McCurrie but he was highly impressive back then. He was a well-built, explosive hooker from the north of England, the life and soul of every party and the fastest player in the squad over 20 metres. Soon after that tour he switched to rugby league and went professional with Widnes. He was even capped for Great Britain but then, for some reason, his career faded. As for Rollitt, well, things did not quite work out for him either. He graduated from Cambridge University but struggled with injury as a Wasps and Bristol player. I heard recently that he had just won his first international cap – playing for Arabian Gulf against China, believe it or not.

By 1991, I was attending the England Under-18s final trial at Nottingham. I had added a few pounds and was now fully grown, standing proud at 6ft $2\frac{1}{2}$ in. The others, however, had also carried on growing. Rollitt was 6ft 5in. And then there was Simon Shaw.

I had never come across Shaw before. He was massive. I still remember a newspaper picture of him and one of the other locks, Barry-Jon Mather (who went off to play rugby league, returned to union and was then capped by England at centre), standing next to a lamppost. Shaw was 6ft $8\frac{1}{2}$ in and $18\frac{1}{2}$ st at the age of seventeen, bigger than any senior international in Europe at the time. (Wade Dooley, in the full England team, was a stone lighter.)

The selectors were intent on keeping Rollitt at 8, so they asked me to try my hand at openside during the trial. I had never played there before. The other guy in the back row was Tony Diprose. Little did I realise at the time how well I would get to know 'Dips' in the future – and little did I realise how inspired the selectors' decision would prove to be. In those days, things were a bit more free-spirited and spontaneous, with fewer game plans and defensive patterns – or, if they did exist, I hadn't been listening – and I somehow bluffed my way into the final squad. Otherwise, I don't remember much about that trial, except that Will Greenwood scored three tries at fly-half and still didn't get selected.

Thus it was, that Richard Hill Mark II won his first England Schools cap – 26 March 1991, against Ireland at Thomond Park in Limerick. You're meant to cherish such moments for the rest of your life, recalling every single detail as if it were yesterday. So apologies to everyone concerned – I don't remember a thing. I know we won and, looking back through some old programmes, I know that I was up against the likes of Anthony Foley and David Corkery, future full Ireland internationals. Daws played, as did Burke and Tim Stimpson. But that's about it. My parents, who supported me and my brother as young rugby players by driving us all over the country, came over to watch. They probably remember more about the game than I do.

We went on to beat France at Northampton's Franklin's Gardens – they had a couple of guys called Fabien Pelous and

Olivier Magne that day – and then defeated the Scots at Aspatria, when I even managed a try. While all this was happening, Richard Hill Mark I was playing a pivotal role in the England senior team's Grand Slam campaign. I would probably have earned a little extra newspaper coverage if I had managed the same – it would have been a unique Bishop Wordsworth and Salisbury double – but it was not to be. After the Scotland game, I was told on the bus that I was being dropped for the final game. My career as an openside flanker seemed to be over barely before it had begun.

Within a few months I was in that pub, admitting to my schoolmates that I had flunked my A levels. While they looked forward to the next chapter in their lives, I was forced into an urgent rethink. I had been hoping to go on to study at Exeter, Cardiff Institute or Loughborough but that all went up in smoke as soon as I opened my results envelope.

Fortunately, my headmaster allowed me back to do retakes. There was a catch, though – no representative rugby. I would have to make do with the school team, with occasional forays for Salisbury. For the first time, books were to come before rugby balls. I agreed, and stuck to the agreement...for at least a few months.

I had retaken Geography in November and, while not exactly knuckling down, handed in a little more course work than usual as I prepared for my Maths and Business Studies exams the following June. After Christmas, however, I was called in by Ralph-Bowman. He had been approached by the England Colts (Under-19s) selectors, inviting me to the final trial. 'What do you think?' I was asked. 'Do you think you can cope with playing as well as working hard?' I pretended to think very deeply for a few seconds before replying that, all things thoroughly considered, I thought I probably could.

Back at No. 8, I got selected to tour Italy, followed by games against Wales, Scotland and France. For the first time I began to get the feeling that I had something to offer at the top level. We drew in Italy, and then beat the Welsh and the Scots before going down narrowly 23–18 to France. One of our selectors said that if he had had to choose one side from the thirty players on the pitch at Bournemouth that day, he would have included only four Englishmen. I, though, was among them.

The day we left for Italy, the manager drew me aside to tell me that my gran had died. It was just before training and we flew out immediately afterwards, so I couldn't phone home until that evening. She had been ill but it hit me hard. To make things worse, I had done very little travelling abroad at that stage. At Colts level, they always told us we were playing for our families, so before the game, the coach told the team to 'go out and play for Hilly's gran'. Italy had a late penalty to win the game and I remember standing under the posts staring at their kicker thinking: 'If you have any respect for my gran you are going to miss this.'

Throughout that time, playing for school, club and country, I did not pick up a single serious injury. All I ever seemed to get was the odd bump or bruise. You just rubbed yourself down and turned out again the next day. We didn't seem to need physios and warm-downs and ice baths when we were young. Today, I simply couldn't survive without them.

(★ (★ (★

At the moment, the Saracens physios are trying to loosen up some of my thigh muscles because my leg extension is a bit behind schedule. I'm still hobbling a little, so I've been trying to concentrate hard on walking normally. As for the current treatment, it's a bit more aggressive than massaging – malicious gouging is probably a better description. The physios look for trigger points, little lumps, and stick in a thumb or elbow. Then they get me lying face down on a bed, with my leg hanging over, and put on a 6kg weight to try and stretch it out. I'm lifting normal weights as well, doing double leg squats while holding 10–15kg dumbbells in each hand, as well as stepping up onto a box and doing pool and bike work.

The one good thing is that there's plenty of moral support if I need it, and not just from Claire. The other day, we held the first function of my benefit year, a gala dinner at Grosvenor House in London. Loads of guys turned out, not just from Sarries. There was Jerry Guscott, Mike Catt, Matt Stevens (whose singing has since received due recognition in *X Factor*), Thomas Castaignede (who mimed, rather than sang 'Thank Heavens for Little Girls'), Kyran Bracken (whose brittle back somehow survived a performance of body popping to the tune of 'Crazy Frog'), Josh Lewsey and Daws and the like (I couldn't perform so I got stitched up in a spoof video set to the tune of 'Amarillo', with reworked lyrics like 'Richard Hillo' and 'Is this the way to the physio room?').

Quite a few of the contributors to my benefit brochure, like Lawrence and Tim Horan, have gone through knee reconstructions themselves and have snippets of advice, telling you what worked for them.

Mind you, two reconstructions is another matter. It's only just beginning to dawn on me that very few people come back a second time. I remember that Newcastle's Scotland flanker Andrew Mower quit the game at the age of twenty-nine after his second reconstruction, following the 2003 World Cup. He had been given a 50 to 70 per cent chance of playing again by his surgeons, but did not make it.

That figure has stuck in my mind since reading a newspaper interview with Fares, in which he put my chances of recovery at 80 per cent.

Fares says he has never carried out a second knee reconstruction on an elite athlete who has gone on to complete a successful comeback. Some have had the second one done, he says, as a retirement gift. He knows a few amateur sportsmen who have got back after two or even three operations on the same knee, but not at the top level. Ronaldo, the Brazilian footballer, is the only case he can think of.

5

RICHARD HILL OF WIGAN AND GREAT BRITAIN

October 2005. I'm seeing quite a bit of Andy Farrell, our new rugby league recruit, in the physio room at the moment. We're involved in a battle to sort out the couch hierarchy. He's accused me of hogging it, although I've noticed his sessions tend to overrun as well.

It's strange, having Andy at Saracens. If things had turned out differently, we might have been team-mates a lot earlier in our careers – playing rugby league at Wigan. Eleven years ago, when union was still amateur, Wigan asked me to switch codes. As it is, I stayed put and it's Andy who's made the jump.

He won pretty much everything there was to win in rugby league. He was a Great Britain international at eighteen – at that age I was still playing for Salisbury – and captain by the time he was twenty-one. In 2004 he won the Golden Boot, awarded to the best rugby league player in the world, as well as the Man of Steel accolade. The one thing he hasn't managed to get his hands on is a World Cup. So when England offered him the chance to try his hand at union, with the 2007 rugby union World Cup in mind, he jumped at the challenge. Since then, though, he hasn't managed to get on the pitch. Having just come back from knee surgery, he injured his foot in a

Saracens pre-season warm-up game and the problem has dragged on and on.

So if I'm finding things hard at the moment, then he must be too. At this rate he'll make his comeback at the same time as me. It could be fun, linking up with him in the back row. He's very friendly with a lot of the guys and a good character but it's hard for him to join in with a lot of the banter at the moment. Games get discussed but he has no union experiences to draw on.

(* (* (*

Wigan approached me in the 1994–95 season. To say that it came out of the blue would be an understatement. It still amazes me to this day. I was doing OK at the time, I suppose, but I was still in my final year at college. Several rugby union clubs had already shown an interest in me, including Bath. Bath, you could say, were rugby union's version of Manchester United. Wigan, though, were the Real Madrid of rugby league.

I had never played the thirteen-man game when I received their phone call. I sometimes watched the game on television on Saturday as a boy – that was about it. As far as I know, Wigan approached me after watching me play eighty minutes of rugby.

It was during the Divisional Championship. It wasn't a massively important tournament, with many of the England players side-stepping the event, but it certainly did me no harm. I was up in London by then but had stuck with my roots and opted to play for the South and South West. When we went up to Sale to play the North, we heard that the place was going to be infested with rugby league scouts running the rule over Andy Northy, a rugged centre from Waterloo, who eventually ended up at Widnes. I thought nothing of it, but I ended up scoring a hat trick of tries in a losing cause.

Soon after, one of my flatmates gave me a telephone message. A reporter had rung and wanted to write an article on me. The 'reporter', it turned out, was a Wigan official. He didn't want to get me into trouble – union players could still get banned for flirting with the thirteen-man game then – hence the smokescreen. I fitted the bill of a rugby league forward perfectly, he said. I was the right height, I could handle the ball and I could run. Had I ever thought of switching? Soon after, I got a call from Jack Robinson, the Wigan chairman.

By then I had spoken to Mark Evans, my coach at Saracens. I was just starting to get involved with England. A full cap did not seem out of the question. There was also the chance of union going professional. Money, though, wasn't the issue. If I was going to do it, it would have been because I wanted to. I never asked what terms Wigan were offering.

The biggest factor was that I had played union all my life. I knew what it was about, how I played, how I ranked, how I needed to improve to win a cap, which had suddenly become very appealing when I realised it could be done. So I said no. A few weeks later, Saracens travelled up north on the train for a game. I got plenty of ribbing from the guys when we passed through Wigan. 'Is that your house, Hilda? Is that where you're going to live?'

As I say, I had already had a few approaches well before then, while still at school. Nowadays, promising players probably get watched from a very young age. It was a bit more haphazard in the amateur era. People would have been aware of me, though, as I progressed through representational rugby.

Richard Hill, the Bath and England scrum-half, had particular reasons for knowing me. I had supported Bath as a kid and remember my dad taking me up to a game at the Rec. Richard Hill had also visited Bishop Wordsworth School to run a coaching session after we reached the final of the *Daily Mail* Under-18 Cup. I had just played for England Under-18s and scored thirty-odd tries for the school that season. The local media took an interest, particularly since Ralph-Bowman had coached both of us. I still have an autograph from my name-sake. 'To the other Richard Hill,' it says.

Earlier, Bath had sent Dave Egerton to my school to have a chat with me when I was seventeen or eighteen. I was invited to a training session run by Jack Rowell at Lambridge. Afterwards, I spent ten minutes on the toilet, unable to breathe, let alone move. They asked me to write down my kit sizes, presuming that I would join. Who in their right mind, after all, would turn down the chance of playing for Bath?

Bristol – just over an hour away from Salisbury – had also been in contact. I got myself involved in some of their junior teams and played a few games. Then, when I was seventeen, I received a phone call on a Friday night. Bristol's first-team had double-booked themselves that weekend and was I available? I wasn't sure if I was old enough or big enough but I did not get the chance to decide either way. My schoolmaster spelt out the law. 'You will play for the school on Saturday,' he said.

Bath and Bristol, the two major powers in the region, would have been my first and second choice of clubs and it was a huge temptation to join up there and then. But by then I had become convinced that I should try to go on to further education, regardless of how bright – or dim – I might be. Rugby was an amateur game. I had to think about my long-term future.

Bath could not offer me any help with my education, so I ruled them out. And anyway, even I was intelligent enough to work out that my playing opportunities would be limited. At that stage Bath had Ben Clarke, Steve Ojomoh and Andy Robinson, all England players, in the back row. It wasn't as if they were in desperate need of some skinny little runt from the sticks.

Bristol, meanwhile, were throwing their net wide in search of new players and were more pro-active in trying to convince me to go there. Dave Coveney, a friend from my Salisbury days, was playing at the club. They had put together a formidable invitational side and I was offered the chance to play for them. As a pretty naïve youngster, I was hugely impressed when their team bus did a detour to pick me up in Salisbury. On top of that, the bus had tables and lampshades. This was state-of-the-art stuff. You didn't get tables and lampshades with Salisbury.

The sticking point, however, remained my education. Bristol said they could get me on an environmental quality and resource management course but that didn't appeal – what does that qualify you for? There were a few people at Bristol who were disappointed that I didn't sign. Their coach, Rob Cunningham, advised me not to go to a London club. 'You will just get lost there,' he said. A few years later Rob moved from Bristol to Saracens. By then I was well on my way to full England honours. 'What are you doing here?' I said to him. 'It's a big place, London. Mind you don't get lost.'

First, though, I had to finish my A levels. Somehow I got through the retakes. I was doing some labouring work when I heard the good news. Perhaps I would have had to continue in that line of work if I hadn't passed. But the grades were good enough for me to scrape into West London Institute (now Brunel University).

It hadn't been on my original list of colleges. I had played England Schools rugby with Paul Burke and our parents had become good friends. It was Paul's dad who suggested West London Institute – he knew the dean of students. Fortunately, there was a place available to study Sports Studies and Geography (initially, they had suggested that I do Sports

Studies and Computer Science but my computer expertise was limited to playing video games).

West London Institute had a fine reputation for sports but because of my late application, there was no room for me on the Osterley campus, which housed the sports students. I was redirected to the Twickenham campus instead, which was dominated by the performing arts. That first year, I shared my floor with a group of ballerinas. They used to do their stretching in the corridor outside my room.

The offers from rugby clubs continued as I began college. There was the chance of playing for Wasps' Under-21 side. Bath also kept tabs on me. I played against Bath University at some stage and Richard Hill – him again – turned up to watch. I was politely invited upstairs for a chat afterwards and again asked whether I would be interested in joining the club. Distance wasn't a problem – some Bath players were already commuting from London anyway. The likes of England internationals Ojomoh, Victor Ubogu and Adedayo Adebayo reportedly all travelled down in a limousine. Again, it was tempting but again, I decided to stay put.

In the end, I didn't join anybody during my first year. I had discussed the matter with the England Colts and Under-21 selectors and they told me not to rush. There weren't many eighteen- or nineteen-year-olds playing first-team rugby at the top level anyway – Daws, playing at centre at Northampton, may have been the exception – and I might have ended up in an Under-21 side or reserve side if I had opted for Wasps or Bath. Continuing with Salisbury seemed the wisest move. It was felt my game needed to become more physical. So why not continue turning out against the likes of Brixham, Torquay, and teams from the Forest of Dean?

Anyway, I've never been one to chop and change ('conservative with a small c and risk averse,' according to Don). I loved playing for Salisbury at the weekend, so I continued doing just that, whenever there was no clash with college games. I would stand out on the A316 on Saturday mornings, waiting for a red sports car – owned by a team-mate who worked in the City – to pick me up.

I began college life, I suppose, as a rugby player who studied rather than as a student who played rugby. My degree work seemed a lot easier than my A levels, probably because I was studying something I enjoyed, but the focus remained on my rugby, and on having fun. The two went hand in hand. In those amateur days there was no hint of the dedication that would be demanded later. Basically, I behaved like any other student. I was a reasonable drinker then – I've gone backwards since – and didn't seem to suffer too badly from hangovers.

Soon I was playing for English Universities, as well as England Students Under-21s, and also took part in the Under-21 Divisional Championship. My main target, however, was the England Under-21 side. In March 1993, in my second term, I made it. Still nineteen, I was selected to play against the French Armed Forces before going on tour to Australia. I was back in my favoured position at No. 8. Even better, my mate Marcus, who was studying in Wales, was also selected. Fittingly, we found out while playing pool at Salisbury rugby club.

Before my debut I roomed with a guy I barely knew – Lawrence Dallaglio. We made up the back row with Dips (a combination we would repeat at full international level a few years later, each of us in a different position). Lawrence, playing at openside, was high profile even then. Just a month previously, yet to turn twenty-one, he had played in England's shock win in the inaugural World Cup Sevens tournament at Murrayfield. Having barely trained together, they had beaten an Australian side including Michael Lynagh and David Campese in the final. That success put Lawrence in a different bracket from the rest of the squad. He didn't make a huge deal out of it, though. I just remember him as a good team man and a guy you respected.

My breakthrough came on the tour to Australia. It was a daunting challenge. England simply did not win Down Under. There was an aura surrounding southern hemisphere sides. It was also the longest tour I had ever been involved in, and the furthest I had been away from home. I'd never left Europe before.

It would be an eye-opener on quite a few levels. Fairly early on in the tour, we stayed at Australia's famed Institute of Sport at Canberra. If we needed an insight into some of the reasons behind Australia's sporting success, we got it there in spades. The place left a huge impression on me. I had never experienced anything like it. The facilities were extraordinary; massive sports halls, full of weights and fitness equipment, experts on hand to help you, swimming pools, Astroturf pitches, hot and cold facilities…and so on, and so on. It was a million miles away from what I was used to.

The other wake-up call was provided by the athletes. We would roll into breakfast at eight or nine o'clock, at which point all the swimmers, who were sharing the same food hall, marched in for their second breakfasts. They had already done one training session, while we, England's finest athletes, had just fallen out of bed and were moaning about what training we might be put through that morning. In all but name, they were professional sportsmen, while we were more like students on a jolly.

We did OK in the end, though.

We lost a few early games, but the key to the tour, of course, was the match against our Australian counterparts. There was plenty of competition for the back row places, but I managed to grab a try in the penultimate game against New South Wales

Country to book my berth. The game was played in Sydney, as a curtain-raiser before a full international between Australia and South Africa, so there was a big crowd.

That game was the making of Kyran Bracken, but boy did I help him to look good! Kyran was a bit of a glamour boy. He had joined the tour after being flown in from Canada, where he had been playing for England A, after Marcus had dislocated his shoulder. Anyway, I made a couple of glaring mistakes when we were going for pushover tries. I lost control of the ball, it squirted out and Kyran ended up scoring. He ended up with two tries and, against the odds, we pulled off a historic 22–12 win. Not only that, but we scored three tries without reply. Any hopes I had of keeping my errors quiet were dashed by Kyran's inability to keep his mouth shut, but it was still a great, great day.

Look back at the photographs of that squad and you see a large number of guys who went on to have highly successful careers. Five of us – Lawrence (with hair), Will Greenwood, Mike Catt, Kyran and myself – were to feature in the 2003 World Cup final. I can barely recognise myself, looking at that 1993 picture – I was so skinny. Then there was John Sleightholme, Austin Healey and Stimpson, Shaw, Dips and Mark Reagan, as well as the likes of Burke, Mark Mapletoft and Darren Crompton.

The only other thing to stay with me from that tour was one of my many nicknames – Hilda. I have no idea – honestly – what I did to deserve it, or why it stuck.

Don Rutherford, the RFU technical coach, later sent out a letter which underlined how important our victory had been. 'You have certainly dented the confidence of the Australians,' he wrote. 'Hopefully those who are now finished with the Under-21 group will move on to even higher honours.'

Ironically, though, I would learn later that I had been

considered something of a disappointment during 1992–93. I thought – and still think – that I had done OK but apparently I had been earmarked to make a major splash at Under-21 level after my success with the Colts. The selectors did not feel I had lived up to that billing. It would take me another year to start satisfying them.

Soon after returning to England, I took the plunge and joined Saracens, in time for the 1993–94 season. In a way, it was an obvious choice. It was just up the road, for a start and the club already had close links with the West London Institute. At any one time we might have had up to a dozen college players there, turning out for the first or second teams or development squad. Andy Lee, a fellow student, was playing fly-half for Saracens at the time and he greatly influenced my decision, especially since we shared digs in my second year at college.

The major attraction, though, was that Saracens had just been relegated, prompting a clear-out of players. The back row in particular had been badly hit. Chris Tarbuck, whose selection ahead of me meant I had to play second row when I first arrived at West London Institute, headed off for Leicester. Eric Peters went to Bath while Justin Cassell, another member of the 1993 World Cup Sevens team, settled for Harlequins. I, meanwhile, wanted to play first-team rugby. Here was the perfect opportunity.

It may sound like I wasn't being very ambitious. Other guys, like Lawrence, aimed high by trying their luck at bigger, more fashionable clubs. He went to Wasps and that worked for him. But I'd argue that going to Saracens worked just as well for me.

First there was a pre-season trial to get through, against Wasps at Sudbury. I was accompanied by two of the ugliest cheerleaders you will ever see, Don and Mark Piper. As my former Salisbury minders, perhaps they felt they were still responsible for me. Saracens also got them a free meal ticket each, so they were happy. I wasn't going to say no. Don, after all, had a car, even if he had no sense of direction outside Salisbury.

As for the game, I remember that Dean Ryan, Wasps' rugged back rower, turned out, as well as Jeff Probyn. I think Rob Andrew and Steve Bates were there and there were some other established top-flight players as well. Just about the only guy I knew personally was Dips. I managed to get in a tackle on Probyn and things went OK generally. The hits were certainly harder, but I just concentrated on doing the basics right. Don and Pipes sat there laughing afterwards – they just couldn't get their heads around the fact that I, that skinny little kid from a few years before, was now mixing it with England internationals. Don would tell me that he felt exactly the same way when I got my first full England cap. When he saw my name on the team sheet on Ceefax he thought it was a mistake.

We drove back to Salisbury and had a few drinks together, wondering if they would invite me back. I might have just played against Australia but the trial still seemed like a major event – it was, in effect, the first time that I had come up against an adult, top-level team.

Soon I got a phone call, inviting me on a Saracens pre-season tour to Scotland, but I was busy doing a bit of summer labouring work to subsidise my college bar bills and decided that I couldn't afford a week away. Fortunately my parents, as supportive as ever, said they would help out.

My Saracens career had begun. And it began, yet again, with my attitude being questioned.

On the pitch that tour, I held my own. I even got told off, for the first and only time in my life, for scrummaging too hard by one of the locks, Mark Langley. I got selected for a Wednesday night game against Gala YM and scored a couple of tries, one from the halfway line after picking up from the base of the scrum. Barry Crawley, the first-choice No. 8, was unimpressed. 'We'll wait and see what he's like when it gets serious,' he said. 'He might need taking down a peg or two.'

And that is exactly what happened when the 1993–94 season started. Not for the first time, my natural reserve let me down. John Davies, the head coach, sat me down for a chat shortly before our first league game against Moseley. Mike Teague, he told me, the former England international and Lion, would be in their back row.

'What will you do if he picks up the ball from the base of the scrum and heads towards you?' he asked.

'Hopefully I'll get in a good position to tackle him,' I replied.

Wrong answer.

Apparently I should have said something along the lines of: 'I'll get right up in his face and smash him backwards.' Perhaps I should have added that I would have danced on his head for good measure and told him not to mess with the new kid on the block. Davies certainly wanted something more upbeat to convince him that I was ready. I suppose it took him a while to realise that I'm not that upbeat a character. To be honest, if you asked me the same question today, you'd get the same reply.

Two years later, I would be declared an unsuitable candidate to play for England. Perhaps, if that assessment had been taken more seriously, I really could have ended up playing with Andy at Wigan.

6

A SARACEN THROUGH AND THROUGH

Late October 2005. I've just been booked in for another opera-tion next month. Actually, I've been booked in for two, one on my left knee, and one on my left shoulder. It's all going to be done in the same session and under the same anaesthetic. I can't help picturing a team of surgeons at the top end of the operating table and another lot working away at the bottom. I'd probably find it quite comical if I were conscious.

I'm pretty relaxed about the news, to be honest. It was always likely that there would be some tidying up to do in my knee, even though Fares hadn't wanted it to happen this soon. Basically, the joint started making a scrunching sound, which got me wondering what the hell was going on in there. I was also getting an odd sensation, as if something was flicking or catching inside. I might not have made a fuss about it, but as Claire and I were walking down the street, I suddenly lost all power in my left leg. It just buckled. There was no pain, it just stopped working for a while, which was a bit disconcerting. I gather it could have been caused by a bit of loose cartilage or debris coming into contact with a muscle.

As for the shoulder, well that's been a long-term problem, which has caused me a bit of pain and restricted movement for

57

the past few years. You just live with it. Whenever it has cropped up before, an injection has usually sorted it out. Using the crutches probably set it off again but this time it seemed a bit more severe. I was driving back from a charity event and I couldn't stretch over to change a CD without dipping my shoulder below the dashboard. I had a word with Fares about it and he referred me to a specialist.

The good news, though, is that the pre-op scans at Barnet Hospital were pretty positive. Fares is very pleased. When I was injured, the two bones inside the joint smashed into each other as the cruciate ligament gave way and got badly dented. Fares had to drill into the damaged area during the initial operation to encourage the bone surfaces to regenerate and that's worked well. Unfortunately the x-ray suggested a screw head might be poking up slightly, which could be causing the flicking sensation. The options are to push it back in, shave it down or remove it altogether. But Fares wants to wait until next month, to give the graft more time to fix itself.

As for the shoulder problem, that's being caused by my muscles, according to the specialist. Apparently they're too big for my skeletal frame. I was quite flattered with that diagnosis – at least it shows I've taken my training seriously over the years. The result, though, is that a tendon has become trapped between the muscle and shoulder bone and has become inflamed. He says the solution is to shave away a bit of bone at the end of the shoulder to give more room for the muscle.

So I'm reassured – things aren't so bad after all. I go back under the knife on Bonfire Night. Before that, Claire and I have decided to squeeze in a holiday. We've always had problems organising our time off together – rugby player and teacher holidays are not exactly compatible – but it's become almost impossible recently. We had planned a break after the Lions tour to New Zealand but that obviously had to be shelved. You could say my left knee has become the third element in our relationship. We're planning to fly out to Cyprus on 23 October – I should have just enough time to watch Saracens' home match against Biarritz in the Heineken Cup before dashing to Gatwick.

The break will be good. It's been a busy time recently. Take last week. First there was the gym work. I've been doing quite a bit on the bike, which kills two birds with one stone by keeping me aerobically fit and working on the flexibility of my knee. Then there's upper body weights and full leg weights – leaning against a gym wall, doing squats with a barbell, leg presses, that sort of thing. I probably started leg pressing with just 40kg but now I'm over 200. That will be 400 when I'm fully fit. It's a bit nerve wracking at the start, but the machines have safety bars on them. I'm also working on fully extending my leg. It's been stuck at about five degrees off straight. At one point we got it down to three and a half, but it's popped back up to five again.

I also had to go up to Leeds to attend a function organised by an Alzheimer's charity – my godmother suffered from the condition – then saw the shoulder specialist, attended a benefit meeting and went to my Auntie Liz's funeral in Cambridge. On Saturday I went to a vice-president's lunch at Saracens before watching the club's amateur first XV play, then on Sunday, game day, I had box duties – visiting corporate boxes before and after the game, talking to people, signing things until my hand fell off.

On top of all that, I saw a careers advisor. Purely theoretical, of course. These advisors visit a lot of Premiership clubs, talking to players, telling them about setting up small businesses and that sort of thing. Maybe at thirty-two it's about time I started thinking about what else I could do, but for now I can't imagine life without rugby. And let's be honest, I'm not exactly used to making major decisions. I left college, became a professional rugby player and have been riding the same wave ever since. At some stage I'm going to have to try and switch to another one. I think I'll put it off for a while.

For now, my only focus is getting fit again. Have I got a lot more rugby to play? I don't know. Cruelly, it's not worked out that way recently. I have always wanted to battle on for as long as I could. I'd love to be still enjoying it and being competitive until I'm thirty-five, although the injury must have put a big dent in that. People keep asking me whether I think I'll ever play for England again. I would love to, of course, but I don't think like that. I can't afford to. It may not be a possibility. It's like the people who want to know what day you are going to start walking again, what day you are going to run, what day you are going to tackle. You make those decisions as you go along. This is a massive period for me, but not in terms of deadlines. If you start putting dates on things, it can become demoralising.

Basically, though, I'm optimistic about the future. If I weren't I'd have checked up on my player's insurance policies by now. If injury ends my career, I'm sure I will get some compensation out of it, but I haven't given that side of things a thought.

One thing I do know for sure is that, when I do quit, I'd like to stay involved with Saracens. Coaching is not on the agenda at the moment, although things could change. I'm not sure I'd want to coach people I had played with, it would feel strange. I'm hoping there will be some sort of role at the club. We've had preliminary discussions about it. I've been here a fair few years now and I think I have something to offer. People associate my face, however battered it may be, with Saracens.

(* (* (*

I joined the club blind, you could say.

When I signed my registration papers, I didn't even know where Saracens played. I hadn't bothered to carry out a recce. I had watched them play Bath in a cup game on television once and thought it looked a pretty good stadium, but I got a bit of a surprise when I turned up for my first evening training session with a bunch of West London Institute students. We drove round the M25 and down the A111 through Cockfosters when the guys started pointing and saying: 'There's the ground.' All you could see was a single shabby concrete stand on the side of a muddy pitch. It turned out the 'stadium' that I had seen on TV had consisted of temporary stands, put up especially for the occasion. To be honest, the facilities at Salisbury were probably better.

Actually, the two clubs had the same sort of feel to them.

Saracens had been founded in 1876 by a group of old boys from the Philological School in Marylebone. They began at Primrose Hill and changed grounds five times in twenty years before eventually settling on Bramley Road, in Southgate in the north of London. When I arrived, Saracens had a bit of a reputation as a 'feeder club' who were good at nurturing talent but poor at retaining it. Invariably, their best players were poached by bigger rivals like Leicester, Bath, Wasps or Harlequins. At the end of the 1980s the team had been promoted, only for future England internationals Jason Leonard, Dean Ryan and Ben Clarke to be lured away. John Buckton, though, who won a couple of England caps at centre, chose to stay.

Not that I was much of a historian when I trundled out for that first training session. All I knew was that the pitch – part of a council-owned park and lying next to a cricket square guarded by a manic-looking groundsman – was pretty boggy. We seemed to be sharing it with a group of grumpy pensioners who were defiantly walking their dogs. The floodlights were along a couple of sides of our training pitch. The only other fixture was a concrete-pillar fence, the sole defence against rugby balls sailing into the road. As for the showers, I seem to remember they were cold.

I took to the place immediately.

Most of all, though, I took to the guys. They were very serious about their rugby but they did not bother with airs or graces. It was their club – a players' club, a family club. On match days, if you wanted to go to the gents, you queued up with the spectators just like everyone else. If they were home fans they would probably let you go first, to make sure you were in time for the kickoff. If they were away fans they probably wouldn't. There were no turnstiles, just ropes around that bit of the park, and there were no match tickets. You gained admittance by buying a programme.

Saracens' home matches attracted around 1,000 people. Afterwards, there was a bar in the clubhouse. Theoretically, there was one section for the club committee, one for the players, and one for the spectators, but it wasn't policed and people just mingled. At the time, I was still a student, so the free barrel of bitter and lager after games was a real treat. Who knows, if I had known about the hospitality, I might have joined earlier. All I remember wanting to do after games at Bramley Road was hang around and talk. I was never in a hurry to get away.

If you had told me then, at the start of the 1993–94 season, that within a few years the club would be regularly attracting more than 10,000 spectators – the record attendance almost reached 20,000 – and would be fielding some of the world's top players, including the most-capped international of all time, the world's top point-scorer in Test rugby and a World Cup-winning captain, I would have presumed your drink had been spiked (and I wouldn't have put it past any of the players to do it).

It had not taken me long to break into the first team – in fact, it happened much faster than I had expected – although first I was asked to switch positions. Coaches Evans and Davies said I should move to 7 if I wanted to make it to the top level. Jack Rowell was in charge of England at the time and he believed in big back rows. I was 6ft 2½in – a good two inches shorter than the likes of Lawrence and my new Saracens team-mate Dips – and I wasn't exactly bulging with muscle either. My lack of height and power would not matter at openside, but it would at 6 or 8. Looking back, it was an obvious decision. Playing at 7 suited me. I wasn't a particularly physical player, I wasn't much of a line-out jumper and I liked running with the ball.

My decision to join Saracens soon paid off. So did my partnership with Dips. We played together for England Under-21s against Ireland at Gateshead at the start of the season, then, a week later, I made my club debut in an 11–9 away win at Otley.

That game was followed by yet another initiation ceremony. The second XV had greeted me by taking me out to the pub and secretly slipping a shot of vodka into each pint of beer I drank throughout the evening. The first team simply made me stand up in the middle of the room and down half a pint of Guinness laced with half a pint of spirits. I recovered enough, however, to earn some half-decent mentions in match reports. By December we were third in the table after winning at London Scottish. Doug Ibbotson wrote in the *Daily Telegraph*: 'When success visits Saracens it invariably signals the onset of an open season for poachers... Accordingly, there was a deal of nonchalant whistling and stretching among Saracens' affable statesmen when, at the Athletic Ground on Saturday, flanker Richard Hill, 20, highly mobile and built like a brick washhouse, scored his first try in senior rugby.' As I remember it, I was built like a tent pole but who am I to argue?

There were several other highlights to my season, including reaching the UAU (Universities Athletic Union) final with West London Institute, which we lost narrowly to Martin Corry's Northumbria, and, rather more bizarrely, making my Cambridge University debut. Cambridge had accepted an invitation to play in the Singapore Sevens in February only to discover that most of their players were tied up with exams. Their coach knew me – I had played with his son at college – and asked if I could stand in. Everyone else on the trip had been at Cambridge at some time or another, so I was the only fraud. The only shirt they had for me was a No. 9 shirt, which was a shade tight. I've still got it to this day. Richard Hill of Cambridge University – sounds good, that.

The biggest game of the season by far, however – indeed, the biggest game I had ever played in up to then, and by a wide margin – came in Saracens' Pilkington Cup quarter-final tie. We had beaten Rosslyn Park in the previous round and we drew Bath, the best side in the country and seeking an unprecedented third league and cup double.

The match drew a crowd of around 5,000 to Bramley Road and was televised. It was a huge event for Saracens. The team hadn't got so far in the competition for almost twenty years. Up went the temporary stands again, with extra seating squeezed in wherever possible. Bath turned up with eleven internationals and a mind-boggling pack consisting of Dave Hilton, Graham Dawe, Victor Ubogu, Ollie Redman, Andy Reed and a back row of John Hall, Andy Robinson and Steve Ojomoh.

We certainly weren't in awe of them, though. For us, it was the ultimate chance to pit ourselves against the best. We went down 23–6 but were far from disgraced. Indeed, we must have got stuck into them because Barry Crawley had to come on four times as a blood replacement; the fans greeting him with huge cheers each time he appeared. The press were pretty generous, saying that we had played some of the better rugby. One of our best chances fell to me but I didn't quite have the legs to outrun Mike Catt after a 50-metre dash.

The season ended in disappointment, Saracens just missing out on promotion but, to be honest, we were nowhere near ready for the top flight. Things couldn't have gone much better for me, though. I had gambled on a less fashionable club and got more than my fair share of headlines because of it. I had continued playing for England Under-21s and ended the season as runner-up behind Dips in the RFU's Young Player of the Year poll. Not bad, I thought, for a fat boy. When Saracens had carried out their end-of-season fitness tests, it turned out that I was carrying 23 per cent fat. Nowadays I would expect to be nearer 15 per cent. I spent that summer trying to cut down on pizzas, biscuits and beer while pounding the playing fields in Salisbury.

There was another special event that year – I started going out with Claire. We were doing the same course and got serious at the end of my second year at college. She was sports mad, which helped. Was it love at first sight? I'm not sure about that. She claims she was tipsy at the time. I tell her I must have been completely legless.

If my first season at Saracens was good, then my second one was even better. I can't say that there was one single reason why I stayed at the club throughout my career, but that 1994–95 season had a lot to do with it.

It wasn't just that we won promotion. More importantly, we were a very happy squad. There were all sorts – teachers and actuaries, builders and policemen, salesmen, lawyers and students. We came from all over, from London and Southend, Cambridge and Loughborough (Dips used to commute down from university) and even Wales. I can remember every player from that first-team squad, which is more than I can say for some of the teams I played for. We weren't just a club, we were a bunch of mates and we stuck together for two or three years. Our fancy dress parties, in particular, became legendary. The squad only began to disband when the game turned professional.

Perhaps I might have considered leaving if we had not been promoted that season, but the situation never arose. I had joined Sarries because I thought being there would help my career, but I rapidly developed a great affection for the place. I have never seriously looked at joining anyone else. I have been spoken to by other clubs, but the furthest it has ever gone is two phone calls, and that was with Wigan. I have never followed up an offer, and never got down to talking money. I've never felt the need.

Buckton had been the main man at the club for years, not only because he had played for England, but also because he had decided against moving on to a more fashionable outfit. He was hugely loyal and a lovely guy. A tall, gangly centre with a good pair of hands, he seemed able to glide through holes in defences. He always performed and was universally popular. To this day he turns out for his own team, the John Buckton XV, against our veterans' side.

Then there was the skipper and scrum-half Brian Davies, another man with an unquestionable love for the club. Several times a week, regular as clockwork, he would drive along the M4 from Barry in the south of Wales, to London, to take part in training sessions and matches. The trek – it must have been around 300 miles – never seemed to bother him. He was another nice guy and someone who would give you advice whenever you asked for it.

He wasn't the only one commuting from Wales. John Green, a fellow back rower, also did it for a period. He would turn up for training just late enough to miss the warm-up. We would just be getting down to the nitty-gritty when Greeny would suddenly appear from nowhere, do two hamstring stretches and announce that he was ready. Some winter nights it would be freezing and he would stand there in his Neath shirt, cut off to the shoulders, and a pair of shorts when the rest of us were wrapped up in thermals. He was a hard boy, Greeny.

For commitment, however, nobody got close to Barry Crawley. There was no such thing as a lost cause for Barry and he proved it in no uncertain manner later that season by breaking his neck while playing against London Irish. He was a committed tackler but got it wrong for once. The physio persuaded him to go off but, Barry being Barry, he refused to take the shortest walk to the clubhouse because that would have held up play. He went to the nearest touchline instead and walked all the way around the pitch before getting changed. He said he felt fine in the bar afterwards but eventually someone got him to admit that, actually, his neck felt a bit sore. He was carted off to hospital and immediately put in traction. He wanted to play again but eventually accepted that he should quit. He would have been mad – but then he was mad – to play on. I think his dad had been paralysed with a neck injury after being knocked over by a freak wave in the sea.

Then there was Dips, a forward with ball skills to match any back and with whom I forged a decent partnership. As up-and-coming breakaway forwards, we hogged a few headlines in our first couple of seasons together, probably more than we deserved. Mind you, Gregg Botterman, our 'international' hooker, managed one or two of his own after somehow wangling himself onto the England bench for the Grand Slam decider against Scotland in 1995. The official reserve hooker had got injured while the other contenders were away on tour with England A. Gregg was the only option left, really. We all thought it was hilarious but were thankful that he did not actually get on the pitch, otherwise we would have had to listen to it for the rest of our lives. That said, Gregg has been known to bring up the subject occasionally.

The fans used to have a song for him, sung to the tune 'Bread of Heaven', which went something like: 'Nothing rhymes with/Nothing rhymes with/Nothing rhymes with Botterman/Nothing rhymes with Botterman.' Mine went to the tune of 'Robin Hood': 'Richard Hill, Richard Hill/Flanker in the scrum/Richard Hill, Richard Hill/Destroyer on the run/He's strong and he's tall [well, relatively speaking]/Can't get past him at all/Richard Hill, Richard Hill.'

Anyway, we won our first couple of games that season before losing away to Wakefield. That, though, sparked a winning run that lasted almost until the end of the season. We weren't putting teams to the sword, but we were certainly being clinical. We went top of the table in October when we beat Dick Greenwood's Waterloo 27–5. Dips and I cashed in on the publicity after our coach, Mark Evans, told the press: 'I would eventually like to see Diprose and Hill in the England back row with Ben Clarke. With Jason (Leonard), that would give me four of England's pack. I'd be happy with that.' It seemed a good joke more than anything. I was still an England Under-21 player and a full cap seemed miles away.

Approaching Christmas, we were four points clear at the top of the second division. That period was to see my rugby fortunes rocket. Everything happened so much quicker than I had expected. I was still a student and had not been looking further than having a solid season for the England Under-21s. Suddenly I was called up for the South and South West senior squad to play in the Divisional Championship. I hadn't even dreamt of playing at that level that season. It was a massive step up, a totally different world, even if a lot of the top players were missing. The team had won the title the previous season, with the likes of the other Richard Hill and Stuart Barnes as inspiration. I had gone along to the first training session presuming that I would be used as little more than a tackle bag.

We lost all our games, against London, the Midlands and the North but, despite playing in all three positions in the back row over the three games, which I found pretty daunting, I managed two tries first time out, and then that hat trick against the North which was to provoke Wigan's interest.

Before I could get my breath back, I was selected for Emerging England's squad to take on Canada in December. That was another big step, and then came another a month later. Claire was flicking through Teletext when she suddenly saw my name in the newly announced England A squad.

Her first reaction was to be annoyed that I hadn't told her and, ready for a fight, she set off to find me. She checked my usual haunts – the gym, the sports fields and the refectory – without success. As a very last resort, she went to the library, where I was making one of my rare appearances. (Claire, though, likes to say I was reading a comic rather than one of my course books.)

'Have you got something to tell me?' she said.

'No,' I replied.

'Are you going to tell me about England A?'

'What about England A?'

It may sound naïve, but getting picked came as a complete shock. Until then, I really hadn't actively thought that I was in contention for an international cap. I felt there were plenty of No. 7s who were ahead of me, people like Clarke, Ojomoh and Neil Back (who was the England A openside at the time), while Rory Jenkins of Harlequins and Derek Eves of Bristol were also big rivals. But as Clarke and Ojomoh were being tried out in other back row positions, it suddenly dawned on me that, in theory, I could be a single training session away from a full cap. 'Jeez,' I thought, 'the next step's the England team!'

That season, I sat on the bench and watched Backy buzz all over the field against Ireland and then France. In February, however, he was rested and I was given my England A debut, alongside Lawrence and Dips, against Italy at Gloucester. I celebrated with a try, set up by Sleightholme.

It was time to start getting serious.

Let's be honest, there was plenty of room for me to improve the way I approached the game. Rugby culture in the mid-nineties bore no comparison to what it has become. At the start of the decade, England teams had been meeting up for internationals on Wednesday and, not so long before that, it had been on Friday, the eve of the match. I suppose you could call it amateurish, but then that is exactly what we were – amateurs. We were fit and dedicated, but it has to be said that the pub played an important part in the sport at the time.

It wasn't just the players, though. The whole organisation could be pretty amateurish, too. England squads would meet up for weekend training sessions on a Saturday evening and train from Sunday morning until early afternoon. If you were in the senior team you would stay at the grandiose Petersham Hotel and train at Twickenham or the Bank of England ground. If not, you were at the nearby Richmond Hill Hotel and would head off to, say, St Mary's College. On arrival, it was possible for players to discover they had been belatedly dropped or promoted from one squad to another. They might even pass each other with their kit bags as they walked along the road, heading to the other hotel.

At one of my first squad meetings, I remember our manager Peter Rossborough getting us to play a letter game. He was discussing England A, and went on about A standing for ambition, attitude, application or whatever. Not everyone bought into this sort of thing, especially if it meant meetings dragging on and on. Steve Bates, the Wasps captain, stood up and said: 'R is for Roebuck, as in the pub, and that is where I am going if anybody cares to join me.' And pretty much everyone did.

I was no different. I certainly remember tip-toeing into the hotel room I was sharing with Martin 'Cozza' Corry at around six o'clock in the morning after a lengthy session and then getting up two hours later to train, having washed my teeth several times while trying to look as fresh and uncrumpled as possible. We lived it up, knowing that the senior team was behaving in exactly the same way a few hundred metres up the road. Half the time, the coaches came along as well. There are plenty of teetotallers in rugby union now, but I can't say I knew many back then.

I was heading for a reality check, however. Things were simply going too well for me.

At Saracens, we soon wrapped up the Second Division championship with a couple of games to spare. At college, West London Institute pulled off an outrageously lucky win in the British Universities Championship final. Swansea outscored us by four tries to one, had two more disallowed and hit the post with two kicks at goal but we still won 31–30, Andy Lee slotting over the winning points with the last kick of the game. (Later, Andy and I shared a house with Craig Yandell, a Saracens teammate. He had played for Swansea that day and would moan about how they had been robbed. We used to agree, and then slip the match tape into the recorder to remind him of all the details.)

I even got a game for the Barbarians against Cardiff that season. So a reversal in fortune was only to be expected, I suppose.

England A were due to fly out to South Africa to play Natal and I had expected to be selected for the squad behind Backy, but Rossborough phoned to tell me John Hall was being taken instead, to give him a chance to prove his fitness before the World Cup (he didn't make it). Me being me, I said fine, fine and fine during the appropriate pauses. I'm not one for public shows of emotions or letting people know what I'm feeling but, in retrospect, I wish I had asked a few questions and made it a bit more difficult for him. I felt I had taken my chances that season and played OK. You could say I was annoyed.

The consolation was my selection for the A tour of Australia and Fiji starting in May, but that was to prove an even greater disappointment. The coaches on that trip, indeed, came to the conclusion that I would not make it as an England player.

I was one of three opensides selected. Backy was heading for the 1995 World Cup, so I was up against Eves and Jenkins. Dips, Chris Sheasby and Cozza were also selected for the back row. Due to the make-up of the squad, I knew I'd be asked to play out of position at some stage. I wasn't very happy at the idea. I wasn't confident about playing at 6 or 8 at that stage and it didn't seem to me to be the ideal way to prepare for a Test match.

I had left home fully expecting to play against Australia A, but things went badly wrong when I was selected to play at blindside, rather than openside, against New South Wales Country. The pitch had been heavy before the start and rain hammered down throughout. I played badly, the team played badly and we lost.

I became convinced that I would not be selected to play Australia and I did something that I had never done before and have never done since. I went 'off tour'. You could say that I reverted to my student behaviour. I wasn't the only one. Towards the end of the tour, the training sessions concentrated exclusively on the first team. The result was that the rest of us were left to get on with things on our own. One session con- sisted of us being told to kick the ball to each other, which I couldn't see would help improve my skill levels as a flanker. It was clear that, with a week left, there would be no further opportunities to change the selectors' minds. So whenever the chance arose I would go out with the guys for a couple of drinks, invariably ending up in City Rowers bar in Brisbane.

We lost several games in a row and a crisis meeting was called. Unfortunately, the meeting could not have been worse timed. We had been on a boat trip around Sydney Harbour earlier that day and, for some mysterious reason, Darren Garforth had been put in charge. He was, of course, one of the squad's senior players, but he was better known for being a senior drinker. We arrived for the meeting rather worse for wear.

Rossborough was pretty angry. He sat us down in front of a whiteboard and started drawing a graph. 'You are up here for shagging and drinking, and down here for the standard of rugby you are playing,' he said. 'What do you want to be remembered for, being the best shaggers and drinkers or the best rugby players?' Fortunately nobody replied but I'm sure a few of the squad were thinking: 'Can't we be remembered for all three?'

In the end, the squad got things together just in time to beat Australia 27–19 in the most important game of the tour. Jenkins had a good game as I watched from the stand. The same team was selected to play Fiji immediately afterwards, going down 59–25 in sweltering, sauna-like conditions in Suva.

Looking back, I blame myself for not getting my mindset right. I allowed my disappointment to show during that tour, at least to myself. I had never been in that sort of situation before. On the way home, Rossborough and Keith Richardson gave me my end-of-tour report. All I remember them saying was a few nondescript things. Later on, though, I was told through the grapevine that they didn't think I had the mental capacity to play for England.

I was surprised. Obviously I would have preferred to have been told face to face. Then I might, just might have told them what I thought had gone wrong on the tour. On the other hand, I might just have said fine, fine and fine.

Back in England, I confided in my club coach. Evans was always very good if you wanted a heart-to-heart chat. I told him I had not enjoyed the tour and that it had gone badly. He pointed out, though, that I had not even dreamt of playing for England A at the start of the 1994–95 season. And we were about to embark on a new adventure, playing in the top division against the country's leading players and with the game on the brink of turning professional. It was just a case of looking forward and not back, he said, while making sure I proved Messrs Rossborough and Richardson wrong.

I had deferred my college finals because of the England A tour to Australia and by the time I got back my fellow students were already celebrating their results. I joined in the partying – it would have been rude not to – before sitting my own exams in September and coming out with a 2.2. By then, however, I had shelved any ideas of becoming a teacher or gym instructor. Saracens had put me in contact with Pinnacle Insurance, the club's main sponsors. The idea was to set me up in a part-time job which would be flexible enough to allow me to train and play for Saracens.

My brilliant new desk-bound career, however, was to last all of three and a half months.

7

REVOLUTION!

November 2005. Things are looking up. I've had a holiday with Claire at last, the surgery went well, it seems I'm on track for a March comeback and England manager Andy Robinson has been in touch. It seems 2005 is heading for a happy ending.

Andy texted me when we were in Cyprus. He wanted to know if I could carry out a little 'spying' for him by going to watch New Zealand play Wales at the Millennium Stadium, in the run-up to England's match against the All Blacks. I enjoy doing this sort of analysis, but unfortunately my operation was planned for the same day, so I had to say no. Still, it's nice to know that I haven't been completely forgotten. Some of the England physios have also been in touch. It's mainly out of personal interest really, since I have no connection to England at the moment, just to Saracens. But they said they would like to see the knee, which is always good – it means another assessment and some fresh opinions.

I took it really easy on holiday. In fact, I've probably never been so lazy before. Normally, I sneak off for a few runs or gym sessions when Claire's back is turned. If there's equipment around, I can't help myself sometimes. A few years back, when we were in Tunisia, Claire woke up early one morning and heard some familiar grunting and panting. Looking down from our balcony, she saw me running around on the small roundabout at the entrance of the hotel (it had been the only bit of grass I could find) while bemused guests and taxi drivers looked on.

This time, the idea was to limit myself to two bike sessions, although in the end I added an impromptu one with weights (after a German gentleman ignored my towel and jumped the queue for the bike). For the rest of the holiday I lounged by the pool, trying to stretch out my leg.

The surgery took place on 5 November, as planned. It was the usual protocol – being asked all the same old questions by the nurses, then meeting up with the same gang who have done my previous operations; Fares at the helm, Craig the anaesthetist, etc., etc. Rahul was the exception. He popped in to say hello and explain he would not be there this time, because of a school reunion.

Anyway, Fares was happy with what he found. He chipped off a bit of bone that was growing over one of the screw heads and then tightened up the screw. He tidied up the cartilage, removed some scar tissue – that allowed my knee to straighten again immediately – and that was that. The bone surfaces in the joint, he said, looked good, and March remains the target. If I get back by the start of the month, I'll be five weeks ahead of schedule, which will be great. Since then, the flicking sensation has gone and the knee has felt a lot freer, even if I'm still nowhere near to running on it. Nobody, though, has criticised my walking recently. The shoulder surgery also went well.

I went to a benefit do at Lord's cricket ground shortly afterwards for Rob Howley, the former Wales scrum-half and my former Lions team-mate. My arm was in a sling, which caused a lot of confusion. At least it meant I didn't have to talk about my knee for once. Perhaps I'll wear the sling more often, just to vary the conversation.

(★ (★ (★

At the start of the 1995–96 season, there was only one rugby conversation going on and it concerned professionalism. The International Rugby Board had accepted the inevitable after the 1995 World Cup and announced the end of amateurism. In England, though, the Rugby Football Union decided to impose a one-year moratorium, to see how things would pan out. It was a confusing time for everyone. Some players thought it would never work. 'Where's the money going to come from?' they asked. Others, with higher profiles, were being approached to play in a breakaway circus funded by the Australian media magnate Kerry Packer. Full internationals would reportedly earn up to £200,000 a year from Packer, with £100,000 for A internationals. I was a bit disappointed nobody approached me. Ultimately, the plan never got off the ground, but change was afoot.

Not that it seemed imminent from where I was sitting, in a corner of the Pinnacle Insurance offices and earning something like £7,500 a year for a two-and-a-half-day week (plus as much tea as I could drink).

I was more interested in getting in Sue and Linda's good books than Packer's at that point. If you could get the office secretaries on your side, I worked out, you were halfway there. I tried to keep everybody else happy – particularly when arriving late from an early-morning gym session or sprint training with Mike Yates, the father of Olympic middle distance runner Matthew – by making lots of rounds of tea and coffee. Claire and my family found it hard to imagine me working in an office, and perhaps I wasn't a natural – I didn't even have a job title for the first few months (Richard Hill, sales operations assistant, for the record) – but I did my best. They even let me loose on writing some point-of-sale leaflets and going on the odd client visit.

Despite all the talk of professionalism, the start of the season had seemed like any other. Most of the guys were still in full-time jobs, squeezing their rugby into their spare time. As a part-time employee I was one of the luckier ones, as was Dips. He worked for NCP car parks. He claimed to be some sort of management trainee but we pictured him in a toll booth, wearing a yellow Day-Glo jacket.

Our pre-season trip took us to Ireland, where we played Shannon. I was a bit worried at the time, because we had recruited a young guy called Kris Chesney. He was very, very big and very, very quick. Later he would become a Lomu-sized winger, then a useful lock. At the time, though, he was seen as a potential No. 7, making him my immediate rival. Fortunately, Kris was also very, very green. His tackling in those days was not the best. He tended to slow people rather than stop them, and was thus nicknamed 'the sleeping policeman'. He had plenty to learn in other departments too. If you had not played in a midweek tour game, you were invariably put through some 'dirt tracking', a tough physical session that left you with hands on knees and lungs on the floor. We all started groaning at the prospect one day, but Kris seemed delighted. 'Fantastic, I can't wait,' he kept saying. The coaches were hugely impressed with his attitude, but not for long. It turned out that our new arrival thought dirt tracking meant riding around on cross-country motorbikes.

The scale of our challenge in trying to survive in the top flight became immediately apparent. Our first game? Away at Leicester. My boyhood hero Dean Richards lined up against us, as did Backy. They strangled us in typical fashion and we returned to London beaten 31–3. That set the tone. Victories were in short supply. We also lost to Harlequins but, with the England coach Jack Rowell in the crowd, I at least came out on top in a private battle against Rory Jenkins that day, while Dips got the better of Chris Sheasby at No. 8. Jenkins and Sheasby had got ahead of me during the summer tour to Australia, so I was pretty motivated. I came off quietly pleased, even in defeat. 'Not so bad for a guy without the mental capacity to play for England,' I thought.

Reading the newspapers at the time, you got the impression that all hell was about to break loose, transforming the game overnight. The biggest story was that Rob Andrew, the England fly-half, was about to leave Wasps to become development director at Newcastle Gosforth, with a massive salary funded by Sir John Hall, the millionaire owner of Newcastle United Football Club.

The rumour mill soon began turning at Saracens, too. There were whispers of a mysterious sugar daddy. One day people would say Alan Sugar was about to buy us up, then Arsenal Football Club (to think that I could have been Thierry Henry's club-mate!). The marketing men at the club even had the idea of approaching the Sultan of Brunei for support after noting that his crest, like the Saracens one, sported a star and crescent. I'm not sure he's got back to them yet.

Amid all the wild speculation, we just kept on playing and, for the most part, losing. By October only Gloucester and West Hartlepool were below us. Then, on 6 November, a special general meeting was called at Bramley Road. We were all told to attend. It was important.

Those who managed to get a space in the packed old pavilion that Monday evening were told that a mystery benefactor was willing to invest £2 million in the club, as well as underwrite a £500,000 share issue. To put that in perspective, Saracens operated on an annual turnover of about £250,000 at the time.

For quite a few of the players and coaches, it was a no-brainer. No one really knew what figures would be involved, but here was a chance to be paid to play. Some clubs had handed out unofficial boot money and expenses in the past, there had been help with finding jobs and there had been perks like cars shared between players, but that was about it. For me personally, the timing could not have been better.

Some club members were suspicious, of course. We were, after all, a fairly cosy outfit, with a membership of around 1,500. Our ground was less than impressive, with its battered main stand housing a mere 300 people, but it was still home. Professionalism would change the club forever.

Despite their concerns, though, the meeting voted unanimously to accept the proposal. Newcastle was already being transformed, Richmond had found a backer and it was a case of join in or get left behind. It was only then, after the vote, that Nigel Wray's name was unveiled. The meeting spilled over into the bar, Wray was called with the news and he joined us. There was a buzz about the place as he entered and started shaking hands. I had never heard of him or his multi-million-pound property company, Burford Holdings Plc. Apparently he had once played rugby for Hampshire, as well as Old Millhillians. What he offered was financial clout, acumen and vision.

'For too long,' he told us, 'Saracens, despite their League One status, have been regarded as a feeder organisation for other high profile clubs…I want Saracens to be playing against Toulouse in the semi-final of the European Cup, under lights in front of a capacity crowd.'

It sounded exciting, of course, but it wasn't quite that simple. As players, we all realised that it would mean different things to each of us. Some guys had good jobs which would not allow them to sign up as professional rugby players. Some did not feel confident to gamble everything on a playing career that might not last. Others appreciated rugby as a part of their lives, but not all of it.

It was much easier for me, a couple of months out of college, to make a decision. But even for the younger players, there was one remaining question. We were bumping along at the bottom of the table, after all, and our new owner wasn't going to be satisfied with that. The professional era was due to start the following season and there was bound to be a clear-out of players. After the initial euphoria, most of us spent the rest of the evening wondering about our futures. I'm sure some guys who loved the club like a second home gradually began to realise that 6 November 1995 marked the end of their Saracens involvement.

Our debut as Saracens PLC came that very weekend, when we hosted Leicester, one of the powerhouses of Europe and a side we had never beaten before. They were vying for the championship with Bath. They rested a few of their top players – it was only Saracens, after all – but paid the price when Andy Lee put over a penalty to seal a famous 25–21 win and send around 6,000 home fans into a frenzy of delight.

Wray must have been equally delighted as he looked on from the stands, but it was arguably an even more special occasion for Dave Brain.

Dave was a 6ft 10in, 20st policeman from Cambridge who, hard as he tried, never got any further than the 2nd XV. A lovely, funny bloke, his only claim to fame had been to lose a tooth during an evening training session at a murky, boggy, Bramley Road. Reverting to type, he immediately lined everyone up in a row and ordered us to tip-toe across the pitch in an unsuccessful forensic search for the offending article.

When Leicester arrived that day, we had an injury crisis. Presumably the tea lady had forgotten her boots, because we had to call Dave up for his debut. After the game, he simply could not believe what he had experienced – there he was, having played a central role in one of the most monumental days in the club's history.

In a way, what happened next symbolised the change over from rugby the amateur pursuit to rugby the professional enterprise. Dave had a good job and was committed to it. He also realised that he had surpassed himself that day. 'I know my limitations, I know what standard I am,' he said in the bar afterwards. 'Beating Leicester! I could never get close to matching that again.' And with that he headed off on the mother of all benders, leaving the most committed of our drinkers far behind, and was never seen at the club again.

It's sad, but a lot of the old traditions soon died after that. I would have loved to have kept a lot of them – chilling out in the clubhouse with a keg or two after a game, for instance – but it would have been impossible, considering the demands of professionalism. When I look back, I've loved both sides of the game, the social side of my earlier years and the great achievements and hard work that came later. I was lucky to get both. Years later, I would get a reminder of what the amateur game had all been about, when we travelled to play Dinamo Bucharest in a European Cup game. Our kit had got lost in transit, so our hosts, despite being so hard up after the collapse of the game in Romania, pulled out all the stops for us. They managed to rustle up boots for our entire team – some of those boots had steel toe-caps – and they even got a dentist to make up mouth guards for us late in the evening. Their pitch had more weeds than grass. The game turned out to be an early 60-point victory.

Shortly after that Leicester game, Evans called me into the back office with Dips and slapped two contracts on the desk. We were, I suppose, the club's two most prominent young players. We were both playing representational rugby for England

and would be targeted by other clubs. Evans said he did not want to lose us – how did £25,000 a year as full-time players sound? He listed all the advantages of staying put, including the fact that we would probably hog all the press headlines. He needn't have worried. Dips sought out some professional advice for us – we ended up meeting this guy called John Partridge in a service station on the M1, which makes it sound all a bit dodgy – but we were both happy and settled at the club. Wray's backing could only improve our chances of playing for England. Anyway, to me, it sounded like a fortune. Crucially, the club agreed that it would regularly review our salaries, as the market rate for players became clear. It was not long before we were earning £40,000.

We weren't the country's first professional rugby union players – Mike Catt of Bath beat us to that honour – but we paved the way at Saracens. Technically, though, we could not be paid to play until the following season, so we were paid our salary for 'promotional work'. We were asked to rent a house together in Enfield, to try and establish a sense of community as the club went looking for new signings.

Things were a bit strange, during that transitional period. The rest of the squad had held onto their jobs to see which way the wind blew, so Dips and I had no one to train with for most of the week. We'd try to hold a skills session every Tuesday, but it often meant roping in people who were not part of the first-team squad to make up the numbers, which wasn't exactly ideal. Otherwise we spent our time in the gym, on our new Ergo rower (Dips's girlfriend, and now wife, seemed to use it a lot more than he did), messing about on our PlayStation or drinking tea and coffee while waiting for developments.

They weren't long in coming – although when they were announced they threatened to leave us in a highly embarrassing situation.

Wray's intervention may have inspired the team to beat Leicester but the effect was short-lived. Off the pitch, all the talk was about finding a bigger ground and strengthening the team. On it, though, we didn't win again until the end of March.

God knows what our next signing made of our wretched form, or indeed, of Bramley Road during an English winter. He didn't have the same excuse as me, of signing up without having seen the place. Having been approached by Wray, he agreed to come over and have a look at the club for himself. Michael Lynagh, he of a world-record 911 Test points and whose last international cap had come just six months before, was camouflaged under a big hat, wrapped up in a thick scarf and overcoat and smuggled in to watch a Saracens home game. Nobody spotted him. Fortunately, we must have put on a reasonable performance that day because the former Australia captain decided to play out the final years of his career at the club.

Even today, it seems an amazing catch. After Wray got involved, the coaches were asked to draw up a wish list of players and someone had thrown in Michael's name. The reaction had been something along the lines of: 'Dream on...'

The official announcement came in January 1996 at Café Flo, in the City of London. I went along with Dips. Michael's name had leaked out, yet it still seemed incredible. It was hard to see what could have attracted him. Big players were meant to go to the fashionable clubs. Everybody was absolutely thrilled. Well, nearly everybody. Andy Lee, the team's resident No. 10, managed to keep smiling. 'Lynagh? Doesn't he also play at centre?' he kept saying.

The Ireland flanker Eddie Halvey was also signed – he joined me and Dips in our Enfield digs – along with Wales lock Tony Copsey. Then came Philippe Sella who, prompted by

Lynagh's arrival, agreed to join the Saracens bandwagon from his home town club of Agen. It was another breathtaking sign-ing. Sella had played 111 times for France, a world record at the time.

I remember him walking in from the back of a press confer-ence, wearing a bowler hat and saying something like 'Eye ear Zarreez ar lewking fair a center?' (Apparently it was an attempt at Cockney – he must have been coached for hours, since he barely spoke a word of English at the time.) It was announced at the same time that the team would ground-share with Enfield Football Club the following season.

The only fly in the ointment, however, was the looming threat of relegation. We had a string of injuries and things were reaching crisis point when we lost at home to Harlequins in February, leaving us needing to win four of our last five games to avoid dropping straight back down to Division Two. The club management must have been sweating blood at the prospect of Lynagh and Sella playing against Wakefield and Blackheath the following season.

In the end, the rugby gods – or, rather, the RFU, with a lit-tle prompting from the English clubs – smiled on us. Our rele-gation fight went down to the very last game, only for us to lose 17–10 on a baking day in front of 12,000 baying West Countrymen at Gloucester, but by then a campaign was under way to expand the top division from ten clubs to twelve. As part of that campaign, it was argued that it would be unfair to enforce relegation, with clubs trying to plan and prepare for their first full professional season in 1996–97. The RFU agreed – having the likes of Sella and Lynagh (and Hill and Diprose, of course) playing in the top division would have been a big draw card for television and sponsors – and so Saracens were saved from the drop.

I would have stayed with the club anyway. Dips, who had

been with Sarries since school, felt the same way. There was a relegation exit clause in our contracts but, with the likes of Lynagh and Sella in the team, we felt sure that we would jump straight back up without significantly damaging our England chances. I was told later that Lynagh had not yet signed a Saracens contract but was determined to stand by his verbal agreement with Wray, even if it meant playing in Division Two. That sounds just like Michael.

Our narrow escape probably made us even more determined to bid goodbye to amateurism in time-honoured fashion. Our end-of-season tour took us to Bermuda and I have to say I knew about only half the people on the trip. It was open to everybody, and pretty much everybody came. Some of them were friends of players, others were friends of friends of players. Judging from their performances, some had not played much rugby or, at least, not for a long time. It was a good old-fashioned rugby trip, one that every club player would recognise. If anyone was disappointed, it was our hosts. They had hoped for Lynagh and Sella but they did not come. Instead they got Old Uncle Tony Copsey and all.

There were only a couple of rules, as I remember. No drinking beyond midnight on the day before a game, and training to be held each morning. Those rules became pretty flexible as the tour went on (i.e. lots of drinking beyond midnight and not much training in the mornings). Brian Davies started the revolt one evening by emptying his glass one minute past midnight. What was good enough for our captain was good enough for us – any small excuse.

Still, in between our moped races along the island's meandering roads and our acclimatisation sessions with the local brew – Dark and Stormy it was called, a mixture of light and dark rum with Coke – we acquitted ourselves pretty well, playing some half-decent rugby. We beat a select team first, with

Me with my little sister Fenella and elder brother Tim. I was two when Fenella was born, and my only comment was: 'Don't want that!' Things have improved since then.

My DIY hasn't got any better over the years.

Butter wouldn't melt…

An early rugby trophy in my childhood days in Salisbury.

An early shot of me in action for Salisbury. I made my senior debut for the club at sixteen and weighing barely 13st – and I would have stayed there if they had played at a higher level. (John Palmer)

The graduation team at West London Institute. Because of an England A tour, I had to celebrate passing my finals before I'd actually sat them. It would have been rude not to.

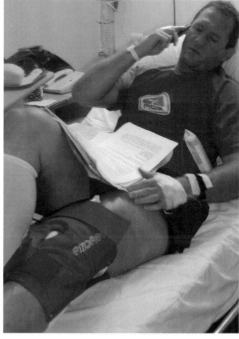

With Don Parsons on his wedding day in August 2005 – I'd not been the best best man, at least when it came to the stag do, and this picture shows why not.

With Fenella, Claire, Dad and Mum after winning the World Cup.

I proudly show off my MBE to Claire.

My gran on her 100th birthday, which she celebrated during the 2005 Lions tour.

Tony Diprose and I show we've got what it takes to make a success of the Saracens – amateur rugby traditions at their finest.

Nigel Wray welcomes Saracens' third professional recruit: someone called Michael Lynagh. Nigel invested £2 million in the club at the start of the professional era. Beforehand the club's annual turnover was just £250,000. (Colorsport)

31 August 1996, Saracens v Leicester – the first game of a new professional era, as I look to avoid the attentions of the Tigers defence, including Dean Richards, one of my rugby heroes. (Colorsport)

Partners in crime, Dips and I keep a watchful eye on the Sale scrum.

oving in to stop Andre Joubert during the first Lions Test against South Africa at Cape Town, hich we won 25–16 to show we were no pussycats. (Colorsport)

aul Wallace and I celebrate winning the second Test, and thus the series, in Durban; he was ot the only one to celebrate in full style. (Colorsport)

Battling with Daniel Herbert for a high ball during the first Lions Test in Australia in 2001 – all that lineout practice put to good use. (Getty Images)

Martin Johnson, the best captain I ever played for, prepares to offload during the second Test. A few seconds later I was caught by Nathan Grey's elbow, and my tour was over. (Colorsport)

Just a few minutes into the first Lions Test in New Zealand, and I hobble off the pitch with cruciate ligament damage. Since then I have been battling to play again. (Getty Images) everyone in the squad being subbed on at some point. Then there was a match against a club side, before the 'international' against Bermuda. They put on a great beach party for us before that game, offering us beers and rum all night only for us to realise late on that they were sticking to soft drinks. Still, by the next afternoon we had sobered up and managed to win again to cap one of the great Saracens trips.

I suppose we were a bit irresponsible at times. There was Dan Zaltzman, our lock, being stopped on his bike by the police for wearing a paper bag on his head (we had all been assigned a moped and helmet each, but one of the helmets got lost somewhere along the line so the last man out of the night-club each night had to improvise), and me, rather worse for wear, paying a passing tramp to kick-start my moped outside one of the nightclubs as I tried to find my way home. Handcuffing the Botterman brothers together probably wasn't too sensible either, not when they were on their mopeds any-way. Mind you, they crashed only once.

That's the sort of thing amateur rugby players get up to. Now it was time to be professional.

The 1996–97 season would be a landmark campaign for me. It was as if everything suddenly began to fall into place. Within twelve months I would be transformed into an England player, a winner of a Triple Crown, and a British Lion.

The revolution at Saracens clearly played a major part in my own personal revolution. The recruiting had continued during the off season so that, when we reconvened, our ranks had been strengthened further by Ireland internationals Paul and Richard Wallace and Paddy Johns, while Kyran Bracken and Roberto Grau of Argentina were on their way. From a personal point of view, I was also delighted to see my old friend Marcus join us from Bath, even if he found Kyran standing in his way again.

The sudden changes were difficult to take in at times – indeed, it may have taken us an entire season to come to terms with them. From being an unfashionable club, Saracens had suddenly become the team to watch. Lynagh and Sella, of course, were central to that. People may have suspected at first that they were little more than PR signings, both past their best and in search of one last lucrative pay packet. That may happen occasionally but, in my experience, most players who come to England with an international background retain a massive pride in their performance. Michael and Philippe certainly did. As a pair, they were completely different characters.

Michael, for all his achievements, shied away from the limelight. He was a world icon but, once off the pitch, preferred a quiet life. I could relate to that. I remember the squad going to the Sports Café on Haymarket for a couple of drinks soon after his arrival. He began as the centre of attention but I noticed that he soon drifted off towards the corner. That's where he felt comfortable. He was never rude to anyone who approached him, but he did not seek out attention. He was a top bloke.

He was not at his best, that first season, largely because of injury. The following year, though, he was brilliant, dictating the pace of games and orchestrating our play. He was a good playmaker and an outstanding kicker.

Philippe, in contrast, was the life and soul of the party, even when he barely understood what was being said. His character shone through from the very start, as we headed up to Scotland for our pre-season tour. We stopped off at a hotel in Newcastle, where Philippe was ordered to sing 'La Marseillaise' in the bar. He belted it out without a care in the world. Michael was a lot less comfortable and forgot half the words to 'Waltzing Matilda'.

Then, in Stirling, Philippe was dressed up in a beret and a string of onions placed around his neck. He was given a map of Aberdeen and, on a particular command which was repeated all evening, he would have to approach one of the locals and ask for directions back to France while pointing at his map. He simply loved it. I can still remember him continuing with the gag until the early hours. '*Excusez-moi*, Ah am lust, culd u pleeze elp me,' he would say, to the bemused locals.

Basically, he was a club man, a player's player who enjoyed the group ethos. He was also a great signing. You just had to marvel at his enthusiasm on the pitch, as well as off it. Watch a video of Philippe – he puts in a big tackle and is straight back on his feet to make the next one. He punched above his weight when he tackled too, picking people right off the ground. Fortunately, I never experienced it, I just admired it.

I don't think Michael would mind me saying that tackling wasn't his strongest suit, although he and I never had any problems defending the channel between us at Saracens. I'm still not sure how we got away with it. But he knew when he had to make a statement. He was tested in his very first training session at Bramley Road, when he was paired in a tackling session with one of our hookers, Charlie Olney. Charlie was well built, enjoyed his weight training and was mobile. He lined Michael up and decided to go route one. Michael didn't exactly knock him backwards but he got him down.

Considering our newly acquired wealth and star status, it was not surprising that a lot was expected of us. That expectation only increased after our opening game of the season when we saw off Leicester at our new Southbury Road home in Enfield. Before kick-off, the new era began with dancing girls, people dressed up as cartoon characters, people on stilts and even a jazz band. In the old days at Bramley Road, the warm-up act had consisted of an evil-smelling burger van and a bunch of grumpy programme sellers. It was a whole new world. More importantly, we fielded seven internationals that day, more than our opponents. A crowd of around 6,000, a Saracens record, saw us win 25–23, with Michael kicking seventeen points. We even had the luxury of allowing them to score two late tries before running down the clock with a series of five-metre scrums on their line, a tactic which Leicester themselves had employed for years.

Sadly, however, we were unable to build on that start. Our form was never much better than erratic. Perhaps it was unrealistic to expect immediate success. We had some serious players but it took time to gel.

Our coaching staff also had to get used to the new Saracens. Suddenly Evans and Rob Cunningham found themselves in charge of a much larger and more powerful squad. Relationships had to be established. I still remember a rather comical situation involving Tim Wright, one of our assistant coaches, suggesting one afternoon that Michael might like to adjust his kicking technique. Tim was a great guy who had come through from grass-roots rugby and he was a good coach, but you couldn't help wanting to burst out laughing. Michael, ever the diplomat, handled the situation perfectly, apparently listening respectfully and at no stage referring to the world record 911 points he had scored for the Wallabies in seventy-odd Test matches. As I remember, he did not change his kicking too radically, despite Tim's input.

We were a shade unlucky with injuries as well. Crucially, Michael damaged his shoulder in our second game against Wasps and struggled to regain his form. He also grew frustrated with our highly structured game plan, which may have suited players of a certain standard, but not a guy of his talent. He was criticised once for attacking down the blindside rather than following the script and going open, to which he responded bitterly: 'You are asking me to play with my eyes shut.' You had to sympathise with him.

I, however, was gaining on all fronts. Playing in the First Division the previous season had given me confidence that I could play at the top level. Granted, we had nearly gone down, but I had not been disgraced whenever I had come up against potential England rivals. Now, I was benefiting from playing with Michael and Philippe. You learnt just by watching them prepare for a game, and how they responded afterwards. Philippe was a great one for visualising matches and reviewing his performance afterwards. He was also perfect to play off in midfield, since he could offload the ball off either shoulder with such precision. All I had to do was break fast and get up to him as he went into contact. Michael was also a good distributor, and much better than many people realised.

The other thing that played into my hands was the great debate raging over England's No. 7 position. Most of us had expected Dips to be the first in line for an international call-up. He was a highly successful captain of England A, and was now also Saracens' skipper. But finding a new openside flanker seemed to be the priority. England had been seeking a long-term replacement for Peter Winterbottom since his retirement in 1993. Ben Clarke made a go of it for a while, before five or six other guys were given run-outs. For some people, Backy was the outstanding candidate, but Geoff Cook and his successor as England coach, Jack Rowell, felt he was too small. It was an era when big was beautiful, even if Rowell aspired to play a more open style of rugby.

That autumn, Lawrence was the man in possession, in a back row completed by Tim Rodber and Chris Sheasby. They swept Italy aside in November, but then struggled to see off Argentina 20–18 and were jeered off the pitch. The press began trawling through fresh candidates and my name cropped up. Ironically, though, my cause was best helped by a New Zealander, even if he did not know he was doing it at the time.

Shortly before the autumn internationals, England had hosted the New Zealand Barbarians at Twickenham and gone down 34–19. John Hart, their coach, said our back row was out of kilter. 'Size is OK but speed, skill and strength are the critical elements in the modern game. The skill and speed factor is the combination you have to get right,' he said. I can't deny that I was pretty pleased to read those comments. Privately, I had been hoping 1997 would be the year to push things and suddenly the No. 7 shirt seemed to be up for grabs.

Back at Saracens, meanwhile, another press conference was called, to welcome another signing. This time, none of us had a clue who it would be. Shortly before the event at the Trocadero in Piccadilly Circus, Dips and I were told that the club hoped this newcomer would be a particular help to our international aspirations, but still the penny failed to drop. Five minutes before the start, a woman walked in and sat at the front. All of a sudden Dips said: 'Hang on, I think I know her.' He had recognised Nerine, Francois Pienaar's wife.

Francois made an immediate impression. For a start, he seemed to be a completely different size from anyone I had come across before. He seemed to dwarf us. Part of it may have been his presence. Everyone could recall the image of Francois receiving the World Cup from Nelson Mandela only a year or so before, uniting a nation in the process. Then, somehow, he had fallen out of favour and suddenly – with Mandela's blessing – he was in London with us.

As Wray put it to the press: 'Who would have thought not so long ago a grubby little club in north London would have Lynagh, Sella and the World Cup-winning captain?'

Francois, though, took time to settle. He was not fully fit when he arrived and played only intermittently that season.

And he also had issues with the way the team played and was coached. It was not long before Rob Cunningham departed, leading to Francois becoming player-coach.

For me, though, the season was only going to get better.

Firstly, I got into the England squad. Backy, the other out-and-out specialist No. 7 and just back from a six-month suspension, was also included. It was going to be a simple choice between the pair of us. On the day before the announcement of England's Five Nations team to play Scotland, Saracens hosted Harlequins and won 28–20. I had not been told, but Rowell was in the crowd. Afterwards, he asked Jason Leonard what he thought. The question at the time was whether I could play a tight game, as well as an open one. Jason must have put in a good word for me – he was a former Saracen, after all – and by the time I left the ground, I had been told on the quiet that it might be worth keeping close to a phone the next day.

It was fitting that, at the time, I was sharing digs with Marcus, the same guy with whom I had kicked a rugby ball about in Salisbury all those years ago. It didn't really work out for him at Saracens and he moved back to Wiltshire to go into teaching, but it was good to have him there when I won my first cap.

Anyway, when the news came through it was a bit anti-climactic, since I learnt of my selection from Mike Scott, Saracens' team manager. 'Congratulations,' he said. 'Congratulations on what?' I replied. I thought I had won the club raffle. I don't know how Mike found out before me, but two minutes later, Rowell called. I was twenty-three years old, 15st 12lb, quiet, reserved, wet behind the ears and about to play for England.

Immediately I rang Claire and my parents. Then the media headed my way. So I phoned Marcus – he was working as a part-time gym instructor – and he dashed home to help me clear up the flat and hide the pizza boxes under our beds. Within a few weeks I was even doing my first photoshoot, advertising a local brewery near Salisbury called Hopback.

Looking back, it was also nice to prove those few people wrong who had questioned my temperament. I've never given too much away – just ask my mum – and I still don't now. On the field, people complained that I played with a blank expression, that I somehow seemed disconnected from what I was doing. Well, I've never been a shouter or a bawler. On the pitch – or off it, for that matter – I don't like people to know if I'm upset, or struggling or in some sort of pain. I'd rather keep my opponents guessing. I think more clearly when I'm calm. Jumping up and down does nothing to increase my motivation. I once read the phrase 'Speak softly and carry a big stick; you will go far'. I don't carry a stick around with me very often but I agree with the gist of it.

Ironically, the subject had come up at Saracens that very season. Perhaps Francois's arrival had something to do with it. Francois's a talker, one for passionate speeches and banging the table with his fist. So God knows what he made of me. Anyway Evans, who had been championing my England cause for some time, suddenly started worrying that I was giving the wrong impression. He suggested I work on my body language, to try to look more enthusiastic. I was a bit confused, since I was playing well enough, my work rate was high and my error rate low. I told a few of my team-mates what Evans had said. 'Forget it,' was the reply. 'Look at Michael Jones and Josh Kronfeld. They don't jump up and down and wave their arms. Your opponents know how hard you hit.' That was good enough for me, and it has been ever since.

Everyone was delighted for me, of course. Well, everyone except for a certain Mrs Hill of Salisbury. My parents had just changed their phone number and, by coincidence, it was passed on to another Mrs Hill. She was inundated with calls of congratulation. My dad phoned up to apologise in the end. She was fine with us, but not very happy with the phone company. As for my old friend Don, he couldn't believe the news. I managed to get tickets to the game for quite a few of my family and friends, but Don had to turn the offer down because Salisbury were facing relegation that season and had a match on the same day.

It might have been tempting to get carried away by some of the press coverage – the *Sunday Times*, clearly unaware of those pizza boxes, went as far as to suggest: 'Ever wondered what the model professional of the millennium will look like? Look no further... The new breed is here, and goes by the name of Richard Hill' – but Rowell made sure that I kept my feet on the ground. In public, he was talking me up. Behind closed doors, he liked to keep you guessing. We were sitting around at one of our first team meetings when he suddenly turned to me and asked: 'Now why have I picked you, Hill?' Jeez, I thought, what am I meant to say? I felt like I was back at school. I began mumbling some sort of reply but he cut me short: 'Hm, we'll see.'

Not that I needed much reminding that I was a novice. All that week, leading up to the game, I found myself among guys who I had watched on television as a boy. I knew a few of them from the Under-21s, but some, like Will Carling, I hadn't met at all. I remember being very, very nervous, but I soon settled. You sometimes hear of teams that almost resent newcomers, but it wasn't the case with that side. Will was a particular help. He had done so many great things as captain, but he was very relaxed and jovial.

We trained at the start of the week at Bisham Abbey while staying at The Compleat Angler in Marlow, by the Thames. As soon as I turned up I was presented with a set of kit, a track suit, polo shirts, T-shirts and training gear, which was very special. We trained on the Monday, Tuesday and Wednesday, with an emphasis on keeping the ball tight. We would be split into two groups and Jack would throw the ball to one lot who had to try and drive it through the other pack. I can't remember much emphasis on throwing the ball wide, despite Jack's public commitment to the fifteen-man game. He knew he had a powerful pack and probably found it hard to move on from that. He probably had mixed feelings about me, too. I was supposed to help improve the continuity between forwards and backs but, if anything, Jack used to criticise me at that stage for being too loose. Work in the tight wasn't exactly my forte then.

I made my debut alongside Lawrence at 6 and Tim Rodber, who I had never played with before, at 8. My main job against the Scots was clear – get Townsend. Gregor was a mercurial fly-half who I had played against at schools and club level, so I knew a bit about him. He was in a rich vein of form at the time. To be honest, I knew there wasn't much I could do to prepare. Gregor's greatest strength was that he played by instinct rather than to a pattern. Paul Grayson, our fly-half and Gregor's team-mate at Northampton, told me: 'I play with him every week and I still have no idea what he's going to do next…if you give him an inch, he'll take seventy yards.'

I was nervous all week, but I slept OK the night before. Oddly, I tend to sleep worse the night after big matches, because I'm always thinking over what happened during the game. After breakfast I just milled around in my room, avoiding the papers – I'm not an avid reader and I'm not convinced reading them before a game is that great an idea anyway. There was a team room on the first floor, overlooking the Thames, with a pre-match meal of soup and sandwiches. We gathered there around three hours before kick off. I tried to relax by watching 'Grandstand' on telly.

Suddenly we were off, heading for Twickenham by coach. Everything was new to me. It was the little details of the day that I would remember. Why, for instance, was the driver going this way – we ended up driving past my old halls of residence – when there was a more direct route? Then, when you got off the bus, they had ropes to keep the fans back as you headed for the changing rooms. I'd never seen that before.

I had been warned that the stadium noise might get to me but there was hardly anybody there at that stage. I had a quick walk around the pitch, and then went through a preliminary warm-up with Lawrence. We returned to the changing rooms for a team talk. There was also a scrummaging machine down there in those days. By this point you could really start to hear the noise. I began to realise what I was heading into – Twickenham, with 75,000 bellowing people inside. Phil de Glanville gave a final talk – I'm afraid I don't remember a single word – then came the knock on the door and out we went. I don't know if I looked around, but I do know I was bouncing with nervous energy during the national anthems. I just tried to keep on top of everything, calm myself down and look as if I was in control. But, in truth, I had never heard such a loud crowd before. In the stands Claire and my mum, who along with Dad have seen more of my matches than anyone over the years, were close to tears.

As for the game, it all passed in a flash. I remember being annoyed early on when I arrived too early, chasing a high kick, and took out Kenny Logan in the air to give away a stupid penalty. A minute or two later, though, I managed to get hold of Gregor and throw him into touch, and at that point I felt I was in the game. For a while it was close, but we cut loose in the final quarter to win 41–13, a record winning margin for the Calcutta Cup. At one stage we scored three tries in a five-minute burst – the team had managed only three tries in the entire Five Nations campaign the previous year – so it was not surprising that we got some pretty good reviews.

I came away feeling pretty happy, having kept Gregor fairly quiet. After the match, Jason Leonard went over and did a swap with Ian Smith, the Scotland openside, and then handed me the shirt, so I ended up with both No. 7s. The rest of the evening soon disappeared into an alcoholic haze.

I was presented with my tie in the changing rooms, then it was onto the team bus on the way to the banquet. As the new cap, I was asked to stand up and sing a song. God knows why I sang 'Help' by the Beatles – it's got a few nasty high notes and I don't exactly have a great voice. I'm not even sure I knew all the words. It may sound mad, but I was more nervous about singing than playing the game. They made you trudge up the coach aisle and screamed 'Sit down! Sit down!' from start to finish.

Then came the alcoholic initiation, when you have to share a private drink with every other player in the squad. They choose the drink, you match it. So I got through red wine, white wine, beer, lager, Guinness and, I imagine, the odd spirit thrown in for luck. By the end of the evening, having received my cap, I spent a while in the Gents, a standard outcome of such initiations. There have been worse performances. Steve Ojomoh was in such a stupor by the time of the banquet that when he was publicly congratulated on his debut by the RFU President, Steve's neighbour had to lift up his hand to acknowledge him. Then there was Iain Balshaw who quite audibly relieved himself in a metal wine bucket during the speeches, all the while shouting 'Jar Jar Binks' at Daws (apparently, Matt bears a passing resemblance to the floppy-eared creature from *Star Wars*, although I'm not sure Jar Jar would be happy with the comparison).

Austin Healey, who made his debut in the very next game,

was in such a bad way that he spent a couple of hours being attended to by the doctor and physio behind an impromptu curtain, lying flat out on a chaise longue and with a wine bucket strategically placed just under his head. He had blood-shot eyes for weeks afterwards. He didn't like red wine, so, thoughtfully, we all drank red wine that evening, except for Keith Wood, the Irish hooker, who bought him a pint of gin and tonic. I think we almost killed him, which some people, in retrospect, might consider to have been a missed opportunity.

Claire somehow managed to get me into my hotel bed after the dinner. I was pretty ecstatic by then. I knew I had done OK although the greatest compliment came in the *Guardian* news-paper, which referred to 'the most authentic openside display seen in an England shirt since the era of Peter Winterbottom'. I had admired Peter, so I was pretty happy to share the same sentence as him.

The other thing I remember was the 'team recovery session' early next morning. Things weren't exactly professional yet, when it came to recovery. There were no such things as ice baths, for a start. I had been told how important it was to attend so, despite feeling horribly tender, I stumbled out of the Hilton after a couple of hours' sleep and into Hyde Park. I had been duped. Only a handful of guys turned up and most of them had been on the bench. We set off on a run and I seem to remember Graham Rowntree, a prop for goodness sake, charging off into the distance. I fell so far behind that the masseur was sent back to fetch me.

Our next game was against Ireland, at Lansdowne Road, and we went even better by winning 46–6. I had never played there before. It was an intimidating place. For the first half I could hardly hear the line-out calls, but the crowd went quiet early in the second half, which was satisfying. The pattern was similar to the game against the Scots as we came away with

England's biggest win in Five Nations history. Again we upped the pace in the final quarter, scoring 29 points (including four tries) in the last eight minutes. Everything seemed to be going for me at that stage. Austin came on for the final few minutes at scrum-half and put me over for a try in the left-hand corner.

I played against two of my club mates, Paddy Johns and Paul Wallace, that day. Paddy was a lovely family-orientated man. He had played rugby a long time and his fingers all seemed to point in different directions at the same time, he had broken them so often. We often wondered how that affected him in his work as a dentist. Anyway, fairly early on I fell over onto the wrong side of the ruck and waited for the inevitable kicking. It didn't come. I looked up to see Paddy standing over me. He lifted his boot, then growled: 'Now don't you be putting yourself there again – otherwise, you'll be getting it.' It was a generous gesture.

We missed out on a Grand Slam, though, by losing 23–20 at home to France. After making slow starts in our previous games, we charged out of the blocks and led 20–6 with twenty minutes left, only to run out of steam.

I probably should not have played. I had twisted my ankle while training at Saracens just before and was barely able to run for most of that week. Backy was called up as a replacement but was then sent back to the A side. A friend of mine asked him how my ankle was and he replied gruffly: 'Not good...but he'll play.' And, having just got into the team, I was determined to do just that. It hurt like hell, especially after I managed to twist it again inside the first five minutes, but I wasn't about to let it show or affect my game. I must have got away with it because nobody noticed.

At least we closed on an upbeat performance, a 34–13 win at Cardiff Arms Park based on another late surge. The game also served as a send-off for Will Carling and Rob Andrew, who came on as a late substitute. Rob had officially retired eighteen months earlier, but had been lured back to help out one more time by Rowell. It was also Jonathan Davies's last game for Wales, so it all got a bit sentimental at the end as the three walked off together.

Jerry Guscott, in the meantime, set up a try for me in the second half. I thus became the last Englishman to score a try at the Arms Park, on my first and last visit, before it was demolished and replaced by the Millennium Stadium. I had played four internationals, and scored two tries. It would have been nice to keep up that strike rate.

My perfect season, however, was not yet quite over.

I had already heard that I was in the preliminary sixty-two-man squad to tour South Africa with the Lions, which was a massive bonus, but there would be one more surprise. I was getting changed after the Wales game, looking forward to a night out with the lads in Cardiff, when Les Cusworth tapped me on the shoulder. 'How do you fancy going to Hong Kong?' he said. Lawrence had pulled out of the World Cup Sevens squad with 'flu and I went in his place. I had played my fair share of sevens and although we did not win, it was a huge experience.

I couldn't have scripted the 1996–97 season better if I had tried.

8

A LION IN AFRICA

People love lists. They're always asking you to put things in order. What was your best or worst moment? What was your best or worst match? Who was your toughest opponent? It's not always easy. There are always specific circumstances relating to each situation. I had some pretty good moments with Salisbury, as it happens, but people wouldn't think I was being serious if I mentioned those.

In terms of career achievements, though, it's simpler. I think my three highs would have to be the 2003 World Cup, winning my first England cap and the 1997 Lions tour to South Africa.

By the time the next Lions set off, in 2009, it will be twelve years since they last won a series. That proves how hard it is to do. I have been on three tours in the famous red shirt and I tend to rate them in order of the success we achieved; 1997 at the top, 2001 in Australia second – even though that probably represented my best playing performances – while 2005 is, let's be honest, best forgotten.

The Lions were always the ultimate for me. As a teenager I remember following the 1989 series on TV and wearing the tour T-shirt until it became threadbare. There was something compelling about selecting the best players from four rival countries, removing them from their comfort zones and trying to forge them into a unit in a matter of weeks.

I wasn't even an England player at the start of 1997. If you had asked me in January about the tour, I would probably have answered: 'Yes, won't it be great, watching on TV.' By the end of February, though, I was beginning to wonder. Suddenly, I was playing against people who were expected to go to South Africa and I was doing OK. As the rest of the England squad began to discuss the Lions, I realised that even I could be in the frame. Why not? Why shouldn't I be?

Initially, a sixty-two-man list of 'possibles' was published and, to my delight, I was included. Phil de Glanville, though, had been omitted. Usually, the captain of the strongest Home Nations side would be seen as a contender to lead the party but Jerry Guscott, who Phil had kept out of the England side that season, was preferred. Obviously the coaches had their own thoughts about how we were going to play.

We were invited to a gathering of all the players. Eventually the squad would be cut right back to thirty-five. I found myself quietly looking around and thinking: 'Well hang on, I didn't play too badly against him. And I didn't really notice him…'

I'd like to say that I sat gnawing my nails until the final letter came through, but it wasn't like that. It landed one morning, along with a bunch of bills and junk mail, and I opened it without realising what it was. It took me a few seconds to take it in. Jeez – I was going to South Africa! I was going to play the world champions.

There were some pretty bold selections. With just four caps, I suppose I was one of them. Will Greenwood hadn't been capped at all. There was also a bunch of players who had started in union, switched to league and were then making their way back, the likes of Scott Gibbs, Alan Tait, Scott

Quinnell, John Bentley, Allan Bateman and Dai Young. Martin Johnson, meanwhile, had been awarded the captaincy despite his lack of experience – I think he had captained Leicester a few times and that was about it. The Lions tour manager Fran Cotton, though, liked the idea of a 6ft 8in lock knocking on the door of the Springboks' changing room before kick-off rather than, say, a 5ft 9in scrum-half. It would make a statement in a country where forward power is revered.

Johnno certainly had presence. I didn't really know him back then, although I admired him. He didn't talk a massive amount. If one sentence will do, one sentence will do. A conversation between R. Hill and M. Johnson would have been a non-starter. But he was a good judge of character and expressed himself more as he became comfortable with his role. Basically, he led by example, in training and on match days, and everyone followed. But he also knew when to ease off and give his players some slack. And when he spoke the coaches tended to listen.

It didn't take him long to earn the respect of the Scots, Irish and Welsh on tour. What you saw was what you got. Most of them probably already knew from painful experience that whenever you played against Johnno you had to front up. He was prepared to fight his corner, for himself and his team, and do whatever it took. He did just that in South Africa, playing throughout with a groin injury and needing injections to deal with a partially dislocating shoulder. In short, you could see even then why he's the best captain I have ever played under.

The name on the final tour party list that most caught my eye, though, was that of Neil Back.

It did not take me long to work out that he and I were the only specialist openside flankers selected. He hadn't been on the original list but managed to battle his way onto it, a pretty impressive feat since he was not part of the England squad at the time. Theoretically, the Test spot would be a direct choice between the two of us, even though there was always the possibility of another back rower switching to openside.

Over the years, Backy and I have become good mates but that was hardly the case then. Put simply, I hardly knew him and that situation was unlikely to change because we didn't talk to each other. At that stage, he was burning with indignation that England were not selecting him. I was his obvious target, which made things even frostier. He was quoted a few times in newspapers, questioning my effectiveness after others had praised one of my performances. I tended not to respond in public. It's not my way. Despite that, I could understand where he was coming from. Maybe I wouldn't have gone to the press, but who's to say that I wouldn't have had the same thoughts and expressed them to close friends if our roles had been reversed? You might criticise him, but it also underlined the passion of the bloke, and his desire and motivation to win at all costs. So it wasn't really dislike between us, more ultra-competitiveness. And I was as competitive and bloody-minded as he was. I had been behind Backy in the pecking order before, with England A for instance, and had wanted a crack at him. Now it was his turn.

Playing against each other for our clubs around that time, we would both indulge in the odd bit of gamesmanship, with a trip-up off the ball here or a shove or shirt pull there, but we managed to keep things civil with the Lions, even if we circled each other warily. The situation could only benefit the team, though, even if it made things a bit awkward.

Before setting off, the squad had drawn up a set of 'Lions Laws', which were in effect an agreed code of conduct. One of the laws, printed on a yellow laminate card, was that it was the responsibility of a player who had missed out on Test selection to go up and congratulate the guy who had been preferred. If we obeyed that command at all, Backy and I would have done it through gritted teeth. I had managed to keep him out of the England side, but I was aware that I would have to prove myself all over again to our new coaches Ian McGeechan and Jim Telfer.

People often discuss the difficulties of blending different nationalities and different playing styles under one banner, but it didn't seem much of an issue when eighteen Englishmen, eight Welshmen, five Scots and four Irishmen met up in Weybridge for some bonding sessions before the eight-week, thirteen-match trip. There were a few accents I struggled with, but that was about the extent of it. There was a large English contingent but it did not feel like a takeover, particularly with McGeechan and Telfer in charge. And guys like Quinnell, Tait and Townsend had already played in England, so the boundaries had come down quite a bit.

Traditionally, rugby team-building had been done in pubs. This time, though, a group of experts were brought in to run a series of activities designed to break down barriers and get us to work together. There were physical tests, assault-course relays and canoe races and the like, in the grounds of the Oatlands Park Hotel. One lengthy evening drinking session at the White Swan in Walton-on-Thames was probably just as effective, though, especially after Fran Cotton put his credit card behind the bar.

Perhaps the key thing which united us was that we were being given absolutely no chance of winning the series. Some critics thought we would struggle to compete in the provincial games, never mind the Tests. The Lions concept, it was argued, belonged to a bygone amateur age. As I remember, we were 5–1 against winning a single Test against the World Cup holders. McGeechan himself did not hide the scale of the challenge – we were about to play the equivalent, he said, of ten Five Nations matches and three World Cup finals.

I remember the squad discussing the situation on several occasions. We didn't like being written off and felt we were worth more than that. The key, everyone agreed, was to stay united, whatever happened. Francois Pienaar had warned me about how passionate South Africans were about their rugby, with Currie Cup teams regularly drawing crowds of 20,000. The Lions had last visited seventeen years ago and there was a huge sense of anticipation. The important thing for us was to stick together and relish rather than fear the challenge.

Our hosts had their own problems. They had a new coach in Carel du Plessis – their sixth in five years – and a new skipper in Gary Teichmann, Pienaar's successor. But they were still regarded as massive favourites.

I soon realised just how rugby-mad South Africa is. Shortly after our arrival, something happened which rarely occurs in England – I got recognised in the street, and not just once but several times, both by Lions fans – they were arriving in droves – and by the locals. It's not as if I demand to be noticed at the best of times, but in 1997 I was pretty quiet and unassuming. South Africans, though, as Francois had said, love the game and read everything they can about the players.

Was I confident? Well, on the one hand, yes. With two guys in the running for one place, I realised that I had a good chance of featuring in the Tests. On the other, though, I knew I was little more than a novice at this level. Looking back, I barely said a word at any of the team meetings throughout the tour. When I did, it was only in response to direct questions. The thought of addressing the group, which included people who had achieved so much, made me come out in a sweat. I didn't want to say the wrong thing. Generally, I succeeded in keeping a low profile. I think I did just one press conference all tour, and that was only because it was my birthday (the guys thoughtfully presented me with a cake, tried to push my face into it, gave me the smallest slice and then threw me into the swimming pool). In a way, I was happy just to be there. Of course, I wanted to play a big part, but I believed other people's experience was more relevant than mine.

I was very keen, though, to play in the first game, just to get my tour under way. I got my wish when I was selected to play against Eastern Province, or the Elephants as they were known, in Port Elizabeth. It was a good nickname. Right from the start, we were struck by the size of the South Africans. Physically, they were a completely different ask.

We got presented with our shirts shortly before the game. I remember being very nervous, probably more so than before England matches. I was leaning up against a chair during the presentations, thinking: 'Jeez, let's go, let's get on with it!' We had known the team days in advance but the time just dragged. I'm a bit better now but in those days I used to go very, very quiet during a build-up. People probably think I'm morose, but I just like to retreat into myself. Perhaps that's where I get my reputation for being miserable. It seems ridiculous to think of it now, but it took me and Claire years to work out why we always seemed to argue on Fridays. I was getting psyched up for playing on Saturday, she was getting relaxed at the start of the weekend. It wasn't the ideal mix.

Different players handle pre-match nerves in different ways. Take Austin – he just fizzes all the time, wise-cracking right up to kick-off. Then there's my approach. After the tour, they sold a video of the Lions trip. There's a bit from the changing room just before one game when Jason Leonard grabs me around the shoulders and shouts straight into my face. I just looked back blankly. He probably thought he was helping me to get in the right mood. Lots of players opt for a lot a chest punching and slapping and shouting but it's not for me. Some like getting into tight huddles and crunching their heads together. I always do my best to hold mine out of the way. Perhaps I did that sort of thing when I was young, because I thought it was normal, but it's not normal. It makes no difference to my performance at all. I do get psyched up, but more quietly. I also tend to start it earlier than some, normally a couple of days out. I then try to relax a bit in the build-up, to make sure I don't overdo it. In the final hour before kick-off I rarely utter a word to anyone.

Another thing. When you see fly-on-the-wall tour videos, there are invariably rousing speeches made by the captain or a senior player just before the off. McGeechan and Telfer were masters of the art. I'm sure it inspires people but I rarely listen to a word of them. Ask me what had been said two minutes later and I wouldn't have a clue. By then, I'm deep in my own little world.

We went into that first game with a strong side and a back row made up of Lawrence, Scott Quinnell and me. Rob Howley and Gregor Townsend, both likely Test starters, were at half-back with Gibbs and Guscott, who had played together in 1993, at centre. Neil Jenkins, normally considered a fly-half, was being tried out at 15, a gamble which turned out to be a masterstroke.

Before our arrival, the South Africans had praised our pack but rubbished our back play. We won that first game at Telkom Park comfortably enough, scoring five tries to one, and afterwards their players and press changed tack. You could see why. They had given us a rough ride in the scrum, which was a worry, but we had run the ball superbly. Their hooker and skipper, Jaco Kirsten, got the ball rolling. 'We can take them up front,' he said.

The pattern repeated itself for the second game, then the third. Against Border, we went with a back row of Rob Wainwright, Backy and Eric Miller and won 18–14 in horrible, muddy conditions. I was delighted to get back in for the encounter against Western Province. They were seen as the first major test of the tour. We won again, 38–21, but once more our scrum wobbled.

Most people expected the heart of the Lions Test pack to come from England after our domination in the Five Nations. Against Western Province in Cape Town, there were seven English forwards. Johnno was playing his first game of the tour. Everything was set up for us to start bossing the South Africans around. Instead we got shunted backwards.

We looked fitter than our opponents, and finished with a flurry of late scores – I managed to set one up by sliding in, football-style, and hacking the ball on for John Bentley to score – and our handling was slick. But we realised we had a problem up front that needed to be sorted, fast.

It may have come as a shock to us but it probably didn't to Cotton, McGeechan and Telfer. They were certainly concerned, but when you look back it's clear they had selected their squad to play a particular game – a highly mobile running game. There hadn't been much talk about game plans or tactics yet. For the most part, we had worked on the basics. But it soon became obvious the plan was clearly to drag the heavy South African forwards about from one side of the pitch to the other in an attempt to exhaust them. If we couldn't go through them, we would have to go round them.

Geech was coach at Northampton but I didn't know much about him. He was a great analyser, 'Mr Video', always reviewing matches and passages of play. He loved spontaneous play as long as it was based on intelligence – 'if it's on, it's on,' he'd say. I didn't know much about Telfer either, and it was probably best that I didn't. He was about to show his true colours. As a combination, they worked very well together. It wasn't so much a case of them playing good cop, bad cop, since Geech could certainly be forthright. He was not a pacifier – he knew when to be tough and when to back off. Telfer, though, was an out-and-out hard man. He got the absolute best out of that group of players – what he did was outstanding, to be honest. But I don't think I could have coped with having him as my full-time boss. He was simply too full-on.

He was certainly full-on after Western Province. I had picked up a slight calf strain, which kept me out of a few games, so I missed the brunt of it, but Telfer decided emergency action was needed if we were to have any chance in the Tests. Some truly frightening scrummaging sessions followed.

He had a perfect ally in Nigel Horton. The former England lock had helped devise a hydraulic scrum machine which pushed back against you. As one of the tour sponsors, Horton followed us around, living out of a truck containing his machine. Telfer proceeded to get the guys to pack down against it, push like mad, run around a set of posts and do it again. And again, and again, and again. Basically, he gave the guys a flogging. He also demanded that we get lower in the rucks and threw a net over us to try and adjust our body positions. I think one session consisted of something like forty-six scrums in as many minutes, each engagement accompanied by a stream of Telfer abuse. 'Attack boys, attack! Get lower and keep it tight!' There was no doubt about his passion. He was responsible for the forwards and felt this was the way he could influence results. Had he been forty years younger, he would probably have got stuck in himself.

People often look back at tours in search of defining moments which tipped the balance one way or the other. Ask rugby fans to recall the 1997 tour, and most will mention Daws's try in the first Test, or Gibbs's tackle on Os du Randt in the second. Both, of course, were unforgettable. But nobody who took part in those Telfer scrummaging sessions, one of which was held immediately after a game, will ever forget them. I'm not sure I have experienced anything like it, before or since. The result was that our scrum improved out of sight. By the time we got to the Tests, it was no longer a major issue.

Next up were Mpumalanga and we crushed them 64–14. The pack was so solid that it allowed the back row to attack around the fringes, with Rob Wainwright grabbing three tries. By now the journalists on tour were trying to predict our Test XV but this result made it much harder for them. Tours often split up fairly early into likely first and second XVs but, as Tim Rodber, captain against Mpumalanga, said: 'There's no such thing as dirt-trackers on this trip.' Everybody believed they had a chance of making the Test 22. There is no better way of ensuring a happy squad.

The only negative was a ligament injury to Doddie Weir, which put the Scottish lock out of the tour. Marius Bosman, who was later fined, kicked him below the knee and seemed to bend the joint backwards. For me, it was a callous act. I was sharing a room with Doddie at the time. He was a lovely, lively character and it was heart-breaking for him. Rob Wainwright appeared with a bottle of whisky and they went off to drown their sorrows.

Spirits sank even lower next time out. Another English-dominated pack – the whole front five, plus Lawrence – took to the field against Northern Transvaal only to lose 35–30 despite a spirited fightback. Telfer was seething and accused us of being no better than the average British or Irish tourist on holiday abroad. 'The first thing they look for is a fucking English pub, the second thing they look for is a pint of Guinness and the third thing they look for is a fish and chip shop,' he said. It was about time we started accepting where we were and how our opponents were playing. Honest players, he said, sought to improve but 'dishonest, weak players are always complaining…

If I tell a player he's too high, or he's not tight enough, he's too fucking high, he's not tight enough, and that's it, and I'm the judge, and not the player!'

I'm not sure I was complaining at the time, but I was confused. I had expected to play against Northern Transvaal but the selectors opted to try Eric Miller at No. 7 instead. As far as I knew, he had never played in the position before and it made me wonder whether I was being rested or whether they were unhappy with what they had seen. I didn't feel confident enough to go and ask what was going on.

That defeat, though, acted as a positive in the end. We had had some reasonable results while not playing particularly well and it was probably the wake-up call we needed.

By now, there were three Saracens in the tour party and it would soon be four. Paul Wallace had sneaked in via the back door when fellow Ireland prop Peter Clohessy pulled out injured at the last moment. Now Dips, having just been capped against Argentina, joined us as Scott Quinnell was forced off tour through injury. Soon Kyran turned up.

We had bounced back to beat Gauteng 20–14 – a morale-boosting result made special by John Bentley's spectacular 50-metre run past about half their side (although I couldn't help thinking that we could have scored an awful lot quicker if Bentos had passed the ball) – then took on Natal, the Currie Cup winners.

This was a game everybody wanted to play in. It had been billed as the fourth Test. More importantly, there were only two games and seven days left before the first Test. Fortunately, I got the call, alongside Lawrence and Eric.

Our 42–12 win, scoring three tries without reply on the shores of the Indian Ocean, was huge, but there was a price to play. Rob Howley, looking every inch like the first-choice scrum-half, dislocated his shoulder and was ruled out of the tour. Still, the scrum had felt solid and Jenkins had kicked twenty-four points. Rob's misfortune was Kyran's opportunity, although his love of fancy holidays nearly cost him the chance. Kyran was sunning himself in the Caribbean at the time and hadn't left a contact address. He was tracked down only after a dozen frantic phone calls to hotels in Tobago.

The Emerging Springboks, a potential banana skin, were then seen off 51–22 and everyone got ready for the real business – the first Test. I was quietly confident I had done enough, although Backy had played some good stuff. Everyone's nerves were on edge as selection approached on the Wednesday morning. I can't believe there were many people who felt absolutely sure of making the team. We had been consulted about how the announcement should be made and we had decided we wanted to be told in private, so that people could deal with the feeling of elation or rejection before appearing in front of everybody else. So it was agreed that a letter would be slipped under each player's hotel room door early in the morning. Some guys did not sleep too well as a result. Bentos, for one, ended up sitting by his door for hours. When we all convened in the team room, he had huge bags under his eyes. At least he made the bench. I thought I would also be waiting nervously for the noise of the envelope brushing across the carpet, but actually I slept OK. I was absolutely delighted to be picked but then realised I had to brave breakfast, not knowing who else had made it. Bit by bit, you pieced the team together by looking at the other guys' expressions and asking around.

There were two extraordinary stories behind the selection for the first Test team. They both involved Irishmen. One got all the luck and the other none. Eric Miller seemed set to complete a fairytale when the selectors decided to go with him at No. 8. He was twenty-one and, like me, had only just been capped. In the run-up to the game, though, he caught 'flu and took some medicine bought for him by his father. When the medical team found out what had happened, they checked what he had taken and discovered it contained illegal substances. Eric, therefore, could not be included in the team, otherwise he could have faced a ban. Worse was to follow. In the second Test he ran on as a substitute and immediately tore a muscle which ruled him out of the rest of the tour. He hasn't been capped by the Lions since.

On the other hand, things could not have gone much better for my club team-mate Paul Wallace. He had made the tour only as injury cover. Along with fellow prop Tom Smith, who had made his international debut only a few months before, he looked destined to spend most of his time in the midweek side. Wally would certainly have enjoyed himself, whatever happened. But both he and Tom ended up doing a phenomenal job, breaking into the Test side and making their reputations along the way. They were midgets compared to the Springbok front row – Wally was about 5ft 10in and $17\frac{1}{2}$ st compared to the 6ft 3in, 20st Os du Randt – but they were able to pack down low and get under their opponents. They were also canny, playing the rules to their advantage, as well as being mobile and good ball handlers. Surrounded by the best players in the British Isles, they stepped up to the next level without blinking.

Not that Wally, who like Tom started all three Tests, was fazed by his success. He stuck to his philosophy of partying as hard as he played. The management treated the players like adults while making it clear that we would be held responsible for our own personal performances, but I'm not sure they quite knew what Wally got up to. I suppose you could call the 1997 Lions one of the last amateur tours. Most of us had only just turned professional but we were still in a transitional period. Some guys had barely changed their approaches at all. That is not to say they were not fully committed but, until told otherwise, they stuck to their old habits. So when they went out on the town, they really went out. Wally was able to train and drink, train and then drink, right up to the top of the tour drinking charts. The only tell-tale sign, for those of us who knew him well, was that he would become very vocal and enthusiastic in training following a heavy session the night before. Back at Saracens, it was not unknown for him to visit the Eros nightclub in Enfield on Saturday night, fall asleep in a corner and wake up refreshed just in time for the start of Sunday's festivities. To this day, I don't know how he managed it.

Our team for the first Test at Newlands in Cape Town was genuinely representative of the four home unions, with six Englishmen and three from each of the other countries. Keith Wood, the Harlequins and Ireland hooker, became a Lion as his father Gordon had done almost forty years before. As for the game, under floodlights and under the shadow of Table Mountain, well, it became the stuff of legend. Cotton had handed out the shirts and everybody had started clapping spontaneously, it was such a special moment. I lined up with Tim Rodber and Lawrence in the back row. Personally, I did not know much about our opponents, Gary Teichmann, Andre Venter and Ruben Kruger, although I had heard that Kruger tackled wildebeest or antelopes as part of his training, a bizarre story which I never quite managed to discount. South Africa being South Africa, we knew it was going to be physical and so it proved.

The deciding moment of the game, however, was not physical at all, for the simple reason that no one got a finger on Daws. We were a point adrift with less than ten minutes to go when he scooped the ball up from the base of a scrum and went blind down the right touchline. Shadowed by three or four Springboks, Teichmann and Kruger among them, he shaped to lob the ball one-handed back infield. And with that his pursuers stopped in their tracks, anticipating an interception. Only the ball never came, it stayed stuck to Daws's fingertips and he cantered over unopposed, dancing in celebration as he went. I'm not convinced it started out as a dummy. Probably Daws just improvised. But it was no less extraordinary a piece of skill for that. Just before the end, Tait crossed in the other corner and we were home and dry.

The elation afterwards in the changing room was huge, even though we knew nothing had been decided yet. But we had won 25–16 and put an end to South African claims that the Lions were mere pussycats. There were celebrations that night – you have to enjoy your victories, after all – but by the next day we got straight back into our routine. As Bentos told a team meeting: 'You've won fuck all yet!' And we hadn't (mind you, his message would have carried more weight if he had not crawled back to the hotel in the early hours that morning).

The other great memory from that day was the Lions fans. I don't think any of us had ever experienced such support away from home. They had come over in their thousands, stuffed into cars and camper vans, following the tour from venue to venue, wearing their red shirts and face paint and singing their English, Irish, Welsh and Scottish songs. I didn't know at the time, but several people I knew were part of the trek. After the second Test, I even came across a couple of guys who had played junior rugby with me. Those fans gave the tour a special feel.

The next Test was only seven days away. So most of us settled down in Durban, while the rest flew up to Bloemfontein to take on Free State. Cotton would call it the finest performance he had ever seen from a midweek team as they ran out 52–30 winners at altitude. We watched it on television and the guys played some great stuff, throwing the ball about and increasing the squad's self-belief. The only negative was an injury to Will Greenwood, who was knocked unconscious after hitting the rock-hard ground head first. At one stage they were considering a tracheotomy – cutting a hole in the front of his throat to help his breathing – but fortunately Will came round in time.

Many of the midweek games served up some excellent running rugby. The second Test, though, was all about manning the trenches and scratching out a win in any way we could. There were not a lot of changes. Ieuan Evans had damaged his groin, allowing Bentos to win his first cap. I felt under pressure, though, after discovering that Backy had been selected as a replacement. As an out-and-out No. 7, he could only really come on in place of me. Telfer felt Backy could provide a different threat out wide while his presence would at the same time force me to play out of my skin if I wanted to stay on the pitch. It was a sort of blackmail.

After another rousing McGeechan speech – 'We've wounded a Springbok. When an animal is wounded it returns in a frenzy. It doesn't think. It fights for its very existence. The Lion waits, then, at the right point, it goes for the jugular' – we kicked off and it was immediately clear that he was spot on. From the start we saw a more physical and more niggly South Africa team. There was certainly a lot more use of the boot, with lots more people being trodden on and kicked, than in the first Test. I think they were genuinely angry that we had beaten them. Not only that, they were playing by far the better rugby. Struggling for possession, we just hung on, trying to work ourselves into positions where we could force them into making mistakes. We had, after all, something that the Springboks did not – an awesome kicker.

Neil Jenkins wasn't our first choice as a fly-half and he wasn't a natural full-back either, but you just had to play him because of his kicking. Give us the slightest opportunity and

The Ginger Monster came up with three points. South Africa, meanwhile, were scoring tries but failing to build a winning score.

Just before half-time, I got kicked on the calf. During the break it started to feel quite sore, so I had no qualms about being substituted with just over twenty minutes to go. The finale was dominated by a couple of images – a bullocking charge from Scott Gibbs and Jerry Guscott's winning drop goal.

Scott looked a bit like a librarian off the pitch. He wore glasses and could be quite quiet at times, preferring his own company before rejoining the party. On the pitch, though, he became a cult figure. He was powerfully built, almost as wide as he was tall and had explosive pace over twenty yards. Jerry, his midfield partner, used to call him a pocket battleship and 'the fastest prop in world rugby'. In Durban that day Scott broke through on an inside pass only for Os du Randt to come steaming across at him. There was an almighty collision and du Randt crashed to the ground, dazed, while Scott spun out of the attempted tackle and smashed further up field. There was a gasp from the crowd and probably from everyone watching on TV as well. It was one of those moments you never forget.

Then came Jerry's winning drop kick right at the death. We were tied at 15–15 when Backy stole a ball from a ruck, Keith Wood hacked the ball down the left touchline and we got a line-out near their 22. A couple of phases later and Daws was passing out the ball to Jerry who chipped the winning points over.

I still remember how it felt when the final whistle went. There was this sea of red in some sections of the stadium but in a way it was quite a private moment, being with your mates as the sense of achievement sunk in. We had been so comprehensively written off, even in Britain. Even after the first Test people argued our win had been some sort of fluke. But now it was 2–0 and the series was over. I was twenty-three years old, barely out of my rugby apprenticeship. I can't really compare my feelings after that second Test with those that followed my England debut – they hold different places in your heart. I don't know if I could choose between them.

We got changed and joined up with fans and friends enjoying their braais (barbecues) around the King's Park ground before moving on to a nightclub. Some of the guys went out onto the beach that night with their duvets and crates of beer. By the morning half the bottles had been emptied and the other half stolen by local drunks. Walking back to the hotel along the seafront that night, I gave Claire a call on my mobile, just to share the moment. She asked me about the game and the celebrations and then asked: 'Where are you now?'

'Oh, I'm just walking home,' I said, 'along Mugger's Mile.'

After all the excitement, the tour wound up in something of an anti-climax for me.

Telfer thought I was a more conservative choice than Backy and, after being forced to play it so tight in the second Test, he wanted to show a more expansive side in the finale. I'm not sure I agreed but I had to accept it. On top of that, I had not been able to train for a couple of days because of my damaged calf. I have always enjoyed playing in teams which run the ball and I reckon I was just as quick to the breakdown as Backy. He had a lower centre of gravity, which made him good at stealing ball, but I felt I knew what I was doing in those situations as well. Still, perhaps it was a fair reward for some of the performances Backy had put in on tour. I shook his hand and that was that.

To this day, it is the only time that I have ever been dropped from an international team. The only consolation was that I didn't play on a losing side in South Africa.

We went down 35–16 at Ellis Park. We had talked about trying to make history by becoming the first side in a century to whitewash the Boks but they were far better on the day. About a third of our thirty-five-man squad were injured by then, which didn't help. Perhaps, having already achieved what we had wanted, the boys could not quite lift themselves one more time. With less than a quarter of an hour to go, we were still in the game at 23–16 but we ran out of steam.

Still, it was a huge achievement and one I could never have hoped to enjoy so early in my career. Leaving South Africa was strange, in a way. You forge intense personal bonds with your team-mates over a short time and then suddenly it's all over and you go your separate ways. As a rugby player, you are involved with so many teams like that. You tend to get to know people well for a short period and then do not see them again for years. Then you bump into them again, on the pitch or at their clubs, and it all comes back. Or, as McGeechan put it – and this time I must have been listening – 'When you meet each other in the street in thirty years' time, there'll just be a look and you will know just how special some days in your life are.'

9

BACK PROBLEMS

December 2005. This month has been as depressing as last month was uplifting. I've been very low, to the extent that Claire has been worrying about whether I could be heading for some sort of mental breakdown. Normally she just tells me to pull myself together and get on with it.

I had been hoping to forge ahead after the operation and for a while things went well enough. I managed to increase the extension in my leg and was back to walking normally. I even risked a couple of short trots across the road, to avoid being run over. It wasn't exactly running, but it felt good.

The trouble started with what seemed like a slight niggle. I was doing a bit of training alongside one of our young associate professionals, Andy Edwards, who suffered a similar knee injury to mine earlier this year. We were enjoying a bit of banter and perhaps I overdid it a bit, trying to keep up with him. Andy is hoping to get back playing next month and was doing about 220kg leg presses. I was on 140kg and, not to be outdone, kept adding weights. It did not hurt at the time but it was very sore the next morning. I thought it was just the muscles firing themselves up again after my three- or four-week break around the operation, so I backed off during the next few days but the pain increased on the inside of my knee.

I went to see Fares, who hoped the problem might disappear with some hefty physio on my scar tissue. I got hardly any sleep over the next few nights, though. There was a sharp shooting pain, like sciatica, in my left calf and buttock, and then my back seized up. The knee also felt sore. Claire, wisely, headed for the spare room.

There was an improvement over the next few days and I managed to do some single leg bodyweight squats which I couldn't do a few weeks ago. The trouble is, every time you feel a twinge you start worrying. Is that a pain or not? Will it get worse again? Some days the knee hurts, other days it doesn't, for no apparent reason. It drains you, mentally.

The answer is to try to find diversions. Being involved in organising events for my benefit year has helped. My mate Marcus's stag do should also have been perfect, but it didn't turn out that way. It was a day-long affair, which started in a country pub outside Salisbury, followed by clay pigeon shooting, skittles and another pub session before the finale in a nightclub. It was great to catch up with some former Salisbury team-mates and friends but in the end I had to miss out on the nightclub because of the nagging pain in my knee. While the guys carried on I headed for home, along with the other old codgers in the party who felt they couldn't handle a late night out. Fares said it was time to shut down my training for two weeks – no leg weights, no bike or swimming, no body weights exercises, no machines, nothing.

So here I am, idle. Last month everything seemed to be going so well, it was just a case of recovering from the surgery and then putting the foot on the pedal. A March comeback is now out of the question. I'll have to aim for early April. I know I shouldn't be setting myself long-term targets but I have, and they don't seem achievable at the moment.

For a younger player, missing a month would mean nothing. For me, though, it's another month without rugby and one I'll never get back. Every game I miss is a game off my life. Another month without that feeling of running onto the pitch and hearing the cheers from thousands of supporters. You can't replicate that. It's hard to explain the buzz it gives you. Imagine walking down into a tube station at rush hour and everyone suddenly turning around and applauding you. It's probably something like that.

There's another worry at the back of my mind. My contract runs out on 31 May. They gave me a one-year extension last year and I'm hoping for that again but I haven't heard anything yet.

Still, you have to put your problems in perspective. The other day I went to the Rugby Writers' Annual Dinner. The main speech was given by Andy Ripley, the former England No. 8. He was a fine athlete. Now he's got cancer. He spoke about not burdening people with your problems when life deals you bad times, of coping with dignity and of seizing opportunities. He was talking about his situation, of course, but every person in the room was thinking about themselves. It certainly affected me. When people ask me how things are going with my knee I tend to say not very well. I do burden close friends with my grumbles and Claire gets it the worst. I'll try to be more upbeat. It'll probably last about a day or two.

I've just bought an ice machine, to help with reducing the swelling on my knee. If things go wrong, well, it will be useful to have around when we throw a party.

Looking back, the only time I've felt half as frustrated as this would have been in 1998, when I injured my back. That stopped my progress in my tracks. My debut year had been fantastic, but the second year turned into a nightmare. I was playing a lot of rugby at the time, so perhaps I had it coming.

(⋆ (⋆ (⋆

England's match against Australia immediately after the Lions tour can't have helped. Put simply, that game was the biggest joke ever. We had just finished an exhausting time in South Africa, loads of guys were knackered – Johnno, for one, had to pull out to get his groin sorted out – but someone still had the bright idea of sending us straight from Johannesburg to Sydney for yet another game. It was crazy, and it still is. We seem to play about twice as many games as the guys Down Under. Even crazier, a handful of guys who had not been with the Lions flew out from England. They arrived about four or five days before the rest of us and had no one to train with.

On the way to the stadium, I was among several players who fell asleep on the bus. They woke us up, shoved us out and, not surprisingly, we blew a gasket in the final twenty minutes and lost 25–6.

The next day, as we headed for the airport, Rowell came down the team bus shaking our hands and making obscure wisecracks at our expense. 'Glad you've lost your puppy fat,' he said to me. I did not think anything of it at the time but he was, in effect, saying goodbye. The game was going full time. Jack, though, had extensive business interests. Within a month he had resigned as coach.

I already knew that I was facing a major challenge from Backy with regards to my England place as the 1997–98 season began. The key would be to begin well with Saracens and thus convince Jack's successor, whoever that might be, that I was still worth my place. I had been signed up as a columnist by the *Evening Standard* newspaper, which led to me being persuaded to blow my own trumpet a bit in public and to respond to some of the things Backy had said about me in the past. I wanted to try and emulate Peter Winterbottom, I said. 'My target for this season is to make the England No. 7 jersey mine...I wouldn't say Backy gets to situations quicker than me.' In another interview I added: 'The open game is my sort of game, too. Rolling mauls don't turn me on. The English game has got to speed up.' And I went on: 'This season...I have produced the kind of form that proves I can be the England No. 7.'

As a prediction, it couldn't have been more wrong.

My first focus, though, was on my club. It was a hugely exciting time to be at Saracens. With Nigel Wray's backing we were hoping, along with the likes of Newcastle, to break the Leicester–Bath duopoly of English rugby. The feel-good factor from the British Lions successes had rubbed off and our squad looked stronger than ever, despite being slashed almost in half. There were new signings, among them Australian three-quarter Ryan Constable, former South Africa full-back Gavin Johnson and Argentinian prop Roberto Grau. We also recruited Danny Grewcock from Coventry. All told, we now had more than a dozen internationals.

There were big changes off the pitch, too. Peter Deakin, who had helped revolutionise rugby league's Bradford Bulls through his marketing expertise, arrived to do a similar job on us. He introduced cheer leaders, the 'Saracens Starlites', music for each player as he ran on the pitch or scored and even a remote-control car to bring on the kicking tees. Close links with local schools and clubs were forged. A handful of our fans had started sporting fezzes so there we were, 'The Fez Boys', with Will Smith's 'Men in Black' as our anthem ('Here come the Men in Black, the galaxy defenders...'). Most importantly of all, though, we moved out of London to Watford Football Club's ground at Vicarage Road, giving us a massive capacity of around 20,000.

Some people thought it was all about gimmicks, but soon we

were battling for top place in the league with Newcastle. Lynagh returned for his final season and was simply phenomenal. Sella was as enthusiastic and hard-working as ever. We certainly had a pretty useful middle five that season – Pienaar, Hill, Dips, Kyran and Lynagh, with Sella one man further out.

By the time the autumn internationals approached, Clive Woodward was in situ as England coach. There had been speculation that it could be Bob Dwyer, Graham Henry or even McGeechan, but Clive came out of left field. He had done well at London Irish and then taken charge of Bath's backs, but otherwise I didn't know too much about him. I wondered how I might fit into his thinking. Early on, I got invited to his house near Marlow with Dips, which seemed like a good sign. He wanted to discuss the back row and back row tactics. You got the impression that he wanted his players to take a much more active role in the team's future direction. It was a very different approach from Jack's. He had been much more distant and headmasterly.

Clive gradually became a manager of change rather than the coach of a team. He knew who he wanted as his right-hand men and quickly beefed up the England back-up staff. New Zealander John Mitchell arrived as forwards coach; Phil Keith-Roach was recruited from Wasps as scrum coach; while Phil Larder, a one-time rugby league man (who would have a huge influence on me) was defence coach. Clive liked to look at the big picture but he also seized on the small things. Straight away, for instance, he wanted our Twickenham changing room overhauled. It had been a fairly Spartan, breeze block of a place, but Clive wanted to personalise it and make us feel as though we belonged. The main changing area was broken up into individual changing slots, with a wooden plaque in each, sporting the player's name and the red rose of England. You'd know when your time was up with England, people said, because you would receive your name plaque in the post. (At the end of one Six Nations, a few of the Leicester boys unscrewed Austin's and sent it to his home.)

Another of Clive's strengths was that he was not frightened to challenge the norm or to experiment, on or off the pitch. He was determined to change the way England played. Nobody felt too secure to start with, especially after Clive announced he would select according to current form and that the entire squad, captain included, would be revised each month.

Not that he got things right immediately. His first game in charge was a drab 15–15 home draw with Australia. Clive made twelve changes to the team which had lost in Sydney. Lawrence replaced Phil de Glanville as captain and five players were given their debuts, among them Will Green and Andy Long in the front row. I was delighted to get picked but was acutely aware that Backy was on the bench, watching my every move. It felt a bit like that Lions second Test all over again. My main memory of the game was our poor scrummaging. Andy, who was only twenty at the time, and Will took most of the flak for that. They recovered, of course, but to this day neither has started another full international.

Next up were New Zealand, my first game against them. They were being touted as one of the most complete sides in history, so it was no surprise when we went down 25–8 at Old Trafford, although we didn't cave in quite as the bookies had predicted. The game began with Richard Cockerill's confrontation with Norm Hewitt during the haka. He walked right up to Hewitt and glared at him, infuriating the All Blacks. It was the first time I had faced the haka at close quarters and it was quite daunting. They said Cockers was being disrespectful, but I don't think New Zealanders should be surprised that their opponents, having got themselves charged up for a match, want to front up in some way.

It was also the first time I had played against Lomu, all 6ft 5in and 18st 8lb of him, and he was pretty daunting too. After the game we upset the New Zealanders again, by going around the stadium to applaud our fans. They seemed to think we were taking a lap of honour despite having lost and got terribly wound up about it, but we were just saying thank you for the crowd's support. We've hardly ever played away from Twickenham – in fact I think it was the first international staged outside London since the Second World War – and the atmosphere was incredible.

Personally, though, I remember that day for a different reason. It was the first time that Dallaglio, Back and Hill came together as a combination.

Backy had begun on the bench but Clive announced at half time that he was coming on. I thought that was the end of my day's work but, to my surprise, Clive pulled Dips off instead. Gradually it dawned on me – if Backy was coming on he would have to play openside, which meant I would have to play at No. 6. There had been no forewarning before the game that this could happen.

We made a mistake in the back row early in the second half and gifted them a try from a five-metre scrum. That was an eye opener. If we were going to work together as a trio, we would have to work at it. And Backy and I were going to have to start talking to each other.

Clive's baptism of fire continued the following weekend as we lost 29–11 to South Africa. It was a record England defeat at Twickenham (although, to put it into perspective, South Africa had just crushed France, the Grand Slam champions, 52–10 in Paris). Backy began at openside and Lawrence and I switched between the other two positions, depending on the situation. Lawrence, for instance, used to like attacking off the base of a scrum. Not everyone was impressed. John Taylor, writing in the

Mail on Sunday, said: 'At the top level you need one real power-house in the back row. Three flankers, including two open-sides, does not work.'

Shortly after the game, Clive rang me up. He had been watching my face when he had announced I would play at No. 8 and thought I had looked unhappy. I told him I would have preferred 7 but I was ready to play in any position. To be honest, it hadn't crossed my mind before that I would be good enough, let alone big enough, to play at 6 or 8 for my country. For a start, it would mean seeing off the likes of Tim Rodber and Ben Clarke. I probably felt very vulnerable because of the switch. Clive, though, said he wanted to persevere with the combination. Over the years, it would mean a change of style in the way I played.

The autumn series ended with a re-match against the All Blacks at Twickenham. It turned out to be a classic, to the extent that it was sold as a Christmas video that year, even though it ended in a 26–26 draw. I suppose we were still in Clive's idealistic period. Asked how he wanted England to play, he would say: 'I haven't got a clue what the game plan is. It's up to the players. My job is to get them organised and on to the pitch.' For several years he talked about playing what you saw – 'heads-up rugby', he called it. I really liked the idea, although you needed a basic structure. Against the All Blacks that day, that is exactly what we did. We played it as we saw it and the result was a thrilling, wide open game.

A lot of commentators said it was the most exciting exhibition of rugby they had ever seen from England. We certainly put together an awesome first half. David Rees, on the wing, showed the way by chipping Lomu and re-gathering the ball before scoring. A couple of his teeth were knocked out as he went over. I got the second try in rather embarrassing fashion after a mazy run from Will Greenwood. He threw a pie at my feet, I managed to scoop it up on the half volley and flopped over the line, grounding the ball before a defender picked me up and held me up in the air. Worried the referee hadn't spotted my touchdown, I was left hanging there, trying to get the ball down again. It was real Tom and Jerry stuff.

New Zealand, though, seeking a record twelfth win in twelve starts that year and with Zinzan Brooke playing his last game, changed things around after reaching the break 23–9 down. They tore into us and looked the most likely side to win by the end.

At that stage, it was probably my best game in an England shirt. In the changing room afterwards, though, there were mixed feelings. On the one hand, it was a huge success. We hadn't lost, we had scored tries and we had played some good stuff. Their coach, John Hart, said he had never seen an England performance like it. But the truth was that, in four home Tests against the southern hemisphere giants, we had not managed a win. It wasn't exactly something to shout about and, a year away from the next World Cup, showed how far behind we were.

Back at Sarries, things were going superbly. We put 50 points on Bath near the end of the year for a seventh win in a row. That was Bath's worst league defeat in ten years, played out in front of a record crowd of 11,000. The previous season, we were averaging around 3,500 a game.

My season, however, was about to fall apart.

A fortnight later we lost 22–21 to Leicester, courtesy of a last-gasp drop goal from Joel Stransky, but I missed the game with back trouble. I kept telling myself it was only a small problem, but it took me five weeks to get back.

I returned for the Five Nations but we lost again, 24–17 on our first visit to the Stade de France. We probably tried to play too much rugby behind the gain line while struggling up front. It was our seventh successive game without a win, so I suppose we were all under pressure, but I was certainly aware of it, with the media again questioning why we weren't playing a bigger, specialist No. 8 like Dips or Rodber. As forwards coach, Mitchell was equally unhappy, saying: 'Some of these guys are lucky they've been given a second chance…We need a physical presence.' I couldn't help thinking he was talking about me.

Perhaps my less-than-perfect back was hampering me, but I needed a big game next time out against Wales. I wasn't too confident. Privately, I felt I was too small to be playing at 6 or 8. At that point, I didn't jump in the line-out either, which limited what I had to offer.

As it happened, we scored eight tries in a 60–26 rout. Bateman scored two early tries for Wales but we finished with an avalanche of points, scoring 28 in the last fifteen minutes. I was subbed off in the second half but felt I had gone OK. Little did I know, though, that it would be nine months before I pulled on the England shirt again.

To be honest, there had been signs of something not being quite right for some time. I had been suffering from recurring calf and hamstring problems early in the season, which then seemed to gravitate to my back. In one Sarries training session, I had gone into an unopposed maul and suddenly crumpled to the floor in agony.

Things came to a head in February, during our Tetley's Bitter Cup quarter-final against Richmond. On the previous evening we had gone to a cinema for a private viewing of the film *Jackie Brown* but my back was so painful that I could not sit down. I ended up lying in the aisle, my drink and popcorn at my side. I was still lying in the aisle when we were bussed to the game the next day, with people stepping over me to get out. The adrenaline kicked in during the warm-up, though, because I suddenly felt fine again and took to the field chewing a couple of painkillers.

We seemed to have the game wrapped up in the second half, allowing Francois to substitute himself and head off to join Nerine in hospital for the birth of their first child. Richmond scored two tries in injury time to make it a much closer affair, but we won and headed for the bar. Within minutes, though, my back had gone again. I was probably in as much agony as Francois's wife. I spent the next week wearing a TENS machine – normally used by expectant mothers to help deal with labour pains – before an MRI scan confirmed that I needed an operation for a bulging disc.

So I missed the end of Saracens' most successful – some would argue only successful – season of the professional era. It is probably one of my biggest regrets. While my team-mates were winning the Tetley's Cup and taking the league season to the final day before losing out to Newcastle, I was spending my time at the Southgate Leisure Centre, doing rehabilitation exercises under the admiring gaze of a group of pensioners with whom I shared the pool. They weren't admiring me, they hadn't got a clue who I was. It was the flotation belt I was wearing – they kept asking me where they could get hold of one.

I'd only ever had one serious injury before, when I needed a groin operation back in the 1993–94 season (that was one of the more painful diagnoses I have ever undergone, involving a Harley Street consultant, my nether regions and his finger. I reckon I would have yelped even if the groin hadn't been torn). In those days, back surgery was a much bigger deal. You knew far fewer people who had recovered from such operations. Still, I was in so much pain, unable even to sit or sleep, that it was a massive relief to go under the knife. Claire said I had a huge smile on my face after coming round from the anaesthetic and realising the pain had gone. Years later, I came across a jar at home containing the part of the offending disc. I threw it away immediately. God knows why I had taken it home in the first place. All it had caused me was trouble.

So my season ended with me wondering what the future held. I wasn't established in the England side and I knew that I would be absent for at least six games, more than enough time for someone to make the position their own. I knew that Rodber, who I got on well with, was still out there, as was Clarke. When I had won my first cap, all I had wanted was to get a second – there can't be a much worse feeling than being capped just once and joining the OCWs (One Cap Wonders)…well, apart from not being capped at all, of course. After that, I had set my sights on ten. I was now on eleven. All I knew was that I wanted more.

Anyway, France duly wrapped up the Grand Slam while Saracens finished the season in style. Arguably the most memorable league game came in April when we beat Newcastle at home 12–10 to keep the league race alive. The match attracted a crowd of 19,764, a record for an English league game away from Twickenham. There was a nice twist in the final minute when Marcus, playing instead of Kyran, flung out a pass to Lynagh, who put over the winning drop goal from 40 metres. Rob Andrew, who had done the same to Lynagh and the Australians in the 1995 World Cup, and a fresh-faced Jonny Wilkinson – who would in due course get a pretty famous drop goal of his own – were forced to look on.

It hurt, missing that game. It hurt even more, missing the cup final. We took on our long-time rivals Wasps on a glorious summer's day at Twickenham, and obliterated them 48–18. It was exhibition stuff. I remember seeing our fans, in their fezzes and scarves, clambering into coaches and cars on their way to Twickenham and it suddenly hit home how big an occasion I was missing. Our guys lived up to it, Sella scoring the first of seven tries while Lynagh, with a superb sense of timing, produced one of his very best performances.

The guys could barely believe the scoreboard at half time. They were leading 29–6. Francois managed to keep them going by telling them: 'You will never get an opportunity to do this again. The chance to take a team apart in a cup final – I'm telling you, it will never come again in your lives.' It was also a huge day for guys like Botterman and Lee, who were approaching the end of their club careers after ten years of service. I still have the picture in my head of Dips raising the cup to our fans after the final whistle.

It was the club's first major piece of silverware in 122 years and seemed to promise so much. I was really chuffed for the guys, although it was quite hard to take from a personal point of view. I didn't really feel part of it, having missed the semi and final, so I avoided having my picture taken with the trophy. I didn't feel I deserved it. I hoped one day I would achieve the same thing myself. With Saracens, that has never happened (well, apart from winning the Old Millhillian Sevens, but that's not quite the same thing).

The last match of the season, against Northampton, doubled as a farewell for Sella and Lynagh. Both teams formed a guard of honour before kick-off, which shows how respected they were. Michael looked embarrassed as he trotted out, while Philippe was beaming. They had both done wonderfully for Saracens, as well as for Australia and France, and I admire them both totally. They went on to become the first two names inducted into the Saracens Hall of Fame, which was fair enough, although I couldn't help feeling sorry for guys like John Buckton, Brian Davies or Lee Adamson (he played 500 games for the first XV) who had stuck with the club through thick and thin.

At least there was one plus point to my lay-off – it meant missing England's controversial 1998 summer tour to Australia, New Zealand and South Africa. I was the first withdrawal from

the squad – I felt I had a fairly good reason, lying on the operating table – but by the time the plane left Heathrow, around
seventeen leading players had been made unavailable for one
reason or another. I'm not sure too many people fancied it
after an arduous season.

Predictably, we got hammered wherever we went, losing by
a record 76–0 against Australia in Brisbane first time out. Some
people might think that Dips pulled the short straw, by being
named captain for that game, but I can assure you he still looks
back on that day as one of his proudest moments. Steve
Ravenscroft, another Saracens stalwart, feels the same. He was
an intellectual guy, a practising lawyer and the club's last part-
timer. Put simply, he typified what we were about. He had been
so proud to get the chance to play alongside Sella towards the
end of his career. He won his only two England caps on the
Tour of Hell but still looks back on those games as a momentous honour.

Despite that, quite a few reputations were destroyed on that
trip. It might have done mine no good either, had I been fit.
Mind you, a few guys came through the ordeal: M. Dawson, D.
Grewcock, J. Lewsey and J. Wilkinson, to name but a few.

10

NEARLY MEN

My memories of the next two seasons blur into one, which is perhaps understandable. They followed an eerily similar pattern. With England, the line on the graph pointed steadily up but, when it came to the crunch, we missed out on the big prizes. At Saracens, things went in the opposite direction. Considering the backing and resources we had at the club, as well as our great start to the professional era, it's no great surprise that we have been branded underachievers ever since. You have to face facts – we expected, and were expected, to build on our Tetley's Cup win and it didn't happen. I hate that word, underachievers. It's repeated all the time and it really gets to me. The worst thing about it is that it's true.

England, over the next few seasons, got a fair amount of flak as well, after failing to win a Grand Slam or make an impression in the World Cup. Some parts of the media painted us as chokers. This time, though, I disagree. Sure, we took a few years to mature as a side, and to produce consistent performances. Sure, it took us time to learn certain lessons as players. Clive would say the same about himself. The simple fact is that other teams outplayed us at key times when we had been expected to win – it's hard to accept, but it's not against the law. But we didn't choke. It's an easy accusation, but not one that has ever been made to my face. I shouldn't think it has been said to Lawrence or Johnno, or indeed any member of that team either.

I had returned to club training in June after my back operation and got through a pre-season friendly against Pontypridd with no alarms. I had worked hard and put on a bit of muscle in the gym (something I continued to do over the following seasons) during my enforced break. We then got off to a flyer in the 1998–99 season. Our first home game suggested that we might live up to the tag of title favourites. There had been a big reshuffle of players, with Alain Penaud, the French fly-half, Jeremy Thompson, the South African centre, and Troy Coker, the Australian flanker, coming in. They looked like inspired signings when all three scored tries within the first half-hour of the game against Northampton.

Shortly afterwards, we beat Leicester 22–10 at Vicarage Road, a fixture which drew more than 17,000 supporters. On the back of that, I was recalled to the England bench for the World Cup qualifiers against Holland and Italy. The Dutch ran out to the tune of 'Tulips from Amsterdam' at the McAlpine Stadium in Huddersfield and duly got cut down 110–0. They were only amateurs, but I had no intention of going easy on them when I got on with twenty minutes left. Cozza and Clarke started those games and back row positions were up for grabs. Italy, meanwhile, gave us a fright before we won 23–15, even if it seemed a largely meaningless game with both teams qualifying for the World Cup. The Italians scored a perfectly good try that day, in my opinion, but we didn't have video referees yet and it was ruled out.

The serious stuff began with the autumn games against Australia and South Africa. To my relief Clive reverted to Lawrence, Backy and me in the back row. Clive, indeed, never lost faith in me while he was in charge, which is more than you can say of some journalists. We went down 12–11 against Australia in a pretty forgettable game and Stephen Jones, who never seemed to like the way I played during this period, wrote in the *Sunday Times* that I was 'disturbingly lacking in profile for such a key man in such a key position'. I'm pretty sure he still thought of me as a No. 7 playing out of position and could not see beyond the numbers on our back. I felt I had improved my defence by then, as well as my work in the tight, even if Clive was in no way asking me to turn myself into a traditional, big, defensive blindside flanker. He was looking to expand our attacking game, with everyone contributing. He didn't see any great difference between a blindside and an openside flanker, and nor did I. The game was changing and it became quite common to see two No. 7s in the same starting line-up. Australia, for instance, went for Phil Waugh and George Smith.

One thing that struck me against the Aussies was their non-stop chatter. A lot of it was communication between players, but there was also plenty of sledging. You would go down for a scrum and hear your name being mentioned. I don't know how much of that was kidology, trying to distract you or make you expect a big hit during the next play. The Australians did it more than anyone back then, although it's common every-where now. Hookers, in particular, get a fair bit of verbal atten-tion at line-outs, while front rows like to swap pleasantries. George Gregan always used to sledge quite a bit, although he doubled up as one of the nicest guys you could meet off the pitch. Win, lose or draw, he would come over and talk to you, which is pretty rare.

The game against South Africa would prove to be much more significant. Indeed, it changed an awful lot in terms of our self-belief.

The statistics were heavily against us. The Springboks went

into the game seeking a world-record eighteenth Test win in a row, having just won home and away against Australia and New Zealand in the Tri Nations before knocking over Wales, Ireland and Scotland. We, meanwhile, had not beaten a southern hemisphere side in twelve attempts since the 1995 World Cup. But we put in a pretty big performance up front and came out 13–7 winners. We had always believed we could beat one of the big three southern hemisphere teams on our day but it was another thing to actually do it. They scored an early converted try, but Guscott replied in kind, after Dan Luger had palmed back a cross-kick from Catty, before Daws sealed things with a couple of second-half penalties. Everybody was absolutely elated afterwards. It was a huge confidence booster. The World Cup was less than a year away, with the South Africans looming as our likely quarter-final opponents.

On paper we were ranked about fifth in the world but, with the tournament in Europe, people started to believe that we might have a chance to cause a surprise. Clive told his critics that they should judge him on the World Cup. In hindsight, that was probably a mistake. By about four years.

Our growing excitement, however, did not survive the Five Nations. The only game to stand out for me was our final outing against Wales. Nightmares tend to stay with you.

We had begun by beating the Scots 24–21 at Twickenham, with Jonny Wilkinson making his first Five Nations start in the centre. We led 14–0, then began to misfire and nearly threw it away. We won a little more comfortably in Ireland. Even the 21–10 home win over France has faded in my memory, which is strange considering they were going for their third Grand Slam in a row and we had not beaten them for four seasons. It should have felt momentous but its significance would quickly be devalued.

We weren't exactly playing our most exciting stuff at the

time. Despite Clive's desire to play 'heads-up' rugby, we were probably improving much faster as a defensive rather than as an attacking unit. A lot of that had to do with Phil Larder. He certainly changed my approach. I had thought I was a good defensive player before he came along but I got quite a wake-up call. Years later I remember watching some clips from the 1997 Lions games in South Africa and I was struck – shocked might be a better word – by my tackling. I brought people down but nowadays we would call them 'soak tackles'. The guy gets stopped but breaks the gain line.

Basically, we were all still using techniques we had learnt at school – hit with the shoulder around the thigh, get your head out of the way, squeeze your arms together and then slide down your opponent's legs. Phil, with his rugby league background, very quickly made us question everything, by asking us to consider what we wanted to achieve from each and every tackle. Did we want to knock guys backwards to deny them yardage, did we want to stay on our feet afterwards, what if your opponent was running straight at us rather than at an angle? Did you want to isolate the ball carrier by turning him, thus stopping him presenting the ball back to his team-mates? After that, we began examining our techniques in detail, from the positioning of our feet to our body angles. It all seems obvious now, but his approach was much more scientific.

He also developed a new defensive system for the entire team. Backy was central to this, effectively becoming Phil's general on the pitch. For the first time, our training was changed to reflect the fact that 50 per cent of the game is about defence. That was completely new. So were the handouts that Phil gave us, detailing each player's tackle count. The target was a 95 per cent success rate. Backy and I compared results and took our rivalry very seriously. The whole thing didn't come easily to the team, though, and took several years to perfect.

We certainly hadn't cracked it by the 1999 Five Nations, as Scott Gibbs illustrated at Wembley. I've never forgotten what he did to us, that day. The game was being staged there because the Millennium Stadium was being completed for the World Cup. It felt odd, being the away team in the middle of London, but the Welsh supporters really made the place their own. It was an amazing atmosphere, with Max Boyce and Tom Jones whipping up the crowd.

To be honest, we went pretty well in the first half and for long periods of the second. We had scored three times by the break, with yours truly flopping over after a blunder in the Welsh defence. Neil Jenkins, though, kept them in the game by kicking absolutely everything. We were still leading going into the final minutes only for everything to go pear-shaped. Lawrence was criticised afterwards for turning down a 40-metre penalty shot with five minutes left and opting to kick for position instead, but that's the benefit of hindsight. Almost immediately, Rodber was penalised for a high tackle – it was the sort of tackle he'd have done countless times before without being sanctioned – they booted it back into our territory and suddenly we were facing an attacking Welsh line-out in injury time.

As I remember it, the ball came off the top to Scott Quinnell who fumbled. If anything, that was our downfall. A few of us anticipated a knock-on and a loose ball but he held on and passed to Gibbs who went on a jinking, bullocking run. With a guy like Scott Gibbs, you have to bring him down as early as you can but we did not lay a finger on him. I think he went between me and Rodber, danced to his right past about three other would-be tacklers and scampered in. Jenkins added the conversion, we lost 32–31 and the Grand Slam had gone.

It was certainly the biggest let-down of my career to date. We had expected to win and could hardly believe what had happened. The Welsh fans were going berserk but there was a stunned silence in our changing room. The only consolation was catching up with a few of the guys on the Welsh team that I had got to know with the Lions. Normally I go back over my England matches on video, to see how I performed, but I didn't this time.

Nothing went right that day, not even the presentations to Steve Hanley and Barrie-Jon Mather following their debuts. I had played with Barrie-Jon Mather for England when we were teenagers. He had been a lock, prior to making a name for himself in rugby league, before finally returning to union as a centre. He put his red velvet cap on that evening and the tassel got entangled in the chandelier above his head. He couldn't get it down so it was left dangling there throughout a rather muted post-match dinner.

So the last Five Nations in history ended with an unusual look to it, Scotland at the top of the table and France at the bottom. Few people would have bet on that at the start of the championship. As for us, we had started the season with that memorable win against the South Africans only to end it on a downer.

The Sarries season went the same way. We finished a distant third behind the champions, Leicester, and failed to retain the cup. Looking back, it was no surprise, considering the personality clashes at the club. The worst of them was between my long-time mate Dips and Francois.

Their professional relationship gradually became unworkable as the results went against us. They were in an odd position. Francois was in charge as player–coach but during matches he had to give way to Dips as club captain. Things came to a head halfway through the season at Gloucester. Down 25–6 at half time, we fought back only to eventually lose 28–27. Dips thanked his players for their second-half performance, but Francois was furious about what had happened before the break. Soon after, it was announced he would be taking over the captaincy as a short-term measure. Dips, understandably, was gutted by that and started questioning his own role. He had been in charge since 1995–96 and said if he was going to stand down then it should be permanent.

Their professional relationship never recovered, even though they get on fine socially. Losing the job had a huge effect on Dips. On one occasion they almost came to blows after winding each other up at training. Dips accidentally caught Francois in the mouth as he was holding a tackle bag and Francois hared after him, trying to get in a return punch. Francois had already replaced Evans as coach, and he also had a tricky relationship with Paul Turner. Turner was brought in as backs coach but never got the chance to make his mark and left before the season was out.

Francois, basically, was full-on. His approach was more stick than carrot. He liked to challenge people but some people interpreted it as confrontation. You could not fault his commitment, but I'm not sure his method got the best out of everyone, particularly when we were losing. At times, in pre-season training, his approach seemed almost military. He took defeat very hard and used to say that he hated losing more than anyone else at the club, which was a bit naïve. It can't have been easy, of course. He had arrived as a player and then became a player–coach, which changed the relationship with his teammates. Perhaps he also got frustrated. He had achieved amazing things during his career but it did not quite work out at Saracens. Our long injury list did not help, and Francois himself was not the player he had been, which he may have found difficult to come to terms with.

All that said, I never had a problem with him. He was a nice guy. Sure, he was serious but he certainly had a sense of humour too. The nearest we came to a spat was when he benched me once, after publicly criticising my running lines and saying he would have done better in my place. I had a good game next time out and Francois claimed that his tactic of dropping or resting me – I was never quite sure which it was – had worked because it had provoked a response. I've never forgotten that criticism about running lines – it riled me and I still don't agree with it. Anyway, God knows what he made of me most of the time. When Kyran became captain, Francois wanted me to be more of a leader among the forwards and do more talking, but it didn't come naturally to me. Unlike him, I wasn't assertive. Perhaps he couldn't understand that.

Sometimes he must have felt that the world was against him. That was certainly the case when we played Lydney in the cup that season. I used to play against Forest of Dean sides when I was at school – in fact, I got my first rugby stitches there – so I knew it would be rough. You could understand them wanting to have a good go and to try and pull off a giant killing, but it got out of hand. A fight broke out straight from the kick-off and skirmishes seemed to break out every other minute. I don't normally talk to referees but even I wasn't happy that day. I heard later that there had been a sweepstake to see which of their players could start a fight with Pienaar first which, if true, was out of order. He certainly got punched twice, while Paddy Johns was even grabbed around the neck by someone in the crowd.

If I had any problems with anyone that season, it was with Alain Penaud. He could be temperamental. He had better attacking skills than Michael Lynagh, without a doubt, and could defend better when he wanted to, but you never knew what he was going to do. For the most part, he seemed to think that I should be responsible for tackling the opposition fly-half, thus allowing him to drift across field. Basically, I felt he wasn't interested in what I had to cope with, but just wanted to do his own thing. On top of that, he had his differences with Turner, who wanted him to play a more controlled game. In that regard, I felt for Alain. Players with flair, I think, should be allowed to play. That is why he was offered a contract in the first place, because he attacks. It was no great surprise that he failed to settle and headed back to France after a single season.

Troy Coker left too, while we lost Paddy, Gavin Johnson and Richard Wallace. What we lacked that season, and have lacked ever since, was stability. Things always seemed to be changing at Saracens. It's incredible how many coaches I have played under at the club – John Davies, Mark Evans, Francois, Alan Zondagh, Wayne Shelford, Rod Kafer, Steve Diamond and Mike Ford. As I write, Eddie Jones has been standing in as a short-term caretaker and Alan Gaffney is arriving next season. Each new coach has had different ideas about how he wanted the team to perform, meaning new back-up staff, new players and new tactics. It's been a merry-go-round.

Francois said the 1998–99 season was the worst of his life. I wish I could say the same.

At least I had the distraction of the World Cup to look forward to.

Not that everything ran smoothly. For a start, Lawrence was set up by a tabloid newspaper which ran a piece alleging that he had been involved in recreational drugs in his youth. It came as a complete shock when Lawrence was stripped of the captaincy, thus missing our World Cup training camp in Australia and the Centenary Test against the Wallabies.

That camp, at the Couran Cove resort on South Stradbroke Island just off the Gold Coast, was not quite the fun I had expected it to be. I got the impression that I would be allowed to recuperate with a little light training for a week or two after a long season. Instead I trained pretty much through the entire two and a half weeks, along with the rest of the guys. There were gym sessions, runs, team-bonding exercises like climbing and a triathlon, as well as one-to-one work with the coaches. The idea was to work hard in a relaxing atmosphere. Our idea of relaxing was not always the same as Clive's, though. For a start, most of us preferred the Gold Coast nightlife to our self-catering apartments in the evening, which did not go down too well. Clive's accommodation was next to the water taxi drop-off point, so anyone returning late had to persuade their drivers to put them ashore somewhere else. Leonard and Guscott missed one curfew and tried to convince the management that their water taxi had broken down on the way back and been adrift for a couple of hours.

In retrospect, I think the balance at the camp was wrong. You have to keep things fun to keep people on board. They made a big push on our nutrition, for instance, but in the end everybody got so sick of the boiled food and tasteless nutrition bars on offer that they stopped eating altogether. There was delight one day when sausages were added to the menu, only for us to find that they had been boiled as well.

Clive also wanted all of us to start using computers and to keep in touch via email, a bit like a business community. This must have got out into the press because Brad Johnstone, the Fiji coach, referred to us during the World Cup as a team armed with state-of-the-art laptops driving around in fast cars. If only Brad had seen us at Couran Cove! We spent our time getting around on push bikes, while quite a few of us were computer illiterate and our mobile phone connections crashed continually.

Even one of our rare days off went wrong. We were offered a choice – a deep-sea fishing trip or a golf day. I opted for fishing. Wrong choice. There was quite a swell that day and only two of the twenty starters were left standing by the end. One side of the boat was for rods and the other for people leaning over and being sick. Backy was sick within the first hour. Six hours later we were still at sea and there he was, pleading with our doctor Terry Crystal for another sea sickness tablet. Terry replied that you were only meant to take one. Backy kept nagging until Terry, all green around the gills, blurted out: 'Look Backy, it won't help you. I know, mate, I've already taken four of them myself.'

As for the Centenary Test, well, we went down 22–15 in front of a crowd of around 100,000 in Stadium Australia, Sydney's new Olympic showpiece venue. We played well enough but I remember being impressed by the Wallaby backs. They took their chances so clinically. Ben Tune scored a couple of tries, either side of the break, to take the match away from us. We had never won in Australia before and deep down, we probably did not expect to that time either. That self-belief only began to materialise a year or so later.

I've since read that one of the reasons for our downfall in the 1999 World Cup was that we focused on it too early, so that we were in a state of mental exhaustion by the time it began. Perhaps there should have been a bit more fun and relaxation. I know some guys found the situation very intense. Garath Archer was one. The boys were put through a really hard physical session and Garath, who had been suffering from a bad back, got through it along with everyone else only to be asked to prove his fitness once more. He thought that was ridiculous but he got through the test, then decided he'd had enough, telling us to hand in his computer for him – Clive had always said you had to hand them back if you got dropped. It was hushed up, though, and he was quickly brought back into the squad.

Personally, I enjoyed a lot of what we did in the lead-up to the tournament, particularly when we were with the Marines in Lympstone in Devon. They pride themselves on running the toughest basic infantry training in the British Armed Forces and we were given a very small taste of it, living rough on Dartmoor and doing military exercises like abseiling down cliffs, crossing water obstacles and launching mock attacks on fortified positions. There were helicopter drop-offs and some pretty daunting experiences in a variety of simulators.

One was meant to represent the hull of a ship, with a fire blazing inside. You had to work your way to the bottom in complete darkness as a team, climbing down a series of metal ladders after the leader of the group had memorised the lay-out from a set of instructions. We were decked out in hoods, goggle and gloves – the ladders were too hot to hold otherwise – and you held on to the guy in front so as not to get lost. Dips didn't bend down far enough at one stage and singed his hair, while Phil de Glanville begged to be taken out because he thought he was on fire.

Another simulator represented a sinking ship, which filled up with water as you tried to block up the holes. The most daunting one, though, was a helicopter simulator at the Fleet Air Arm Museum at Yeovilton. About eight of you were packed into it and then it was dropped into a pool and flipped upside down. You had to stay in your positions while it filled up with water and then get yourself out of your safety belts and squeeze out of a variety of exits. To make it even more disorientating, they turned out the lights.

The first time I was so confused that I got out straight away, before it had even turned over. I broke the water's surface and got a stream of abuse from the officers around the pool. Their attitude was understandable, when you think that a mistake on a rugby pitch might mean conceding a try or losing a game, while cock-ups in their line of work are altogether more serious. Dan Luger got into an even bigger scrape when he swam the wrong way as he tried to get out of the simulator and got trapped under a bench. One of the safety divers tried to turn him round but Dan panicked a bit and punched him in the face. The one thing it did teach me was that, if you are ever in a plane and it lands in water, get out quick and forget everything you ever learnt about good manners.

The idea of the week's training, I think, was first to fatigue you, then to see how you responded. It was right up my street. I got a lot out of it, especially when I was asked to lead an exercise. They encouraged everybody to take charge at different points, to help break down barriers within the squad. I think it encouraged a lot of people to speak who would normally have hung back. I thought that could only help us as a group. The other thing that these sorts of exercises teach you is that, even when you think you are mentally and physically exhausted, there is always something more you can pull out of the bag.

As for the Marines, they're a fascinating breed. I loved listening to their stories and watching them work. They were amazingly resilient. They tended to be quite small and slender but would carry these huge, heavy backpacks for twenty or thirty miles. Some of them did it on their days off, for fun. It's a special mentality, and pretty humbling. These are guys who tackle situations the rest of us would do everything to avoid.

As for the World Cup, well, to be truthful, I have only sporadic memories of it. For obvious reasons, it was a lot less memorable than 2003. Somehow it never felt as huge an event. It seemed just like any other tournament, perhaps because it was at home and everything was familiar. It also ended in anti-climax for us.

We began with a 67–7 win over Italy. Jonny, aged twenty, scored 32 points, a record in an England international, but had the decency to leave a few scraps for the rest of us, including a try for me. I went down the blindside and found no one was at home, so I ran in from 40 metres. One newspaper wrote that 'if

Neil Back and Lawrence Dallaglio are the heroic tenors of the red rose opera, Richard Hill is the rich baritone who holds the production together'. As it happens, I couldn't hit a note with a blunderbuss.

We always knew that our second game against the All Blacks was the one that mattered. The winners would earn an easier run to the semi-finals. The losers would face an extra play-off game and a likely trip to Paris to take on the Springboks.

The press, of course, built us up, but we were nowhere near tournament favourites. New Zealand were and they brushed us aside 30–16. For a while, we were doing well and even dominating possession. They led 13–6 at half time but de Glanville scored following a Guscott chip early in the second half and everything seemed set up for a rousing finale. Then along came that man Lomu again, taking a cut-out pass from Andrew Mehrtens, handing off Guscott and then blasting past Healey, Daws and Luger. We had nobody who could do that to their defence. It was the same old story – we were good at getting the ball, but less good at exploiting it.

The price of defeat was three bruising matches in nine days. I had already picked up a cut around my eye, which was nothing out of the ordinary. You get them as a matter of course when you go head first into rucks and mauls (hence yet another nickname, 'Paperface'). I do remember the clout I got in the following match, however.

Tonga's World Cup team seemed to be made up of policemen but they failed to keep their discipline that day. The trouble started when one of the guys from 'the Friendly Islands' took Matt Perry out as he went up for a high ball, tipping him over onto his head. There was a bit of a mêlée. I was minding my own business on the fringes and all of a sudden I caught a glimpse of this guy flying across the pitch towards me. I managed to turn my face away at the last second, which probably saved me from being knocked out. Instead, I copped a glancing blow from their 19st prop Ngalu Taufo'ou. By the time I got up he had been sent off. You never want to be involved when someone gets sent off and unfortunately it ruined the game, which ended with us winning 101–10.

Claire was watching in the crowd with some of her pupils. Normally, she would have been sitting in the West Stand, row 26, next to Ali Back and Alice, Lawrence's partner, but this time she was in the South Stand with her party. She said she could see what was about to happen as if it had been in slow motion and, for the first time ever, swore in front of the kids. There was a hushed silence as they all stared at her.

Then one of them piped up: 'Was that your boyfriend, Miss?'

'Yes.'

'That man just hit your boyfriend.'

'Yes,' was the terse reply. And that was all that was said.

After the game Taufo'ou came up to me and apologised. He repeated the apology later in the season, when playing for Pontypridd against Saracens. He was very polite about the whole thing. Tongans, in my experience, are the most friendly, God-fearing people you can imagine off the field. Unfortunately, I do a lot of my socialising with them on it.

We were now forced into a play-off with Fiji. Like the Tongans, they are very physical and hugely inventive. Looking at them, I could hardly tell the backs and the forwards apart. I began as a substitute but our bench was empty by the end of a bruising encounter which we won 45–24.

We were through to the quarter-finals but it left a bad taste in the mouth. The winners of each of the five groups had qualified automatically, but the rest of us had to play that extra game. That seemed wrong. I couldn't see how you could have a World Cup where some teams had to play more games than others. We had had to play the South Africans four days after the Fijians, while the Springboks had nine days' break.

We got back to our hotel late on the Wednesday evening to find out that Jerry Guscott had injured his groin and decided to retire from the game. He was a special player but sadly there was no time to go out and celebrate his career. We headed straight for the swimming pool to begin our recuperation before catching the Eurostar early next morning. In Paris, there was time for one team-run on Friday and then we were propelled into one of the biggest games of our careers. Eighty minutes later and it was all over. All credit to the Springboks though. They did a job on us that day. They analysed our play and came up with the plan to deal with it.

The killer blow – well, five killer blows, to be exact – came from the boot of Jannie de Beer. He kicked a world-record five drop goals that day, all sweetly struck. He sat deep in the pocket and we couldn't get anyone near him because of the quality of their possession. The worst part was that we didn't feel exhausted afterwards. They had scored freely and we hadn't been able to do a single thing about it. Jannie, who had not even been in their preliminary World Cup squad, kicked 34 points and did not miss a kick all day. Hats off to him.

That night, we went out and drowned our sorrows in a Parisian bar. There were still two weeks to go and we were out of the tournament. Clive must have thought he was out of a job. He had asked to be judged on the World Cup and we had fallen short of England's performances in 1991, when they reached the final, and 1995, when they got to the last four.

Clive, though, was adamant he could still do something with us. It would have been very easy for the Rugby Football Union to replace him, but they stuck with him and it proved the right move. It gave the team stability and gave us the chance to develop as a group.

South Africa went on to lose to Australia in extra time and the Aussies then won the World Cup by beating France in the final. By then, I was back at Saracens and watching on TV. The only consolation was that Tim Horan, the player of the tournament, joined us shortly afterwards at Vicarage Road.

(* (* (*

Ultimately, 1999–2000 was a season of missed opportunities, just as the previous one had been. The World Cup was bad enough, but the Six Nations which followed was even harder to digest. Again, we went into our final game with a Grand Slam for the taking, and again we missed out.

We began without Johnno, who had Achilles trouble. Some young players, though, were coming through. We crushed Ireland 50–18 in our opener. Mike Tindall and Ben Cohen, watched by his uncle George who had played in England's 1966 World Cup-winning football side, made their debuts and shared three tries. With Austin and Catty in the side alongside Jonny Wilkinson, we had plenty of decision-makers among the backs – it was like playing with three fly-halves. It was a few months too late really, but Ireland's coach Warren Gatland said it was probably the best stuff he'd ever seen from England.

Our 15–9 win in France was less spectacular but probably more significant. Conditions were wet, the ball slippery and no one managed a try. If anything, they kept the ball tighter than us. But our defence was excellent. Larder's system was beginning to work at last. The thing I remember above all else was a tackle from Jonny. Just before half time, Emile N'tamack tried to burst past him, only to be smashed upwards and backwards. It provided a huge psychological boost for us. You need someone to make a big tackle like that every now and again. We ended the game in desperate defence, camped on our own line, but it showed that there was a real spirit in the side despite the recent disappointments. There were a lot of guys dancing in delight at the final whistle. For me, it was a first away victory over the French.

I was the subject of a fair bit of mickey-taking before that game. Usually the guys go on about me being tight with my money or just plain grumpy ('show Richard flowers and he thinks of funerals', that sort of comment). Anyway, during a press day I was flattered to be asked to do a one-on-one interview with a French journalist. His English was not too hot, but then nor was my French, so we battled on as best we could. Soon he was asking me questions about their left winger, Christophe Dominici, which confused me a bit. What did I think of him as a player? What were his strengths? I bluffed a few answers before the next question – so how was I going to deal with Dominici? Suddenly it dawned on me; he had asked for Healey and ended up with 'Hilly'. I beat an embarrassed retreat, but not quickly enough. The guys – Backy and Lawrence in particular, the more 'fashionable' members of the back row – nearly died laughing when they heard what had happened.

Wales provided that same back row with a statistical oddity. Each of us scored a try in the 46–12 win over Wales at Twickenham (something we also managed against South Africa two years later at the same venue). Mine, though, was probably offside. I don't quite know how but as I tore the ball off one of their players I seemed to emerge out of the back of their maul. At the time I thought it was OK, but I was less convinced after studying the video. One of my former schoolmasters, a Welshman through and through, wasn't happy either. He always got in contact to complain when I scored against Wales.

We played some pretty good stuff that day, scoring five tries without reply. A couple of second-half sin-binnings helped, although Graham Henry said his side would have needed twenty-four players, not fourteen, to stop us. Brian Ashton, in charge of the backs, was also having a major influence. The bulk of the squad had been together for some time and we were beginning to get some returns for our efforts.

The press had already installed us as Grand Slam winners-elect, even before we travelled to Italy and crushed them 59–12. That left Scotland.

What can I say? Massive favourites, we marched up to Murrayfield, it rained and we lost 19–13. We started the day in search of a Grand Slam, a Triple Crown and the Calcutta Cup and had to make do with the championship instead. Upsets don't get much bigger. We had won all our games while Scotland had lost all of theirs, including a 34–20 reverse against the Italians. That made it even worse than our defeat against Wales the previous season.

We had been in good spirits going in, even after some of the boys were stitched up by a tabloid newspaper. At training, two girls turned up at the university ground where we were training and asked to have their picture taken with them. A guy appeared with a camera, everyone posed and at the last second the girls lifted up their tops. The photographer then legged it. The players pleaded their innocence, although questions were asked the next day when the newspaper came out. The picture showed a couple of the guys looking down rather than up at the camera, with large grins on their faces.

As for the game, well it started perfectly when Lawrence scuttled over for a try off the base of a scrum. Then, just before half time, the heavens opened and the wind started to whip around Murrayfield. We tried to continue running the ball, while the Scots wisely played the percentages. Duncan Hodge burrowed over for a try and had the game of his life with the boot. They played the situation perfectly. My Saracens team-mate

Scott Murray was at his niggling best for Scotland in the line-outs, getting under the skin of a few players and making them lose concentration. To complete the humiliation, I went down with cramp and had to be stretchered off, which felt idiotic. Both my quad muscles cramped up for the one and only time in my life, which in turn meant my legs locked up. I tried to walk, but it was as if I was on stilts.

I don't think I have ever known a more despondent dressing room in all my time playing rugby. Later, we heard we'd also managed to snub the Princess Royal. We had slunk off after the game and had forgotten to pick up the Championship Trophy.

Inevitably, the result led to renewed accusations that we lacked bottle. We were fine beating out-gunned opponents, the media said, but caved in at the slightest hint of pressure, just as we had done in the World Cup. It was more a lack of brains than bottle that day, though. We just got it all wrong.

The season at Saracens was even more deflating. We had the usual influx of new faces, with Alan Zondagh as coach and Horan, Dan Luger and Thierry Lacroix in the backs. It didn't help. We were on a slide by now, which continued for several seasons. As usual, we seemed to get our fair share of injuries. Dan arrived with a groin problem and barely played all season while Thierry injured his knee ligament. Jeremy Thompson, meanwhile, was released early from his contract after wrecking his shoulder.

Again, there was a string of near misses. No excuses, though. Games last eighty minutes. We seemed to be playing for seventy-nine that season. In all, I think we lost five games in the final minute or in injury time. The most painful defeats came against Munster in the European Cup. We went down 34–35 at home, when Ronan O'Gara converted a late try from far out on the right. In the return at Thomond Park, the lead changed eight times only for Ronan to step up again and convert a Keith Wood try with the last kick of the game as they won 31–30. There was a massive crowd that day but it was so quiet for that final kick that Ronan had to repeat his routine when a mobile phone went off.

Almost as bad, we lost to Northampton in the Tetley's Bitter Cup 34–32. At the death Matt Leek, our nineteen-year-old fly-half standing in for Thierry, went for a drop goal. Everyone thought it was over, but the referee disallowed it. Not long afterwards we increased the height of our posts to avoid a repetition.

At least we managed to win our final two games to finish fourth in the league and make sure of a place in Europe. The finale wasn't quite as enjoyable for Francois, though. He was in his last season as a player. His final appearance saw him come off the bench, struggle to keep up, get sin-binned and then get injured. Not the best way to go, for such a great player.

11

—

THE START OF SOMETHING SPECIAL

January 2006. The roller-coaster continues. Last November was great and December awful. Now things are looking up again. I've given up trying to predict what will happen to my leg next. Sometimes, I'm not too sure anybody quite knows what's going on. I mean, how logical is this? We decided to rest my leg for a while to try and reduce the swelling. Result? No real improvement. So Fares decided to force the issue a bit by suggesting I return to the gym and push through the pain and discomfort, to see what happened. Result? It was fine. There have been a few minor irritations since, like a bit of stiffness, but that's all. The mechanics of the body are weird and wonderful. I have done three or four big bike sessions this week and the only thing which hurt was my lungs. My leg presses are up to around 200kg, so that's just another 200 to find. It's all much more positive.

Things are not so great for Andy Edwards, the young guy I was training with recently. He had been out for nine months after wrecking his knee, and was offered a game with Hertford Rugby Club. He came on for the last thirty minutes and was doing fine until the final play of the game, when he slipped while side-stepping an opponent, got tackled and his cruciate ligament went again. He's twenty. I saw him the next morning. What can you do, apart from put your arm around the guy's shoulders? Some of the guys said he was taking it badly. 'Of course he's taking it badly!' I said. 'He's twenty!' He'll need a lot of luck, as well as guts, if he is going to make it as a professional now. I've had a good rugby life so far; even if it were to end now, and touch wood it won't, I've achieved far more than I ever thought I would.

When my knee went the first time, I was sent out to Vermont in the United States as part of my recovery, to train with a knee expert, Bill Knowles. Normally he deals with ski injuries. I got on really well with him and he had a big effect on my recovery. The plan is to try to get him over here soon, perhaps in February, to help with my current rehabilitation. In some ways I am ahead of where I was last time I worked with him. We measured my legs today, around the thigh. There was a $3\frac{1}{2}$ cm difference in circumference between my left leg and my right. When I went out to Vermont last year it was 4cm.

Lawrence is back in the England squad for the Six Nations. Good luck to him. The last time he played for England was back in 2004, before he broke his ankle on the Lions tour.

(★ (★ (★

Lawrence, Backy and I go back a long way. I hadn't realised it at the time, but we broke the world record for a back row playing together in internationals, when we lost to Scotland at the end of the 2000 Six Nations. I suppose that's quite something. I worried about keeping my position for a season or two after linking up with them, but somewhere along the line we became established and took on the identity of a trio. By 2001 or so, we were probably starting to think as a unit. I'm not sure it was telepathic, but we could read each other's games perfectly.

When we first got together, we used to walk through all our moves every week but as time went on we knew each other's positions off by heart.

We're all very different in terms of character. Would we have been friends if we had met up in different circumstances? Probably not. It's a deep bond, but not a natural friendship. We were known as a unit on the pitch but there wouldn't be many people who would claim that they had gone out and seen Lawrence Dallaglio, Neil Back and Richard Hill in a nightclub having a drink together. That would be very rare.

The one thing that unites us, apart from the England cause, is our sense of pride. None of us would be happy performing below par. Things could get pretty tense between us during fitness tests, even if it never showed on the surface. You knew the events you were good at – I quite fancied taking them on over the 3km run – and none of us wanted to let the others have it all their own way during their favourite tests.

Lawrence was very much the hub of the team. He was a natural leader, having been a captain very young in his international career. He aspired to leadership. Even when Johnno took over, he would still be very outgoing and vocal in team meetings. He's very confident and knows what he wants to achieve. He also likes to have a good time when he's not on duty. For Lawrence, there has to be a balance. He's not one for living like a monk, not all of the time anyway.

Backy, in contrast, is much stricter on himself, not so much in training but in terms of nutrition and, of course, drinking. He's very careful about that. He's so competitive, he wants to be number one at everything he does. He'd probably be competitive at stamp collecting. I wondered how he would get on after retiring, but it hasn't been a problem. You find him in the gym as often as before. I think he's trying to develop the perfect aesthetic body. Knowing him, he'll manage it.

In the old days, they used to think of back rows as three guys with specific roles. One was the ball carrier, one was the blocker, the other the brains. Things aren't quite that simple in the modern era. As a trio, I felt we did pretty well in merging all those roles. Backy certainly was a specialist at snaffling the ball away from the tackle area while Lawrence was a natural ball carrier. I felt I was a pretty good reader of the game with a decent work-rate. But we all tried to develop all-round skills. Ideally you want three players who can carry the ball, who can tackle and who are quick.

If we were beginning to come into our own by 2000–01, then so was the team. It was, I think, a pretty special year for us, or at least it was the start of something special. Ask me if there was a single defining moment for that team and I would have to say it came on 24 June 2000, on our tour to South Africa.

We were, of course, the underdogs. England had only ever won two games in South Africa and never a series. But there was a real sense of optimism that we could do something. We also knew we needed to start winning away from home.

We had flown in with a huge party. Clive, in effect, took two teams, one to play in the two Tests and another to contest the provincial games. There were some interesting names on that tour. Liam Botham, son of one of my great sporting heroes, was among them. Sarries, meanwhile, had a healthy contingent which included Kyran, Danny Grewcock, Dan Luger, Ben Johnston, David Flatman, Julian White and Nick Walshe. Sadly, most of them have since left the club.

Clive decided to base the team in Johannesburg for the entire trip rather than tour around the country. We stayed at the Westcliff Hotel, otherwise known as the Pink Palace. It was a series of converted townhouses, on a hillside overlooking a local zoo. I remember struggling to get used to the altitude during the first few days, not so much in terms of breathing, but when playing. I went to catch a cross-field kick in training only to misjudge the flight of the ball completely. It smacked me right on the top of the head and ballooned fifteen feet into the air before one of the other guys caught it and touched down.

The first Test in Pretoria coincided with the Hansie Cronje hearings, which made for compulsive viewing on TV. The game itself was historic in that it was the first hundred-minute Test – there was about twenty-four minutes of extra time added on – but it ended in the wrong result for us. It was also the first of several games that season that hung on decisions made by the video referee.

We had been forced into a late change when Jonny went down with a stomach bug. Johnno, who had taken over the captaincy from Lawrence, had the same problem but somehow managed to play for most of the game before being forced off. Things still went well, only for us to go down 18–13. We felt, though, that we should have won. The game hinged on one controversial incident. Tim Stimpson chipped ahead in the second half, tried to gather the ball over the South African line but was then clattered into by Andre Vos as he tried to grasp the rebound. He was certainly impeded from my point of view, but you could not prove that Tim would definitely have caught the loose ball.

It had been a tough old battle in the back row against Andre Venter, a hard but fair player I have always respected, Johan Erasmus and Andre Vos. I was severely dehydrated by the end and hobbling around with cramp. We had scored the only try of the game but it was a lost opportunity.

The second Test at the Orange Free State stadium in Bloemfontein on 24 June more than made up for it, though, as we ran out 27–22 winners to draw the series. Jonny, having not eaten for three days and having lost half a stone, returned to kick eight penalties and a drop goal. We dominated for most of the game although a late Joost van der Westhuizen try – which also went to the video ref amid doubts that he had grounded the ball – made the final minutes tenser than they should have been. Just before the final whistle, Austin got to a cross-kick aimed at Chester Williams, pirouetted in the tightest of spaces and kicked into touch as he was chased down. Only he could have got away with it – it was one of those Austin Healey moments.

The result, in retrospect, was huge. It was also quite a shock for our hosts. They take their rugby very seriously. I remember one grinning, biltong-chewing Afrikaner fan looking up at our bus as we arrived at the stadium and running his finger across his throat.

We clearly knew how significant it had been for us psychologically because we took loads of pictures of our celebrations in the changing rooms, which doesn't happen after many games. Often, on tour, your best chance of an upset comes in the first game, when there is an element of surprise. But we had shrugged off the disappointment of the first Test, travelled to the heartland of South African rugby, and won.

With hindsight, you have to say it was a fundamental building block on the road to the 2003 World Cup. Before Bloemfontein, I think we had won one game against the southern hemisphere sides in seventeen starts. After Bloemfontein we did not lose a single game against any of the Big Three right up to the Sydney final.

It's hard to put an exact value on self-confidence but those statistics get pretty close to doing so. We didn't mix with the South Africans afterwards – to be honest, they have never been too friendly towards us – but we felt we had put down a marker. We had won away, and won well. With a bit of luck, indeed, we could have taken the series 2–0. Suddenly we had credibility.

I have one other odd recollection of the game. Usually, during internationals, you're so focused on what you're doing that you aren't aware of anything else. You barely even hear the crowd. There are moments, though, perhaps during a pause for injury, when you become aware of your surroundings. During one such break, I found myself looking at the big screen at one end of the stadium to see Francois Pienaar's face beaming down at me. Francois had disappeared from Sarries for a few days during the previous season. We thought he had gone to check out some South African player as a possible recruit. Clearly he hadn't, I now realised. He had gone home to make a crisp advert.

We flew back to Johannesburg that night. Halfway through the flight the captain announced that there was fog over the capital, and we might have to turn back. To cheers, however, he decided to continue. We weren't quite so happy when he had to pull out sharply of his first descent after losing sight of the runway. It was a bit unnerving, but not half as bad as a Sarries flight home after a European Shield game in Bucharest one year. We hit some very heavy turbulence around Gatwick, which caused quite a commotion. Tim Horan, next to me, got out his Filofax and started writing a message to his wife and kids. Oh my God, I thought, this is serious. Mind you, I was happy to start baiting him in front of the entire squad once we'd landed safely.

That South Africa win marked the end of our season, so a court session to impose fines and penalties was held by the squad back at the hotel before most of the guys hit town. The next morning, one of the buggies used to ferry guests around the hotel grounds was found, written-off in the undergrowth. No one owned up. I have my suspicions but the CCTV pictures were inconclusive.

Our new-found confidence manifested itself in a rather

different way a few months later. We went on strike – and came within a whisker of losing our coach into the bargain.

First, though, came another stern examination of our credentials as we hosted the Wallabies in the first autumn international. Home advantage was all very well but they were the world champions, had just won the Tri Nations and beaten France in Paris. The likes of Horan, Jason Little and David Wilson had retired and Gregan and Stephen Larkham were missing, but it remained a huge game. I had played them five times at senior level without winning. It took another contested decision by the video ref to get that monkey off my back.

We were still behind five minutes into injury time, with two Aussies in the bin for persistent infringements, when Iain Balshaw, who had missed the South Africa trip for a groin operation, chipped ahead towards the goal line. It was pretty audacious. I remember thinking: 'What the hell are you doing?' If it hadn't worked, that would have been it, we would have lost possession and the match. But it came off. Dan Luger got to the ball first. The jury's probably still out about whether he had control of the ball as he touched it down with his elbow, but that was one where the video ref came out in our favour, allowing us to scrape through 22–19.

The best bit about the game was that we had not panicked, even while they slowed things down as much as they could. A fair amount of that goes on in the modern game – feigned injuries (though we're not anywhere near as bad as footballers), doing up shoelaces, towelling down the ball and talking to the ref, that sort of thing – but it did not stop us winning the Cook Cup for the first time.

Argentina were to be up next. Within days, however, we had downed tools.

We had been talking to the RFU before the Australia game about our contracts, which had remained unsigned that season.

There was concern at the time about things like image rights, but also over what proportion of our match fees should be made up of win bonuses. Some of the guys argued that while the sport's popularity was increasing, we could find ourselves actually earning less. We felt our concerns were not being taken seriously by the RFU so we threatened to train with our tops inside out, to hide the sponsors' logos. Clive was categorically opposed to that. 'You're either fully focused on your training or you're not,' he said, but promised to organise a meeting with the RFU management board after the Australia game.

That meeting got us nowhere, so a players' meeting was called.

Johnno, Lawrence and Daws, as our representatives, told us what was on the table. It was decided to take an anonymous strike vote, so that no one felt under pressure. Two people voted against, the rest for. I was one of the two (I think Cozza may have been the other).

Let's be honest, I'm not a revolutionary by nature. I didn't want to rock the boat. I was very proud to play for my country and I thought refusing to do so was too strong a statement. I just didn't like the idea of not playing for England again. I was also worried about the future. Money matters to me, of course. But it's never been the biggest issue. I tend not to get too involved in those sorts of things. Saracens have asked me to take a pay cut a couple of times during my career, when things have got tight, and I understand that (mind you, I thought it was completely unreasonable the second time when I learnt the pay cut would allow them to sign Horan and Castaignede – they wouldn't have been coming to play for peanuts).

Anyway, we had decided before the vote to abide by the majority decision and I was 100 per cent behind the group once the vote had been taken. So Clive was told we would not turn out against Argentina. He was less than amused and the meeting got quite heated. We were then asked to leave the squad hotel, so I packed my gear and headed back to Southgate with the other Saracens boys to await developments. We hadn't been in the clubhouse long when Julian White's mobile began to ring. It was Clive, asking if he was available to play that weekend. When Julian said no, Clive warned him it could mean the end of his career. Shortly afterwards, someone else got called. Then mine began to ring. I turned it off.

The young guys in the squad were certainly being leaned on by Clive. Then, for a while, there was a suggestion that a totally new side might be selected from the Premiership clubs, or even lower if necessary. No one, though, crossed the 'picket line'.

By the next morning, everything had been resolved. The crisis had lasted about thirty-six hours. I suppose it was the principle that mattered, rather than the money. I don't think you could say greed was involved – it came down, in the end, to something like £125 extra per player per game. But it showed we were united. It pulled us together even tighter as a squad.

Mind you, it nearly destroyed our relationship with Clive. At the start, he seemed to be on our side, backing our demands. Then he sided firmly with the RFU, saying he could not understand our behaviour. That didn't go down well with the guys, even though Clive vehemently denied he had switched sides. Our mutual trust and respect seemed to have been damaged beyond repair, but at some stage we got together and decided that the most professional thing would be to let bygones be bygones. We could easily have declared that we could no longer work with him, which would probably have made his position untenable. But for us as players, once things had been agreed that was the end of it. You can stay pissed off with someone for as long as you want, but it does not help you in the long term.

We were a bit worried that there might be a backlash from the public when we ran out against Argentina, but we had the perfect man to defuse the situation. Jason Leonard had been picked for his eighty-fifth cap, an England record. Jason's a man of the people – everyone loves the Fun Bus. Out he ran, while the rest of us waited to see what would happen. As soon as he appeared the Twickenham crowd rose to him. If there was a single boo, I didn't hear it. The game, and our 19–0 victory, seemed no more than an afterthought after all the excitement.

We wrapped up the autumn internationals with a far more impressive win, 25–17, against the Springboks. Backy and I ended up in the wars that day. By the twentieth minute, indeed, three of us had gone off for cut heads. Jonny went first, then Backy – he had about twenty stitches, I think, in two layers because the cut on his forehead was so deep – then I needed ten.

The Boks were on our goal line and I was searching for the ball in a pile of bodies when suddenly the back of Mark Andrews' head came up from underneath and split open my forehead. He was a rough customer, Andrews, and played the game close to the borderline. By the time I had got to the dressing room Backy had nicked the best seat and I was shoved in a dentist's chair. Just as they were finishing off my stitches, I heard some more studs coming down the tunnel. 'Not another one,' I thought. But it was one of theirs this time, Japie Mulder.

The strike, as well as those victories over Australia and South Africa, were dramatic events, but they were soon dwarfed by the 2001 Six Nations. Quite simply, we upped a couple of gears and began playing the most open and entertaining brand of rugby I have ever played at international level. We were given licence to throw the ball around. It certainly wasn't the traditional England game and must have caught our opponents on the hop. It was almost as if someone suddenly flicked a switch and sent us into overdrive. Suddenly we were playing out Clive's dream of heads-up rugby, feeding off each other so well that the numbers on our backs became almost irrelevant.

How did it happen? Well, there must have been a lot of factors. Our defence was now firmly in place, so it was easier to concentrate more on attack. Our backline was beginning to excel, with the likes of Jonny, Tindall, Greenwood and Cohen all coming to the fore while Austin provided flashes of the unexpected. Jason Robinson, recently signed up by Sale from rugby league side Wigan, also made a huge impact, so huge in fact that he would be a British Lion by the end of the season even though he hadn't yet started an England match. Arguably, though, Balshaw made an even more stunning impact that season.

Iain was something of a secret weapon. Few of our opponents knew much about him. That did not last long. He made his first Six Nations start against Wales, scored five tries in the next three games and simply electrified our backline. He gave us incredible pace, counter-attacking from the back. Teams are at their most vulnerable immediately after making mistakes in attack. Their alignments are set up to go forward, not back. If, as the defending side, you can get your hands on the ball at that stage and move it away from the contact area as quickly as possible, you are going to be a threat, especially if you have pace out wide. Iain's speed seemed to be the missing piece of the jigsaw. He was devastating in broken play, gliding past people as if they weren't there. But if defences couldn't cope, well we struggled too. It was hard work for the rest of the team to keep up with him. Sadly, though, it only really lasted one season. He was so dangerous that our opponents reacted immediately, organising their defences to neutralise him. Singled out for special treatment, Iain's confidence levels may have dropped.

I will always remember that season with great pleasure. Who wouldn't have done, when you consider that extraordinary set of results: 44–15 away against Wales and 80–23 against Italy, 43–3 against Scotland and, to top them all, 48–19 against France.

I'm sure that we would have gone on to win the Grand Slam if the foot and mouth crisis had not intervened by postponing our game in Dublin. Our rich vein of form had dropped off by the time the game was eventually played in the autumn.

The win over Wales was particularly special since it was also the first Six Nations game in the new Millennium Stadium. We were greeted with a huge noise as we prepared to run out. Johnno, typically, kept things brief. 'Hear that?' he said. 'Let's silence it.' We scored six tries, three of them from Greenwood, and ran them into the ground. It must have been good – we even managed to impress a Frenchman. Thomas Castaignede, my new team-mate at Sarries that season, wrote in the *Guardian*: 'I watched the best team in the world in the Six Nations on Saturday...I think that if the World Cup was played now they would win it.' Perhaps he missed the bit where Rob Howley dummied me and raced away for their try. I hoped that Graham Henry, the Welsh coach who was due to take charge of the Lions later that season, had as well. Phil Larder didn't, though.

Some Welshmen took the defeat pretty hard. On the way to the post-match function, a Wales supporter charged our team coach and head-butted it. There was blood everywhere. At the next set of traffic lights, another supporter ran out and got knocked over by the wing mirror. We sent out the team doctor Terry Crystal to patch him up while the police kept the chanting crowds back.

Next it was Italy. They scored first and we led only 20–17 after half an hour, but by the end we had run in ten tries. Iain ran the full length of the pitch to score one of his two tries while Jason Robinson came on as a substitute and looked the part immediately.

That was a record Six Nations score, and the Calcutta Cup also threw up a raft of new marks – highest score, biggest winning margin and the most tries in an England–Scotland match. Again we exploited space well and dotted down six more tries, with Iain the man of the match as he claimed another two. I jogged over unopposed for mine.

There was no revenge involved, after what had happened at Murrayfield the previous season. The media use the word all the time, but as players you don't concentrate on it. At most, you remember how bad it felt to lose and try to exploit that by making sure it does not happen again.

The Ireland game then had to be called off, because of the foot and mouth crisis in England. It was massively frustrating because we were on a roll. We took out those frustrations on France. It was still close at half time, but then we blitzed them. Again, it was a record score for England against France. At times it was more like sevens. I'm loath to say it, but this may well have been the best game I ever played for England. I don't think anyone has ever played the perfect game – there is always something that can be improved – but I was pretty pleased with that performance.

I even managed a decent try around half time which seemed to spark us into action. Daws took a quick tap and it came to me via Austin on the French 10-metre line. I think they were concentrating so hard on Austin that I was allowed to slip through a gap. It then probably looked like I took full-back Jean Luc-Sadourny on the outside and sped past him, but I can't help thinking that he wasn't too keen on tackling me, which gave me a bit of extra space. So I just kept chugging along. When he did eventually commit himself I was already up

174

to the line. I think I ran about 40 metres, which probably explained my expression of delight which featured in a few newspaper pictures the next day. I normally try not to give anything away to opponents but I couldn't help it this time, clenching my fist in triumph into the bargain. I'm a bit embarrassed about that celebration now. 'Victor (as in Meldrew) doesn't believe it', one newspaper headline ran, the article adding: 'Hill probably celebrated last night by complaining about the coffee sachets in his hotel room.'

So we ended the truncated Six Nations season with four wins and no defeats, 215 points for and 60 against and a record 28 tries. Rob Andrew said it was a shame we could not play the World Cup that October rather than in two years' time, adding: 'I wonder whether history will prove that 2001 was the best year for this particular England squad. Two and a half years is a long time to wait.'

Well, a fat lot of good all that did us when we eventually went over to Ireland, after the Lions tour to Australia, for the final game. You can look for excuses – it was our first game together for six months, by then Johnno, Lawrence and Phil Vickery were injured, while Balshaw's form had dropped off – but the fact is that they beat us 20–14. It was a bit like Scotland the year before. We were handed the Six Nations Trophy after the game and struggled to smile for the cameras.

To be honest, Ireland were up for it and we didn't play well. The Irish guys had also learnt a lot about some of our players and our line-out work during the Lions tour. I suspect they even managed to read some of our calls, because they certainly disrupted us there. We nearly pulled a rabbit out of the hat when Dan Luger broke clear on the right only for Peter Stringer to throw himself across and bring him down with a last-ditch ankle tap.

It was a major disappointment – missing out on all those

Grand Slams were major disappointments. They all felt pretty much the same – wretched.

There were a few more routine accusations of choking from the media – 'Champions by name, chokers by nature', 'Triple Clowns' – that sort of thing. What you have to understand is that we were going well at the time and all the other teams were determined to raise their games against us to stop us winning trophies. I think that was a huge incentive for them. It had been the same for us when we beat South Africa and stopped them claiming that world record eighteenth win in a row at the end of 1998.

Personally, I never doubted myself or the team. On top of that, we always felt we were learning something from each of our losses. It may sound strange, but I really think each one helped us. There were always little details that you picked up on and stored in the memory bank. That Lansdowne defeat definitely influenced our preparations for the next time we played there.

I've always been very much aware that England are a team that others want to bring down. A lot of it seems to be linked to national history. It doesn't sit comfortably with me. Some people really do seem ready to judge you as an individual – to the point of actually hating you – on what happened between countries hundreds of years ago.

I've always found that a bit odd. Perhaps I just don't have a sense of history. On a personal level, though, I have never had any problems. That season at Saracens we had Tim Horan and Thomas Castaignede. They were both great guys and I don't remember them too often harping on about things that happened a century ago.

Unfortunately, they both fell victim to the Sarries injury jinx shortly after joining the club. Tim, indeed, arrived injured and continuing niggles blighted his Saracens career. He had undergone knee reconstruction himself, and he got in touch after my injury, texting me with ideas and things that had worked for him. When he did play, you could immediately see his class. He wasn't necessarily always going at full throttle, but I was always impressed with the way he backed himself. If he thought something was on, he just went for it. It might not always have been the right decision, but sometimes you can turn things into the right decision if you commit to it totally. He was a serious player and a good man to have around off the pitch, always messing about and winding people up. There were two personalities to him; Timmy and Tommy. Timmy was the mild-mannered, polite guy. Tommy was the man with a drink in his hand who turned into a playful lunatic.

We got our revenge on him just before he left England. He invited a load of us round for a farewell drink, just before his furniture was packed up for shipping to Australia. We found some raw sausages in his kitchen which, one by one, were hidden away among his crockery. I never found out whether any of them made it all the way back to Oz.

Thomas, meanwhile, was another player from the very top bracket but he lasted only a few months before wrecking his Achilles, an injury which needed several operations before being put right. We know him as Frank the Tank, after the character in the film *Old School*. He looks so neat and tidy and innocent. Then he has a drink. At one of my benefit functions, he was due to perform on stage at about nine o'clock. I spotted him three hours before, with a drink by his side and, for some reason I can't quite explain, a black sock pulled over his head down to his ears. Frank can impersonate the suave sophisticated French wine drinker, of course, but he's better at it early in the evening.

Without the pair of them, it was another year of expectations turning sour, despite such high points as home and away victories over Toulouse in the Heineken Cup.

For me, though, the worst memory was Dips's departure. He was only twenty-eight but he was not offered a new contract, so he headed down the road to Harlequins. He and Pienaar had never been close, even if they were civil to each other in public. It was a personality clash between two very determined guys and in the end something had to give. Dips had helped me out a lot, especially during my early years at the club. I remember his final game at Vicarage Road, walking around the pitch with him and realising it would be the last time.

12

A SORT OF FAME

In 2001, against all odds, I became famous. Well, sort of famous. For a period I certainly got a lot more recognition than I had before. I'd had quite a few nicknames up to then – Hilda, Hilly, Victor Meldrew, Paperface, Ruben (apparently Ruben Kruger, the South African flanker, and I shared the same receding hairline), Silent Assassin and Unsung Hero. Now, for a while, I became a sort of 'sung unsung hero'. Lawrence certainly thought I got more than enough attention. 'It's now a fact of English rugby life,' he said, 'that Richard Hill is the most over-praised unsung hero in the game.'

It was a limited sort of celebrity, within the rugby community I suppose, and thank goodness it stopped at that. It doesn't sit easily with me. I'd hate to be really famous, or to have to put up with the attention which Jonny got after the World Cup. It's nice being appreciated for a particular performance, particularly by your peers, but I'm not keen on all the extra stuff, even if it does make you a bit of extra money. You can get offered advertisements and public speaking engagements and things like that. I've never made a huge effort to get too many of them, although the public speaking has grown on me. It's a different challenge, it's part of my role and you can meet some very interesting people along the way. Once I get going, I'm told, I'm pretty good at it – I reckon I've been around long enough to know the subject pretty well – even if I do still get nervous beforehand.

Fame's other knock-on effect is that people want to meet you. Normally it's enjoyable, but sometimes they can get a bit intense and over the top. It's as if they want to put you on a pedestal. They can't seem to appreciate you are a normal person who goes home with the same concerns in life. My lawn still needs mowing and my washing still has to be done.

Claire hates it too – the attention, that is, as well as the washing. We're not exactly Posh and Becks, but sometimes I get recognised on holiday and it drives her mad. All she wants to do is relax by the side of the pool and suddenly someone starts to stare, wondering if that's that bloke, you know, whatsisname, the one who plays rugby for England.

It was at its worst between the 2001 Lions tour and the 2003 World Cup, but now it only happens occasionally, mostly around Southgate and Enfield. It's happened more during this injury, now I think about it, because of my crutches. People look harder at you when you are on crutches. Or perhaps I'm easier to spot because I'm moving slower.

I suppose Lawrence was right, to an extent. For some reason I became flavour of the month for a while with the media. Off the pitch, I suppose I present journalists with a problem: I'm not controversial and I don't have any dark secrets. Jason Robinson had a tough background and switched codes, Ben Cohen's uncle won the 1966 World Cup, Johnno almost became an All Black, but what about me? Well, I did fail those A levels, of course – perhaps I should have made more of that.

My position is not even regarded as particularly sexy. The job is about allowing the team to function better, rather than being individually spectacular. I'm not a great flashy midfield runner or try scorer, it's more about tidying up and sorting things out. I don't even have stand-out blond hair like Backy (though it was blond for a few years, as a kid) and I don't pull the sort of gurning faces Lawrence is so good at. To cap it all off, as the second Richard Hill from Salisbury to play for England, I don't even have an original name.

In short, I'm not exactly exciting copy. I've never been massively articulate in those sorts of situations either, so I get a bit guarded to make sure I don't say anything stupid or which could offend someone. Most of the interviews I have done go on about me being a secret weapon or a mystery man. It's as if the journalist thinks I'm important in some way, but can't quite work out why, which is fine by me. There's no mystery, though – the truth is, I'm just a very ordinary bloke.

I seemed to start making headlines during the 2001 Lions trip to Australia. The tour certainly went well for me. I felt I had taken a step forward in my play. It was a watershed of sorts, because for the first time, I think, I was taken seriously at world level, and I was pleased about that. It went over the top in the end, though, when some people tried to argue that I made a critical difference on that tour. There was a bit of that at the World Cup too. I don't buy that. Teams win or lose games, not individuals.

The tour started as it had in 1997 with some bonding sessions, at a beautiful manor house called Tylney Hall just outside London. The dragon boat racing was fun but I was less convinced when we were given musical instruments, with the idea of forming us up into a band. Fortunately I got the cow bells, which were not too complicated. Music has never been my forte. At primary school I used to mime playing the recorder at the back of the class rather than actually risk any notes when we played 'London's Burning' or 'God Save the Queen'. Strange how certain things stay with you. Every time I line up for the national anthem at Twickenham I am not, believe it or not, thinking about national pride and glory. I'm back at school, with a sheet of music in front of me. That bit, between the verses, G, A, B, C it goes... I can remember the notes to this day.

I had been busy even before Tylney Hall. There was more competition for back row places compared to 1997, with more guys, including myself, being able to cover different positions. Having looked at my game, Andy Robinson had suggested I would have a better chance of selection if I could turn myself into a line-out jumper. So I got some of the guys at the club, like Danny Grewcock and Julian White, to give me a bit of last-minute tuition. I struggled at the start. Julian is exceptionally strong and it was a bit unnerving being hoisted so high in the air from below the knees. I got it in the end, but I took some stick to start with. Danny, who worked exceptionally hard on his game, said I looked like a windmill, flapping my arms all over the place and pulling idiotic faces. I also used to kick out, which produced a few expletives from my lifters when I caught them in sensitive places. It paid off, though. From then on I continued as a jumper for Saracens and England. I think I even took a couple of line-outs in the 2003 World Cup final.

In the end, the 2001 Lions are probably remembered for the things that went wrong rather than the things that went right. The bottom line, of course, is always the results. We had been given a reasonable chance of winning the Test series but we lost 2–1.

For a lot of people, the overriding impression was of an unhappy tour. Daws and Austin publicly criticised Graham Henry and the management, saying the training was mindless and relentless. I never saw it that way. It was certainly a very intense tour and some of the training sessions did drag on for much longer than they were meant to. Andy Robinson, I remember, also used to suggest that we might like to squeeze in a bit of extra line-out work on our rare days off, which was a bit irritating. If you wanted a lie-in, that effectively meant you did not have any time to go out anywhere on a visit, since the daylight hours were quite short at that time of year. But my attitude was that it was a shorter tour than previously and I wasn't going out there as an automatic first choice, so it was a case of knuckling down and getting on with it.

One of our few organised trips, to the Great Barrier Reef, did get cancelled when one of our flights got delayed, but I managed to fit in a few excursions. There was Perth zoo – visiting zoos is one of my vices – and there was also a dive into a shark aquarium in Brisbane. I've never been quite the same since watching *Jaws* as a kid but they were pretty tame and well fed, so that was good to do. We were warned they would swim right at our heads, then suddenly rise up and drift over us at the last second. You just had to stay still, with your hands tucked behind your back. Jonny put his hand on a camouflaged shark as he climbed out but lived to tell the tale.

As for Graham Henry, well, it can't have been easy for him. He had beaten Clive Woodward to the post. A lot of the guys would have preferred a British guy in charge and I was one of them. One of your own is always going to have more understanding of our way of doing things. Graham was coaching in Wales, but he had not grown up on Lions tours. That is not to say that he did not put his heart into it. He was very straight – you didn't get much humour with Graham – and meticulous. My impression was that he was a workaholic, analysing our play and our opponents down to the last detail.

He came to the conclusion that we should play a very structured game, which often meant us learning up to six or seven consecutive phases of play, without much room for improvisation. That seemed a bit extreme. England, at the time, were doing just the opposite, so it took some getting used to.

Perhaps the bottom line was that we were not a lucky group. By the end, there had been so many injuries that we struggled to put out a team for the third Test. Things began pretty well, with a 116–10 win over a Western Australia President's XV at the WACA, but the casualties began from the very start. Phil Greening injured a ligament in training before the first game while Simon Taylor managed just half a game before his knee went.

The second game, an 83–6 win over a Queensland President's XV in Townsville, turned into a Jason Robinson exhibition as he announced his arrival with five tries on his Lions debut. Things got a bit more serious, though, against Queensland Reds at Ballymore. They were Super 12 semi-finalists, although they did not play all of their Wallabies. We beat them impressively enough, 42–8, I got my one and only Lions try, off an inside pass from Jonny five yards out – but the game began with a few fractious incidents. I think they were trying to unsettle us and break the game up a bit, although the home press stuck to the party line that it was us who were getting over-physical.

The first hiccup came with a 28–25 defeat against Australia A at Gosford. I didn't see it as a major issue – the same thing had happened before the first Test in South Africa in 1997 – but things continued to go wrong on the injury front. Training for the next game against New South Wales Waratahs, Dan Luger unwisely chose to clash heads with Backy and ended up with a fractured cheekbone. He and Phil Greening, though, made the most of their bad luck by staying in Australia and following the tour around in a camper van, like a couple of die-hard fans. They went home having seen great swathes of the country. I have been to Australia on seven rugby tours and seen a lot of hotels, a lot of gyms, a lot of pitches and one shark aquarium.

The Waratah game, which ended in us winning 41–24, took place a week before the first Test. Our team that day was, to all intents and purposes, the Test side. I was tipped off beforehand that I had not been picked but was told not to take it too much to heart. Lawrence, who was struggling with a knee problem, was being given extra game time to test his fitness.

That gave me a grandstand seat to see one of the big controversies of the tour. To be honest, I was shocked by what happened. The violence began from the whistle, when Tom Bowman was sin binned after three whole seconds after planting a forearm into Danny Grewcock's face.

Now don't get me wrong. Everybody knows Danny is no angel. In fact, it's frustrating at times that he can't control himself better. I honestly don't know what goes on in his head, because he's a lovely guy off the pitch. It's as if there's a switch which suddenly flicks. God knows, he doesn't need it, because he is still damn effective when he plays it hard and fair. But on this occasion he was entirely blameless.

The tension of the occasion was certainly not helped by some coaches, who should have known better, stirring things up beforehand. Bob Dwyer was one, accusing us of playing illegally in the scrum, the line-out, the breakdown. He probably thought we put our jock-straps on illegally as well. After the game, he went on to blame us for a lot of the niggly stuff, which continued when four guys, two from each side, were binned for a brawl.

The worst incident by far, though, came when Duncan McRae pinned Ronan O'Gara to the floor and punched him repeatedly in the face, splitting his cheek open just under his left eye. Ronan was on his back and couldn't defend himself. I couldn't believe what I was seeing. I had played with Duncan at Sarries and felt I knew him well enough. It seemed so out of character. Duncan got sent off and was banned for seven weeks.

I'm sure he would be the first to admit that it's not something you would want to see in the sport, in any sport, or anywhere.

I think he later suggested it was in retaliation, although Ronan is not exactly a dirty player. It was still way over the top. Claire caught up with Duncan and his wife later in the tour but the subject was not brought up. Next time I saw Duncan it was long gone and we didn't mention it. Perhaps it's something he wanted to forget.

The low point of the tour came at Coff's Harbour in the run-up to the match against New South Wales Country. We'd lost quite a few more players in the previous few days – Lawrence's knee had gone again and needed a reconstruction, Catty was out and Greenwood had been sidelined – and perhaps the pressure was getting to the management.

Anyway, a day or two before the game, Graham Henry said it was time to concentrate solely on the Test team. The mid-week guys would still have been hoping to make a final push for Test selection but the training sessions were instead geared towards preparing the Test side for the weekend, with the mid-week team reduced to imitating Australia's style of play before working on their own moves. It's always a tricky balance, trying to keep the back-up players happy on a tour, but this was certainly not a masterstroke. Even before the tour, Graham had made a speech about people in the southern hemisphere not respecting the Lions, adding: 'And I should know because I am one of them'. He meant it as motivation but some guys took it the wrong way.

Worst of all Anton Toia, our baggage handler, had a heart attack and died shortly before the game. He had been swimming back to shore after we had been on a whale-watching trip. He was a great bloke and seemed so healthy. It was unbelievable.

Within a few days, though, I had played in possibly the best game of my career. The first Test at The Gabba remains a career highlight. It began so fast it was stomach churning. After fifteen minutes I thought to myself: 'I'm not going to be able to keep this going much longer.' You already knew you were involved in a massive game. Fortunately, the pace gradually slowed.

In many ways we played the perfect game, scoring early and then repeating that feat twice over in the second half as Australia attempted a comeback. And this against a side which had only conceded one try in the entire World Cup two years before.

The lead-up to the game had been odd for me. I had been switched to openside late on, when Backy was ruled out of the match through injury, but I was quite happy with that. It was an evening kick-off and I felt very calm about things. Mind you, I still felt just as relaxed with three hours to kick-off, so much so that I began to worry that I wouldn't be mentally ready. Willie John McBride came in and gave us a talk on the pride of playing for the Lions before handing out the shirts, and all of a sudden I was in game mode.

So was Jason Robinson. Within three minutes of his first international start he had crossed for a try. With barely any room to move next to the touch line, Chris Latham offered him the outside. Jason said thanks very much, and was gone. It was an amazing bit of skill, like threading a needle. Then Dafydd James scored a second and we were 12–3 up at the break.

Brian O'Driscoll had been in sparkling form and he all but killed off the game straight afterwards with a 40-metre run. He scythed between Nathan Grey and Jeremy Paul in midfield, and then left Matt Burke for dead as he rounded him to score one of the great Lions tries. Soon we were leading 29–3 and that was that, even though they came back strongly to finish at 29–13.

I had a pretty good tussle with George Smith that day. He was only just coming onto the scene but was obviously a very good player. We had watched him a fair bit. His strength was, and still is, over the ball. He wanted to get to the tackle as the second man, rather than make the tackle himself, so he could concentrate on stealing possession. So I decided to try to remove him from contact areas as quickly as possible, rather than actually contest the ball itself, to reduce the threat he posed. That would take him out of the game.

We also noticed he liked tackling high, so that he could fall to the floor with you, then be up on his feet immediately, standing over you, to steal the ball. So I decided to concentrate on driving through him in contact, trying to bump him off in the tackle, before going to ground. It worked pretty well. We had analysed his game and found a weakness. To his credit, though, he sorted it out soon afterwards.

Before the tour, there seemed to be a chance that the Lions' back row might be Lawrence, Backy and me. Instead I played alongside Scott Quinnell and Cozza that day. It was our first time together as a unit and it went well. Martin had joined the tour as an injury replacement and played out of his skin – taking your opportunity like that is what Lions rugby is all about. Until then he had spent a fair while on the England bench but he remained as determined as ever. Martin certainly didn't come over for a holiday.

The support we got added to the occasion. Around half of the 37,000 crowd must have been wearing red. It had almost been like a home game. There we were in Brisbane, and 'Flower of Scotland' was being played on the bagpipes for us – it was a bit surreal.

The press conference, however, did not go as we expected. I was one of the guys chosen to attend. As usual, we got briefed by the press officer on what issues might come up and we were suddenly told that Daws had made some critical comments about Graham and the way the tour was being run, in an English Sunday newspaper. It was quite a surprise. We just wanted to talk about the game. I don't really know why Daws said what he did – I didn't read the article then and I haven't since. All I knew was that we had just won and I was on cloud nine. It was hard to see where he was coming from. Even if I had not been in the team, I don't think I would have made those sorts of comments, just like I wouldn't have said some of the things Gavin Henson said in his book after the 2005 Lions tour. I'm very conscious that team-mates mean a lot to you. There are things best kept within four walls.

It all blew over pretty quickly, though. There was a suggestion that Daws might get sent home, but he was genuinely upset by the reaction it caused, that was clear to see, and apologised to the whole squad. He responded in the best way against ACT Brumbies, the Super 12 champions, by converting the final kick of the game from the touchline to complete a 30–28 win.

Perhaps, if we had won the second Test, all the negatives about the tour would have been forgotten. It all went wrong in Melbourne, though. And for once, I found myself at the centre of the controversy.

The Test was going really well – I had even won my first line-out in international rugby – and we were 11–7 up just before half time when Johnno drove up through the midfield. He passed to me and I failed to take it cleanly. Now once you start juggling a ball, you are laying yourself open for a hit. As I went to catch the ball again, all I know is that I got hit on the side of my face. I remember going to ground and feeling a bit dazed. Right, I thought, am I with it? I found myself wondering who I was playing for, and who the opposition were. There was a bit of blood around my nose, so I had an excuse to go off and sit on the sidelines. I gather I then asked Graham Rowntree the score. Then I asked him again. And again. Anyway, I decided I was fine and ran back on. The rest is a bit of a blur, really. I remember some moments but not others. I began to come round in the changing rooms at half time, where I found myself surrounded by a bunch of medics asking me whether I knew where I was. I got that answer right but did not do so well with the others, apparently, because they ruled that I was concussed and would not allow me back on. So I retreated to the stands after half time and watched the game swing against us.

Joe Roff scored immediately off an interception, another try followed quickly and we were suddenly 21–11 behind and being harried out of the game. We conceded 29 points in that second half. Adding injury to insult, four of us ended up in hospital.

It turned out that I had been hit in the face by Nathan Grey's elbow and had crumpled to the ground. He ran across me and caught me as he went through. Most of our guys seemed to think it was malicious and everything I have read since takes the same line, but I am not sure. Graham Henry said that my injury was a key moment in the tour, and wrote in my benefit brochure: 'It's a fact that we were never behind in the Tests while Richard was on the pitch.' Which was a nice thing to say. But then that is what people do in benefit brochures; they say nice things.

As for the incident itself, I don't believe you can really tell from television pictures what happened. I've seen the clip a couple of times. It looks bad, sure, but you can't really tell (Claire thinks she can, but then she's got a long list of people who she blames for destroying my good looks. I think she was angry that, having come half way round the world to watch me play, she saw only forty minutes).

As far as I'm concerned, the matter was investigated and Nathan was cleared, so that was that.

Concussion meant a three-week break from playing, so my tour was over. I was carted off to hospital with the other crocks – Rob Howley (ribs), Jonny (leg) and Brian O'Driscoll (neck) – and learnt another thing from my scan. My skull is apparently twice as thick as the norm. Stupidly, I told Dorian West about it when we got back to the team hotel at midnight. By breakfast the next day everyone seemed to know. 'Ah, Mr Neanderthal, did you sleep well?' came the greeting.

Rob had also been ruled out of the tour, so we shared a room for the last week. The tour doc, James Robson, said he did not want me going out for forty-eight hours but he agreed to cut that to twenty-four so long as he was there to chaperone me. So off we went and met up with Claire, a bunch of supporters she had got to know, and a few Saracens guys. I was pretty depressed but I gradually accepted what had happened and it turned into one of those great nights. My concussion must have got to me in the end, though. It was probably the only night in my life where I went to bed and left Claire drinking in the bar, rather than the other way around. Ever since, I reckon I have met every single person who was in that bar that night. Everywhere I go, people seem to come up and say: 'Do you remember me? I was in the Novotel hotel when…'

Rob and I spent the rest of the week visiting the set of *Home and Away* (I was a big soap fan in those days), having a few beers and catching up with people we knew. We also met up with Andy Nicol, the Scotland captain, who was leading an organised tour party following the Lions. Little did any of us know, let alone Andy, what would happen next.

By the time of the final Test, our casualty list had got beyond a joke. That week, they were struggling to get enough players together for a meaningful training session. I think we were down to about a dozen fit players. So Andy was put on call for the third Test. He must have been sweating blood – as well as all the beer he had been drinking – at the thought of coming on as he tried to mug up on all the calls. Fortunately, he was not needed. As Johnno put it, that team was held together by sticky tape as they ran out at the Olympic Stadium. They put up an excellent show, though, before going down 29–23.

By now the Aussies were doing everything they could to gain an advantage. For a start, they had handed out loads of free gold caps, shirts and scarves to their supporters in an attempt to match the display of colour being put on by the Lions fans. They had also isolated our fans at the two ends of the stadium, then turned the lights off in those sections in the build-up to the game, which seemed pretty cheap.

From what has come out since, they had another trick up their sleeve. One guy was not officially part of the Australian coaching set-up, but we learnt that he had been following us around during our warm-up games, standing around pretending to be a water carrier or just watching our training sessions while gathering information. Coupled with what they had been able to pick up from television, they had pretty much cracked our line-out codes by the third Test.

This sort of thing happens fairly regularly. People love to get hold of any information which could give them an edge. You hear stories of people leaving line-out calls in the back of taxis and the incriminating evidence being passed on to their opponents.

Right at the end of the third Test, we got an attacking line-out near Australia's line. It was our last chance. The call was made for a throw to Johnno at the front, with a driving maul to follow. It was perfectly set up for one final throw of the dice, but the Australians bravely challenged the throw rather than just defended their territory. If we had won the ball, their ability to defend a drive would have been seriously weakened, with their jumper Justin Harrison and his lifters out of position.

Harrison, however, pinched it and the series with it. It was just as if he knew where that throw was going.

Who knows what might have happened if I had stayed on the pitch in Melbourne and we had gone on to win that second Test? I might have graduated from Unsung Hero to Hero at last. As it is, I didn't quite pull it off. Eddie Butler wrote in one newspaper interview: 'He may not be the heart of the team, like Martin Johnson, or the brain like Jonny Wilkinson. But he is something essential; I don't know, the pancreas perhaps.' Oh well. It's better than nothing, I suppose, being a pancreas.

As I said, I seemed to have moved up a notch after the Lions tour. But if I did ever feel the temptation to believe some of the publicity, I soon got put in my place. Shortly after returning to England, I went down to Salisbury and went for a lads' night out with Don 'Pigman' Parsons and Marcus 'The Rat' Olsen. We decided to go to a nightclub for a few late beers only to find a long queue outside. Rather than pack up and go home, Marcus suggested I should go up to the front and ask to be let in as a British Lion. I wasn't going to do that but said I would turn a blind eye if they wanted to try it. So Marcus marched up and said he was Rob Howley and got let in. 'OK Rob,' said the doorman, 'I've heard of you, in you go.' Then Don got on his tip toes, puffed out his chest and said he was Martin Johnson. In he went as well.

I started walking in behind him only for the doorman to ask my name.

'Richard Hill,' I said.

'Sorry mate, never heard of that name,' came the response. 'Still, if you're with Rob and Martin I suppose you can go in.'

Which just about sums up how famous I really am. Don and Marcus have never let me forget it. Worse still, Don tells me he has gone back since and the doorman has recognised his old mate Johnno, and let him through with a pat on the back.

13

FINE-TUNING

February 2006. It's official – I am not going to be fit by April.

Bill Knowles came over from the States for two weeks of one-on-one training towards the end of the month and immediately made it clear to me that I was not doing anywhere near as well as I had thought. My leg, for a start, was not bending enough. It's at about 120 degrees and will have to get up to around 145 at least, which is itself by no means the maximum but, considering the nature of my injury, is probably the most I can expect.

It's pretty disappointing. Now I'm aiming for 21 May, the date of a benefit match we've been organising between a Saracens XV and a World XV. I would have preferred to get back for a proper Saracens match but the season ends on 6 May, which will be too early for me.

I had hoped to be running almost normally by the time Bill left. Bill was very candid and said I had to accept the situation as it was. That doesn't make it any easier, though. There is certainly no comparison between my recovery this time and when I first did my knee. If I get back for May, I will have been out for virtually eleven months. Last time it was six.

Bill had never seen any film of my injury so we got out the

DVD of the 2005 Lions tour. I had to take the cellophane off the pack – it was the first time I had watched it as well. My first thought was: 'Ouch!' It wasn't good. The joint really crunched up. Let's just say I don't think I will ever be able to get my knee in that position again. Bill said a healthy knee would probably not have been able to handle the impact either.

We managed a lot of pool work during his stay, concentrating on walking exercises and the quality of movement. A lot of it was about trying to push my leg beyond its restricted range of movement without aggravating it. There wasn't a lot of emphasis on strength training, although my left leg is still much smaller than the right one. We have to try and balance them up, so that my running style doesn't become lopsided. Anyway, things went really well. Bill has a good mix of techniques. Best of all, he makes you believe. Then he makes you work hard. By the end of those two weeks, we had found another ten degrees of flexion.

Hopefully, funding permitting, I will be able to go out to the States in April so that we can finish things off. I'm finding it harder to train at the same intensity since Bill's departure, which means working for longer hours to get the work done. Not that Claire is impressed. She says I've never put in a hard day's work in my life.

Lawrence got back in an England shirt this month, returning as a substitute against Wales more than eighteen months since announcing his international retirement. England – I almost said 'we', but that doesn't sound right anymore – did well to win 47–13. I managed to enjoy the game as a spectacle, rather than getting too analytical. Typical of Lawrence, though – no sooner is he on the pitch than he scores. Mind you, I'm not dwelling on the past or on memories. I'm concentrating on myself and what is happening now.

Things are not going well at Sarries. We've gone and lost

another coach, with Steve Diamond leaving. It wasn't very pleasant. I'm a bit detached from the club because of my injury, so I wasn't there when it happened but I gather there was a difference of opinion over tactics. Steve had introduced a 'back-to-basics' rugby based on our forwards, but we lost to Biarritz in the Heineken Cup and have lost eight out of our last ten matches in all competitions.

Eddie Jones, the former Australia coach, has been brought in as a consultant until the end of the season to try to turn things around. Eddie will address the players, then do an analysis of the way we are playing. Things are certainly getting pretty hairy. We're tenth out of twelve at the moment and on the slide.

A trip to Portugal has been organised for one of the weeks when we don't have a game, for a bit of warm-weather training and to lift morale. It will be really good for me too, to feel a bit of heat on my back. The other good news is that the Saracens owners and directors have made a statement, saying they are committed to staying at the club even if we go down. For us, as players, it means we will still be able to pay the mortgage, which is the bottom line. For the club, it should mean avoiding a mass exodus of players, which will improve our chances of bouncing right back up to the Premiership.

Mind you, I have to be offered a contract first. I haven't got one for next season yet. Contract negotiations should be starting soon, but I really don't know if they are interested in keeping me on. The first discussions should take place within the next week or so. Deep down, I expect them to offer me a lower basic wage, and a higher pay-per-play, for a single year. I won't get longer than that, considering what has happened. I'll be thirty-three soon.

(* (* (*

The situation reminds me a bit of the season when Francois Pienaar left in 2002, to be replaced by the likes of Buck Shelford and Rod Kafer and, ultimately, Steve Diamond. Francois was doing everything at that stage, as director of rugby, chief executive and as coach. We had had a phenomenal loss of high-quality players the season before – it was alarming, to be honest. Dips had gone, so had Danny Grewcock as well as Paul Wallace, Julian White and Dan Luger.

It was pretty clear that Francois had taken on too many roles and began to struggle as a one-man band as the defeats piled up after a good start to the season. I remember one team meeting where he began by telling us this story about the monk (i.e. Francois) who plants lettuce seeds (i.e. the players) and who was responsible for providing the right conditions and nutrients (i.e. training, tactics and facilities) to make us a better team. I tended to take notes during meetings, to help me concentrate. Later in the meeting, Francois started criticising one of our recent performances and I wrote on my pad: 'The lettuces have just been blamed.'

In January of that year, the season collapsed. We were knocked out of two cups and then got hammered by Leicester at home. Worse still, another of our imported stars, Jannie De Beer, injured his knee and was forced to retire at the end of the season.

That Leicester game was my 200th for the club. I got a dead leg – I remember some of the Leicester boys like Johnno were telling me to go off – but I plodded on, what else could you do in that situation? By the next weekend, Francois had resigned. To be truthful, it did not come as a shock. Morale was pretty low. We had got to the stage where a fresh face was needed. For a short while, I helped out with the coaching alongside Tim Horan and Kyran, but I was delighted to rejoin the ranks as soon as possible. As stand-in selectors, we had to drop some of our mates, which was not great. I did not enjoy the period; it put me off the coaching side of things.

Nigel Wray must have been more depressed than anyone. He had sunk something like £12 million into the club over five and a half years and got just one cup win in return. We finished tenth that season, precariously close to the bottom, although in the end there would be no relegation, since Rotherham's facilities did not come up to scratch to join the top flight.

I suppose it was refreshing from a mental standpoint for me to join the England squad for internationals during that period. It meant going from a struggling team to a winning one. I managed to separate them in my mind – this is the Saracens block, this is the England block. England were doing a lot more winning than losing, even though we started our season in October by losing that 'foot and mouth' match to Ireland.

I had managed to squeeze in a last-minute holiday with Don and Marcus on the Greek island of Zante before the start of the season – Claire couldn't come because of a school trip – which involved a fantastic snorkel and mask swim among loggerhead turtles. But I still felt pretty tired, post-Lions, and made a slow start to the season despite the break.

I even got rested by Clive for one international, a 134–0 run-around against Romania, because I seemed a bit jaded. That was a period when Andy Robinson was getting us to email our thoughts to him about how we were playing. It seemed to make me get a bit over-analytical as a result. I've always known, ever since my student days, that I am driven more by negatives than positives, which is not ideal. Fear of failure is a big thing with me. So the more analytical I got, the more I found myself concentrating on what I did badly rather than what I did well. The problem was physical – I was pretty knackered, basically – and then became a mental one. It wasn't that I was playing badly but I just wasn't sharp. But my form soon came back.

The two big autumn internationals went well, with a 21–15 win over Australia and a 29–9 victory over South Africa. We saw off Eddie Jones's side without the injured Johnno, Lawrence and Daws, which made a statement. It was also back-to-back wins over the world champions. Johnno was back for the Springboks and made an even bigger statement after that match, saying that it was no longer such a big deal for us to beat southern hemisphere sides. It was just a remark, but it meant a lot. Only a couple of seasons before, we would have gone into these games with hope rather than expectation. Every win against them built up the team's dossier of confidence.

The other big thing, that year – actually, it was probably another of those defining points in the team's progress – was the fine-tuning of our style. That might seem strange, considering the successes we had had the previous season in the Six Nations, giving the ball width and running our opponents off their feet. But, with the World Cup beginning to appear on the horizon, we realised we had to be adaptable. Different conditions would demand a different approach. So would certain opponents. We had to be able to play whatever game was required on the day.

We played some pretty fast and open stuff in the 2002 Six Nations as well, running in plenty of tries. We beat Scotland 29–3 at Murrayfield and saw off Ireland 45–11 to start with – that result took us to the top of the world rankings – then hammered Wales 50–10 and Italy 45–9. Our third game of the championship, however, was the most important – a 20–15 defeat in France.

The game was as good as over before half time. We may have been looking to play fast and positively but France were supremely well organised. Imanol Harinordoquy was at the heart of their best work, scoring the second of their tries within the first twenty minutes. In no time we were 17–0 down. We got one try back just before half time, through Jason Robinson, and Ben Cohen caught a cross-field punt just before full time to make things respectable, but we didn't deserve to win. We couldn't even hide behind the excuse that France had produced a couple of moments of their legendary flair. They hadn't. They just put in a great effort up front, defended superbly and were very direct in their running. They spotted weaknesses in our game and were clinical in exploiting them. Crucially, their flanker Serge Betsen gave Jonny a wretched time. As for us, we were just too lax. For years the England team had prided itself on playing pragmatic rugby, but we failed to live up to that.

Johnno made exactly that point afterwards; we needed to go back to those roots in crunch games, playing it tight where necessary. The stats at the end of the Six Nations confirmed his point. We had outscored France comfortably over the season, with 184 points to their 156, and conceded only 53 points to their 75, but they had still won the Grand Slam. It wasn't rocket science and Clive agreed. He said we had been developing an 'all-singing, all-dancing brand of rugby' but the method was not always working when we were put under pressure. For years, under previous coaches, England had gone through an era of rolling mauls, so Clive had concentrated on taking us to the other extreme. To be successful, though, we knew we had to marry the two approaches.

There were other good reasons to change. Some of our players who had set the championship alight in 2001, like Balshaw, were injured or weren't performing to the same level. Other teams were also getting used to our new way of playing and beginning to counter it. You can have an awesome running game, throwing the ball wide, but there are ways for opponents to deal with that. When that happens, you have to switch tactics again and, say, go up the middle. We had revolutionised our game, but perhaps it had been a case of throwing out the good with the bad. In a way, during that game in Paris, we had looked more French than the French, while they excelled by playing an English game.

We must have learnt our lesson, though. We did not lose another game right up to the 2003 World Cup final, apart from a warm-up fixture against the French in Marseilles that year.

The other plus, that season, was that a number of new players started to break into the squad, among them Steve Thompson, Lewis Moody and Ben Kay.

Steve, a quiet guy, got his debut against Scotland. I'm told he was once a roller-skating international, but I still find it hard to imagine. As a former back rower – before he put on a few too many pounds – he offered good hands and good pace about the pitch. With Lawrence sidelined, Lewis made his debut against Wales, alongside Backy and me – all of us, spiritually, were opensides. Actually, spiritually, Lewis came from outer space – the man is completely fearless, totally enthusiastic and, to all intents and purposes, a lunatic. He even admits it himself. Once he's after a loose ball or chasing a kick, he just becomes transfixed. There is no malice in his play but he wouldn't back down for anyone.

Ben, meanwhile, had done so well that he even kept Johnno on the bench for a couple of games. Against Italy in Rome, during the second half, Clive made a quadruple substitution and on rolled Johnno, Lawrence, Daws and Jason Leonard – four former England captains with 326 caps between them. It must have been a bit dispiriting for our opponents.

That summer, quite a few of us were rested and allowed to miss the tour to Argentina, which was great. The previous season had stretched on forever. It was the first full summer I had had off since my injury break in 1998. Kyran invited me and Kris Chesney to stay at his parents' place for a week in Jersey.

We trained on the beach in the mornings and did some gym work in the evenings. It was nice to relax a bit. Perhaps we relaxed too much. One evening, as we were watching England play Argentina on television in a hotel bar – we had been hoping that our close friend and Saracens team-mate Kevin Sorrell would get on from the bench but it didn't happen – we somehow allowed three guys to challenge us to a scrum. Normally I would run away from such situations so I can only suppose it was towards the end of the night and that we were already pretty merry. Anyway, Ches is 6ft 6in and an 18st lump and our opponents weren't particularly big, so we agreed. As soon as we engaged, though, we knew we were in trouble. Kris and I looked across at each other. There was only one way to save face and, without consulting Kyran, our hooker, we collapsed the scrum into the carpet.

There would be no relaxing over the next thirteen months. Things were about to get serious. The most momentous year of my rugby life – indeed, the most momentous year in the history of English rugby – was about to begin.

During that period, we would play twenty Tests. Three of those matches would be against Australia, two against New Zealand, two against South Africa and four against France. There would be history to be made Down Under and statements to be made at home. All of which sounds so mind-boggling that you wonder how we ever got through it. The secret, of course, cliché though it may be, was to take every game and every day as it came.

So you divide each game or set of games into separate blocks. The first block was pretty daunting in itself – three autumn internationals, against New Zealand, Australia and South Africa. As it turned out, these games would provide three very different challenges. Looking back, they were about as close as you could get to the last three phases of a World Cup –

quarter-final, semi-final and final, one after the other.

I began that autumn on forty-nine caps. Little did I realise that I would be playing my fiftieth back at openside. I remember being amazed that I had got to my half century so quickly. I could remember my first goal in international rugby had been to get one cap, and then being determined to get a second, just to make sure I did not join that sad list of names who only ever got one chance. Suddenly I was on the brink of my half century.

Despite the cause for celebration, I went into that game feeling a bit guilty. I was heading for a team meeting at our hotel in the run-up to the game when Backy came up to me and shook my hand. 'Congratulations on playing at 7,' he said. For a second, I did not take it in. Then it dawned on me. Backy must have been dropped. Bar interruptions for injury, he, Lawrence and I had been together as a unit for five years, dating back to that very first game against the All Blacks in November 1997. Now, though, Backy was making way for Lewis Moody, a younger guy with a different style of play and his understudy at Leicester. We all knew that we were under pressure to keep our places – you were every single game – but the news still came as a bit of a shock. Backy had just reached fifty caps himself. As a courtesy, Clive had let him know that he had been dropped before the selection meeting.

I can't remember if anyone in the press made much of Backy's demotion that day, with an 'end of an era' story, but if so, they did not know the man. One thing I was sure of was that it was not the end of him. It would just make him even more determined. He had set his sights on the World Cup and would be there. That, in turn, left me in no doubt as to where I stood. I would have to step into his shoes as defensive captain. If I did not perform against the All Blacks, it could be a straight swap, Backy for me, the week after. Lewis's selection had changed things for all of us.

New Zealand had a new look to their side as well. They had rested a number of players for that tour, although there is no such thing as a weak New Zealand team. Guys like Carlos Spencer and Doug Howlett played that day, which says something about their strength in depth. Mehrtens, who began on the bench, set the scene for the game by saying something along the lines of England being arrogant and 'pricks to lose to'. I don't know the guy so it's hard to know what provoked that statement. Most of us had never beaten New Zealand in our careers, so it seemed an odd thing to say. At least Mehrtens knew what he was talking about after the game.

It was such a big game in its own right that my landmark, quite rightly, did not get much attention. It was still a proud moment, though. Traditionally, you lead the team out on those sorts of occasions but Johnno was so focused that he almost forgot. He was heading out of the tunnel, then suddenly realised. He turned around, raised an eyebrow and, with a grunt, let me pass. So I ran on to the pitch, accompanied by a spine-tingling rendition of 'Swing Low, Sweet Chariot' – the singing at Twickenham drowned out the haka that day – only to realise I was running straight towards the All Blacks' half. A quick side-step off my right and I rejoined my team-mates, all of whom were following Johnno in the opposite direction.

It was a cracking game. They began well but we fought back around half time to lead 31–14 after Jonny scored a great individual try, chipping over the defence to gather his own kick and touch down. That was followed by a 45-metre breakaway try from Ben Cohen. They came right back at us, though, to set up a grandstand finish. It took a late cover tackle by Cohen on Ben Blair to secure our 31–28 victory. I was pretty relieved after committing a howler which led to one of their tries. I intercepted a pass but then threw a stupid interception pass myself as I was tackled. The ball got to Howlett and he disappeared into the distance.

We hadn't beaten the All Blacks for a decade, but that day was historic for northern hemisphere rugby as a whole, with Ireland beating Australia and France defeating South Africa.

I remember a nice touch from John Mitchell, our former coach who was now with New Zealand, after the game. I respected Mitch. He was a hard-nosed, mentally tough guy and wanted to instil that in us. He played his part in turning me from a pretty loose player to one who was more physical in areas like the ruck clear-outs. We never fully clicked in the major games when he was there, though. It's funny but he always seemed to be on the wrong side during England–New Zealand matches. He was a member of the 1993 All Blacks touring squad when they lost at Twickenham. Then he joined us as coach and we lost to New Zealand in 1997, drew the next game, and then lost in the 1999 World Cup. He became their coach and lost to us in 2002 and then again in 2003. Anyway, I hadn't had the chance to catch up with him after the game but, as we boarded our coach to return to the hotel he ran on and congratulated me on my fiftieth cap. He must have been pretty disappointed with the result, so it was a nice gesture.

Lomu and their openside flanker Marty Holah certainly deserved congratulations that day. Lomu had scored two of their four tries and also single-handedly led to us re-evaluating our defensive system. Basically, he was too powerful to stop from close range with a drift or up-and-out defence, where you move forward while shadowing the man you are marking across the field. From five metres out, the only chance was to charge straight out, more like a blitz defence. As for Holah, I had not known much about him before the kick-off but I certainly did by the end. He gave me a very tough time. After that game I had a long hard look at some of my work around the contact areas, what angle I went in on and how I removed players.

Australia were next up. Clive took a look at the back row and changed things around again. Backy returned to the starting line-up and this time Lawrence got the chop. To be fair, he was still working his way back after his knee reconstruction. It was another warning, though, that nobody had a sacred right to play in an England shirt.

Backy's return meant that I was shunted to No. 8. As for the game, well, it followed a different pattern. We were going well and doing most of the attacking but things unravelled in the second half, when we conceded three tries in eight minutes. We had been leading comfortably and suddenly it was 28–16 to them and we were chasing the game.

There was a bit of bad luck involved in two of the tries – Jonny slipped over to allow Elton Flatley past him, then the ball squirted out of the wrong side of a ruck as we attacked and Flatley again got away down the blindside, running almost the full length of the pitch to score. I missed most of all this, though. I had been forced off after a cut on my stitched-up nose split open again. I felt a bit sorry for Lawrence afterwards. He had come on as my blood replacement just as Australia got into gear. He stayed on just long enough to see them score two tries and then had to go off again. Lawrence hated that situation. It wasn't the best way for him to win his fiftieth cap and he deserved better.

Crucially, we didn't panic. We kept cool and worked our way slowly back to win 32–31. Johnno had got all the players together under the posts after one of their tries and said great teams could handle just this sort of situation. It was another good lesson learnt. We returned to Pennyhill Park Hotel and Johnno phoned out for thirty portions of fish and chips which were smuggled past reception in a cardboard box as a celebration.

The first two games of the autumn had been compelling. The next one, against South Africa, was remembered for entirely different reasons. We won 53–3, a record England score against the Springboks, but there wasn't much talk about our seven tries (Lawrence, Backy and I got one each again) afterwards. Put bluntly, the South Africans lost it completely in a game which would later be branded a disgrace to rugby. I think it probably was.

There had been some early niggle, which led to the referee, Paddy O'Brien, telling both captains to lay down the law to their teams. O'Brien's warning clearly didn't register with their lock Jannes Labuschagne, though. With twenty-two minutes on the clock, he dipped his shoulder and took Jonny out late. By the time Jonny was back on his feet Labuschagne was heading for an early bath.

To be honest, I didn't think he deserved a red card. He certainly caught Jonny in the air as he was kicking the ball clear, but I thought ten minutes in the cooler would have been enough. But O'Brien clearly felt he was in danger of losing control of the game. The sending-off, though, didn't solve anything. Perhaps it made things worse. The violence, well masked though it was, continued. There were punches, kicks, head butts, the lot. By the end, Jason Robinson had a perforated ear drum, Jonny had a damaged shoulder, Daws was in a bit of a mess – he did well to carry on, considering some of the stuff he had to take, including Krige diving over a ruck to get at him – and Backy had a damaged cheekbone.

The weird thing, though, was that I, old Paperface himself, or 'International Rugby Punch Bag' as some of my mates knew me for a while, did not take a single shot. It was a phenomenon, really – I didn't need a single stitch. So it was disappointing when the *Times* newspaper wrote in their match report: 'Richard Hill's face looked like he had spent the afternoon chasing parked buses.' I'm afraid I always look like that. Weirder still, I honestly did not have a clue that anything dodgy had gone on. I knew we had been beaten about a bit, but it was quite normal to need two days to recover after playing the Springboks.

I don't even think many of the spectators would have known either. Johnno also missed most of the dirty stuff. He said later he would have led the team off if he had realised, which is saying something. It certainly wasn't until a few days later, when Sky Sports put together a compilation of incidents that I saw exactly what had happened. I was shocked, and also surprised that no players were asked to account for their actions. I had gone to the post-match press conference blissfully unaware of any controversy and was a bit confused when some journalists started talking about violence. Those questions led to one of those classic sporting quotes from Rudolf Straeuli which you can't help smile at now. He responded by saying that one of his players had taken a blow to the head, adding: 'It takes two to tango and we didn't concuss our own players.' I heard that and thought: 'Oh God, has one of our guys dished something back?' Well, no, as it happened. The TV pictures were clear. Krige himself, who had certainly played a part in what went on, had aimed an undercover punch at Daws, missed and instead caught his own fly-half, Andre Pretorius, on the jaw.

Krige ended his press conference with the emotional words: 'See you in Perth.' The two teams were due to meet again there in eleven months, in the first round of the World Cup. I was a bit surprised by his words, though. We hadn't even begun to think that far ahead. His words also sounded a bit like a threat.

Still, we came away from that autumn campaign with a southern hemisphere Grand Slam. We could now boast eight wins in a row over those three teams, as well as a record eighteen wins in a row at Twickenham. Each side had asked different questions. The All Blacks, with their powerful runners, had seemed down and out but still ran us close. The Australians, as usual, had played a canny, resilient game – in my experience they have tended to be far cleverer than the Kiwis, continuing to compete even when their pack has not functioned exceptionally well. Then there were the South Africans. Normally you would highlight their physicality and strength, particularly in the scrummage. On this occasion, they were simply out of control.

To beat them all, one after another in three weeks, was huge and another major step in the team's self belief. It would have been a bit like the England football team beating Italy, Germany and Brazil over three weekends.

You couldn't forget, though, that we had had home advantage and played them at the end of their seasons. Some of their top players weren't available and the first two wins had been by narrow margins. We knew we were not the finished article. We would only be able to prove that at the World Cup.

We all returned to our clubs – Saracens, now under Wayne Shelford, were at it again, starting the season well, struggling during the autumn internationals and then failing to find any real consistency – but we were soon back together for another major challenge.

France, the Grand Slam champions who had just beaten South Africa themselves and drawn with New Zealand, were first up in the Six Nations. That provided us with the perfect opportunity to build on the momentum we had already achieved. We had beaten three of our biggest rivals and now came the chance to make it four out of four.

The game, which we won 25–17, will probably be remembered as Jason Leonard's day, as he trundled out onto the Twickenham pitch for his one hundredth cap. He was the first forward and only the third man ever to reach the mark. For the squad, however, that triumph was tempered by tragedy.

Nick Duncombe, Jason's Harlequins team-mate and who

had made a big impression in winning two caps the previous season as a substitute scrum-half, died on the eve of the match. Mark Evans, my old mentor and who was now the chief executive at Harlequins, arrived at the team hotel and broke the news to the Quins guys. It was a difficult time for Dan Luger in particular. They had been good friends. Nick was only twenty-one and had been on a warm-weather training trip to Lanzarote when he cut his foot and the wound became infected. It seemed so innocuous, it was almost impossible to understand. As a rugby player Nick, like the rest of us, would get cuts and grazes all the time. We talked about Nick in the team meeting and decided the biggest respect we could show him was to go out and win.

So Jason led us out and we did just that.

Jason's own career had also almost ended before it had really begun, when he underwent major neck surgery – involving a bone graft from his hip bone – way back in 1992. Imanol Harinordoquy, the French No. 8, had given an interview before the game, saying he despised England and all Englishmen, which just went to prove that he had not spent any time with Jason Leonard. The Fun Bus was a throwback to the amateur era. He never really let go of some of the old traditions. He was always looking to share a pint with his opposite number after matches – perhaps it was a way of avoiding the ice baths. Not that he wasn't as fit as the next man – he was another of these guys, unlike me, who could enjoy a late night and then appear for training the next morning as if nothing had happened. A quality bloke, amiable to all and with no airs or graces, I can't imagine there is a rugby country which does not have a strong affection for him.

I still laugh at the story of Jason turning up at Twickenham when they knocked down the West Stand in the early 1990s – he was a builder and carpenter in those days – and trying to make off with one of the massive team baths in the back of his van. He convinced four of the builders to help him carry it out before he was caught in the act by an RFU official.

That win over France had not been particularly pretty, but we were effective for most of the game, forcing mistakes and letting Jonny slot over the penalties as he took his career points tally beyond the 600 mark. We got lax in the last fifteen minutes, conceding two late tries, but we had won. The bad news was that Lewis, who had retained his place ahead of Lawrence after making such a big impression, damaged his shoulder and did not return for seven months.

Wales in Cardiff was another scrappy affair but we came through. Our injury toll, though, was mounting. Half the team who had played Australia in November were crocked, including Johnno. Backy was also among them, so I was shifted around to openside again, my third position in the back row in as many games. I was happy enough to do it although the chopping and changing was not ideal. I was pretty comfortable on both flanks but less so at No. 8.

It was at this stage that Josh Lewsey, with a perfectly timed run, broke into the team. Jason Robinson was nursing a knee problem and Josh quietly took over at full-back. He'd taken his time about it – he'd made his debut five years before, on the Tour of Hell, and managed only a few caps since, all against minor opposition – but nobody could have picked a better time to make their return, around eight months before the World Cup. He still had to show what he could do, of course, and he did that in capital letters by scoring two tries in the 40–5 win over Italy and another in the 40–9 victory over Scotland. One minute he was not even in the squad and the next he was almost an automatic choice.

Just before that Scotland game, Jim Telfer set the 'Dad's Army' ball rolling, even if he did not use those exact words himself. He highlighted the age of our pack, suggesting we might run out of steam against younger Scottish legs. That idea, that we were on our sell-by date, was repeated over and over again in the coming months. We took Telfer's comments with a pinch of salt, though.

True, we had five over-thirties in the pack and it was also true that we had had a rash of injuries that season. Jim might also have thought that the dropping of Johnno, Lawrence and Backy over the previous season suggested the team was beginning to break up, but all three had battled straight back. Perhaps it was a case of wishful thinking. The Scots hadn't won at Twickenham, after all, for twenty years. And what recent evidence was there to suggest that our performance levels were dropping off? We'd reverted to a less expansive, more deliberate game that season, but we still played at pace when required. The proof was in the pudding. We scored four tries against the Scots and one glance at the scorers – J. Robinson (2), J. Lewsey and B. Cohen – will tell you that none of them came from slow-moving rolling mauls. There must have been something for the forwards to do, though, because I got my hands on the champagne for man of the match that day. (I'm not sure I ever saw it, actually. I think Claire must have drunk it with some of her friends.)

Anyway, here we were again, in exactly the same situation as we had been two years before, facing a trip to Lansdowne Road for the deciding game of the championship. There was one significant difference, though. This time, Ireland were also in the running for a Grand Slam, Championship and Triple Crown of their own, having won all their previous games. That helped our cause. The Irish like playing the role of plucky underdog. It can be liberating, having nothing to lose. But this time there was great expectation on them.

Mind you, there was quite a bit of pressure being built up on us too. I don't usually read the newspapers too closely, but the general argument before this game was that it was about time that England won their first Grand Slam since 1995, which was fair comment. Jason had won three of the things. I hadn't won a single one. Also, this was an all-or-nothing game. In previous seasons, we had lost the Grand Slam deciders but still won the Six Nations championship. Defeat this time would leave us empty-handed.

The other question being asked by the media was what effect would another away defeat, and another missed Slam, have on us as a team? If we couldn't win in Dublin this time, they said, then we would have no chance of winning the World Cup in Sydney. One article went as far as to argue that the game would define our lives. If we lost, as we had done in the 1999, 2000 and 2001 deciders, we would be scarred for life. It would confirm that our characters were in some way fundamentally flawed.

Well, I'm sorry, but that was rubbish as far as I was concerned. I may be in a minority of one, but I still don't think it would have been serious if we had lost. Of course, it was a big, big game and of course we were desperate to win. But from my perspective, no, it wouldn't have been terminal. We would all have sworn, and kicked the walls back in the changing room, and we would have copped a lot of bad press. But by then I think we were beyond being psychologically damaged by losing a single game. We had, after all, beaten most teams over the previous few years, often by record margins. I honestly don't believe another defeat would have affected us.

Another big difference between 2003 and 2001 was that our preparation was so much better this time. We had played together throughout the championship, even if we weren't quite at our best. Most of our injury problems were also behind us.

op) I chase after the French ball-
ier in this Under-19 inter-
ional. Fabien Pelous looms
ge in the background.

entre) With Marcus Olsen, my old-
friend in rugby, as the England
der-21s prepare to take on the
nch Armed Forces at
ckenham.

ttom) My England A debut against
y in February 1995. Steve Bates of
sps is to my left, a man who
derstood that while A may be for
bition and attitude, R was for
ebuck, as in the pub. (Colorsport)

Looking alarmingly thin, I take on the Scottish midfield during my England debut in 1997, a game we won by 41–13. (Colorsport)

I touch down for my first England try, against Ireland in 1997 when I scored at the end of the game to help us to a stunning 46–6 victory at Lansdowne Road. (Colorsport)

il Greening, me, Jeremy Guscott, Nick Beal, Phil Vickery, Austin Healey and Martin Johnson
Lympstone, working with the Marines ahead of the 1999 World Cup.

the way to scoring a try (of dubious legality) against Wales in 2000. That day, all the back
w got on the scoresheet. (Colorsport)

On the way to the tryline against France in 2001 – a 40 metre dash that surprised me as much as everyone else.

'The most over-praised unsung hero', as Lawrence Dallaglio called me, visits Twickenham with Kyran Bracken, while the bloke on the right can't quite take it all in.

I won my fiftieth cap for England in November 2002, against New Zealand, but most of the attention was given over to the fact that I had replaced Neil Back at openside. Those who thought it was the end of an era did not know him.

At last! Our 42–6 Grand Slam victory over Ireland in 2003 set us up for the World Cup. (Getty Images)

After picking up a hamstring injury early in the tournament, I was back in action at last for the World Cup semi-final against France. Replacement fly-half Gerald Merceron just evades my diving interception attempt. (AFP/Getty Images)

(*Opposite page*) Let the celebrations begin! After our 20–17 victory in extra-time, the England squad was about to find out that some things would never be the same again. (AFP/Getty Images)

The back-row union of Dallaglio, Back and Hill in tandem during the World Cup final against Australia.

Posing with the cup on the flight home from Australia. We did not know what would be waiting for us when we landed at Heathrow.

Hiding at the back of the bus during our victory parade through central London on 8 December 2003. (Empics)

Standing next to Jonny Wilkinson, I was never going to get to talk to the Queen as she made her way down the line. (Empics)

You could certainly tell that people were up for it. There was a real edge in training that week, with people much snappier than usual, which was a good sign. Clive tried to wind us up a bit, telling Lawrence, Backy and me that we had won nothing yet as a back row. I knew he was right. But, to be honest, I have never needed that sort of help to get up for a game. I can do that on my own, whether it's a club game for Saracens or a Grand Slam decider.

The game began with a minor diplomatic incident.

We were playing right to left in the first half, so, according to protocol, we ran out and lined up on the right for the presentations and national anthems. There we were, minding our own business, when an official marched up and told us to move to the left half of the pitch. Apparently Ireland always lined up on the right – it was their lucky side. Johnno, who was captaining the side for the first time in a Grand Slam decider, told the official where to go and refused to budge. Ireland – clearly a superstitious lot – responded by lining up further down to our right, which must have confused the officials when they came out to meet the teams. I suppose Johnno's stance made a psychological statement that England were not there to be pushed about. That was certainly the line taken by the media. Me? I'm sure I would have done what the officials wanted. That's just how I am. Anyway, we won 42–6 that afternoon, so perhaps Johnno was right – and perhaps the Irish were wrong, it can't have been that lucky a side after all.

I've never really been into superstition. Some guys cross themselves before they run out. Others have boot rituals, or have to hang up their clothes in a particular order. I think Will Greenwood had a pair of lucky socks and Mark Regan relied on a lucky pair of pants – when they wore out, he sent his mum down to Marks and Spencers to buy an identical pair. I remember on the 1997 Lions tour always wanting to be second to leave the changing room behind Johnno, but that was more a case of eagerness rather than superstition.

As for the game, well, the scoreline may have flattered us, but we took control in the second half, playing a mauling, pick-and-go game before creating space outside and scoring five tries without reply. I had a hand – well, a foot – in the first one when we wheeled a scrum and I stuck out a leg just as Stringer went to pass. The ball went loose, Daws sniped through and then put Lawrence in. We had to defend really well at times – before the break we were out on our feet at times – but never gave them a sniff, then brought the hammer out.

It was a good feeling, when the final whistle went. The first block, the autumn internationals, had gone well. Now the second was over and we had made another statement by winning a Grand Slam at last! The next block – away Tests in New Zealand and Australia – would be more demanding still.

I did not give it any thought but for some players, that game would be their last Six Nations start. We went out on the town that night and quite a few of the Irish lads did as well. We had always got on well with them as a side. Many of them had spent time with English clubs, and I had also met many of them with the Lions. That was a good thing about the Irish, they tended to party whatever the result. Definitely not 'pricks' to lose to. By the end of the evening, though, I was feeling pretty sore. With about twenty minutes to go against Ireland, someone had landed on my ankle while tackling me but I was determined to stay on until the end.

Sarries were in the relegation mix when I returned, so I played against Leeds but had to come off early. When I rolled my sock down, I discovered that the ankle had gone completely black. For a while, I was worried that I might miss some crucial end-of-season games for Saracens as well as being ruled out of the summer tour, but fortunately there was no fracture.

It was not a nice time at Sarries. The feeling in the England camp, just days before, had been of elation, but at Saracens people were worrying about more mundane things, like whether they would still have jobs in a few months if the club were relegated. You don't sleep too easily during such times.

We got to our last game of that season against Sale needing a bonus point to be sure of staying in the Premiership. Early in the second half, we secured it with our fourth try and a huge cheer went up. We must have felt like walking off right then and sinking a few beers, but we stayed on to win the game.

We finished in eighth place in the table and went into the Zurich wildcard play-offs, giving us an outside chance of qualifying for the Heineken Cup. We met Leicester in the final, on a sweltering day. The game went to extra time, by which time both sides had fought themselves to such a standstill that, at one line-out late in the game, I looked around and found I was the only Sarrie there, with the rest of the guys strung out all over the pitch, struggling to get up with the play.

Anyway, Leicester nicked the result at the death. I did not realise it at the time, but that match would prove to be a perfect training exercise for the World Cup final.

14

WHITE ORCS

March 2006. I'm back running. Better than that, we've had some discussion over a new contract. And Sarries are winning again. It doesn't get much better than that.

Running again was hugely liberating. I hadn't been in the best of moods just before that. For starters, the club decided at the last moment not to take any long-term injured players to Portugal, which was really depressing. I had really been looking forward to mixing with the players and being part of the group again. My reaction was to retreat inside myself a bit.

The knee wasn't feeling 100 per cent either. I'd gone down to Exeter for a benefit event at Nigel Mansell's golf and country club and it had grumbled all day long, so I took an anti-inflammatory tablet. It helped so much that Fares has agreed to keep me on them for about a week, to see if they keep helping. I don't want to rely on them as the only way to be pain free, but they've definitely helped me do more good-quality work.

As for that run, well, the knee felt so good one morning in the gym that I did a jog on the spot. The next day I was in the clubhouse and I went for a spontaneous run around the table and chairs. It was about fifteen metres. There were quite a few people around who saw it and it felt really good. They obviously were very happy for me. Best of all, there was no pain.

I had agreed to meet up with a few of the guys and their wives afterwards for a coffee, but I was a bit late because I needed a little extra treatment. By the time I got there, they had already told Claire about the run. She was delighted, then after a pause, said: 'Were you meant to do it?' When I replied that no, technically it had not been in my programme, she went on: 'So why did you do it?' You can't win, sometimes.

I've continued doing some runs in the gym, on a strip of flooring which is sprung like a trampoline. It's like a carpet with sponge underneath. I've done a few jumps over a six-inch hurdle and a dive and forward role on the mat. The only fly in the ointment is that I needed to have some fluid drained off the knee and it then returned pretty quickly. That suggests there might be something that has become aggravated inside the joint. Also, I've lost a fair bit of cartilage, so there is less of a buffer inside my knee. I've been warned that this may remain an issue in the long term. The scans, though, seem to show that the bone surfaces have mended well. I would love to have a stint without pain or discomfort but I'm under the impression that I will have to put up with it, during my rugby career and perhaps beyond.

It makes you wonder if I will ever be able to play at the same level again. My style of play has always been based on fitness and a high work rate. It might be tough to maintain that if I'm limited in the amount of training I can do. I've spoken to the club physios about that. I'm certainly going to have to modify my training – that's on the presumption I get that far. I can't be pounding my knee every day, it simply won't take it. I know of other guys out there who have their own tailored fitness programmes because of problems they've had. The key, though, is how you perform in matches, simple as that.

When you think of what medical science can achieve nowadays, it's incredibly frustrating that we can't put our finger on just why my knee is swelling up. You'd think there would be an answer for everything, not just for my problem, but for lots of illnesses from which people suffer. Sadly not.

Anyway, I've kept the faith, even if there are periods when you feel down. Fares has as well – he says he still believes I have the character to make a comeback. I was having a bad patch the other week when a card arrived by post from Somerset from a young lad called Mike Stanton. There was a picture of me with a crutch and my other arm in the sling, wearing a fez. 'Get well soon, Sarries need you back, you are my favourite player', it said. It made me smile and I've kept it.

The other good news is that I now have that verbal offer of a contract for next season. Nothing is signed yet, though. It had been playing on my mind a bit but my agent phoned up and told me the good news. It's for one year and will be based on the number of appearances I make. Considering what has happened over the last year and a half, that's to be expected.

Anyway, the guys are doing fine without me at the moment. After beating Premiership leaders Sale away at the start of the month, to end a run of eight defeats in a row, they've now gone and seen off Worcester to jump right up the table. I'm not quite sure how much credit Eddie Jones can take for the Sale win, since he's only just arrived and only had time to chat to the players once. Mind you, he must have said all the right things and put the guys in the right frame of mind.

He's been doing a lot of analysis since and did some hands-on training sessions in Portugal. I had a chat with him and he asked me for my opinion about how the team was playing. What he says makes sense. Another thing you have to say for the guy – there's a huge amount of respect for what he has done in the game.

(* (* (*

Eddie was in charge of the Wallabies when we went out there after the 2003 Six Nations. He and Clive, as usual, spent a fair amount of time winding each other up in public as the World Cup approached. Actually, I think they respected each other. They may even have enjoyed getting on each other's nerves.

First, though, we had to play New Zealand. There was a fair amount of negative talk in the media before we set off. Quite a few people thought Clive was making a bad mistake in taking on two of the best sides in the world just a few months before the World Cup. If we lost, they said, it would damage our chances in the tournament. Gavin Hastings, the former Scotland captain, said in a newspaper that even a Scot could not have devised a more horrific set of matches for England. There was also talk of player burn-out and that we might give away too many trade secrets (although, with Mitchell as their coach, they probably had more than enough information on each of us).

All I can say is that the whole squad bought into the trip. Everybody who was available went. As far as we were concerned, it wasn't a part of our World Cup warm-up anyway. That was almost four months off. It was a self-contained, two-Test summer tour. We were playing well and we did not fear the challenge. We weren't worrying about what our opponents could do to us. It was an opportunity, indeed, to make them worry a bit about what we could do to them.

New Zealand sides had just dominated the Super 12 that year, playing some really ambitious stuff – a bit like we had done back in the 2001 season. Mitchell, though, told the press he was a bit worried that they were neglecting their bread-and-butter forward play. It was the same sort of debate we had had a few seasons before. Not that I have ever met a soft All Black forward.

We warmed up against the New Zealand Maori. They had just beaten Tonga. Quite a few of their players also wanted to make a good impression on the All Blacks selectors before the World Cup. We went in with a pretty useful side, with Phil Vickery as captain, even if a lot of regulars were left out. Most of that team, though, were already experienced internationals and the rest, like Stuart Abbott and Andy Hazell, have made their mark since. Trevor Woodman also played that day in New Plymouth as we won 23–9 in cold, damp conditions. Their coach, Matt Te Pou, said it was probably the strongest side the Maori had faced in his eight years in charge, which was definitely nice to hear.

The game that really mattered, though, was in Wellington. Just before it, I got the chance to meet up with some of my Kiwi relatives – including Peter Jackson, the director of the *Lord of the Rings* films.

It was the first time I had met him. My gran and Peter's mum are cousins. Peter had visited England and stayed with my grandparents, so he knew all about their house and the beloved croquet lawn. He also knew a bit about rugby – every Kiwi does. Anyway, they were doing some retakes on *The Return of the King* and I was able to help arrange a visit to the set for the England squad to watch some filming. It was fascinating, seeing how they put the film together. We also got shown some extra scenes of Aragon fighting the orcs.

Another of my distant relatives from the Ruck side of the family, Gareth, is also in the film business. I met up with Peter and Gareth again during the 2005 Lions tour, following my injury, and got the chance to go back to the film studios and even get my hands on some of the Baftas and Oscars they had won. (Tom Shanklin, my former Saracens team-mate, came along with me on that occasion and, when we got back, told the rest of the squad he'd just been out to lunch with his friend Peter. Shanks, incidentally, is obviously closely related to Gollum but everyone at the studios was too polite to mention it.)

Anyway, the *Lord of the Rings* connection resurfaced, in pretty comical circumstances, after the Wellington game against the All Blacks. I suppose we may have been regarded as slight underdogs, going in. New Zealand were already being touted as World Cup favourites ahead of us. They had guys like Ma'a Nonu, Daniel Carter, Joe Rokocoko, and Mils Muliaina coming through, and were strong enough to leave out the likes of Christian Cullen, Taine Randell and Andrew Mehrtens. England, meanwhile, had only ever won once in New Zealand, thirty years before.

I think Johnno and Jason Leonard were the only two guys who had ever won over there, and that had been with the Lions. We were unchanged from our Ireland game, though, and on a roll. To win at the 'Cake Tin' in Wellington would be historic and – despite being written off as boring and one-dimensional by the media – we knew we had a good chance.

Most matches get remembered for great tries or kicking displays. Usually it's the decisive score which stays in the memory. This one, though, was all about a key passage of play during which, in effect, nothing much happened. Midway through the second half and leading 9–6 in miserable conditions, we had been reduced to six forwards after Backy and Lawrence had been sin-binned, both for infringing at the breakdown. Typical of those two guys – when things get really tough, they disappear and leave the grunt and grind to me. There we were, defending a five-metre scrum and I was on my own in the back row.

I hadn't paid much attention to all the talk about the decline in standards of New Zealand forward play before the game. They certainly got plenty of possession that game. All I know is that they had eight forwards against our six and that they failed to take advantage. I think they had four attempts at pushing us back over our line and could not do it.

I had to protect the openside, so that's where I went. We could not afford to bring someone like Mike Tindall into the scrum, since we would have been left short behind where the All Blacks were so strong. I had only one option – push hard, break hard and hope.

I think we disrupted the first scrum by wheeling it, and then the second collapsed. The next scrum also ended in a mess and had to be reset before we were penalised for not binding correctly. They took a quick tap but we managed to stop their No. 8, Rodney So'oialo, on the line before winning a penalty of our own. It was a massive moment. As I remember, we then worked our way up to the other end of the field, playing some of our best rugby of the game, and Jonny rubbed it in by putting over a three-pointer. He had an impeccable kicking game in testing conditions. It was so windy that we were having to hold the ball for him when he went for goal.

The other thing I remember was Josh Lewsey coming out of a ruck with a bleeding head after being trampled on repeatedly. Josh began to complain only for Johnno to tell him to shut it and get on with the game. It was later decided that Williams had no case to answer, which was a surprise.

At the final whistle, we had won 15–13. We hadn't played well and we knew it, so there was no euphoria. On the one hand it was an awesome victory, but on the other we were disappointed that we had not played much rugby. Still, there's a value to winning through sheer bloody-mindedness. We had refused to be beaten that day. I remember thinking that if we could win while playing badly, anything was possible.

Johnno would have known more than anyone else that winning in New Zealand is the ultimate. He had spent a year or so playing there as a young man and had even turned out for an

All Blacks Under-21 side. He had a bit of fun in the press conference afterwards when he was asked what had been going through his mind during those crucial scrums on our line. 'Nearly my spine,' he replied. The media kept probing, in the hope of getting him to reveal that he had made some Churchillian speech which had somehow galvanised the rest of us in our hour of need. But Johnno had not said anything at all and he knew nothing needed saying. It was just a matter of shoving with every ounce of strength that we could dredge up.

In a way, it was just a case of going through a routine which we often carried out at training. We usually practised seven-man scrums, you never know when you are going to lose a man during a game. So it wasn't down to luck. It was something we prepared for; mind you, I'm not sure we practised six-man scrums very often.

Now that I look back, a few years later, I realise that that victory is right up there with the best in my career. You collect loads of shirts over your career and give a lot of them away, but some, from matches like this, you like to keep. I keep them in a box somewhere. I've got my shirt and my opponent's from my first game, from my fiftieth, from the Centenary Test against Australia, from Lions games and from the World Cup. I'm not very sentimental but I'll dig them out at some stage and have a look. Hopefully not for a while.

The next day, I picked up the local newspapers and came across one of the funniest post-match analyses I had ever seen. The article said the England pack looked like 'giant gargoyles' or 'a tribe of white orcs on steroids', adding: 'Forget their hardness – has there ever been an uglier forward pack? Small children who stayed up late to watch this Test will be wetting their beds for weeks.' Well, cheers for that, I thought. I suppose it was as near to a compliment we were going to get in a country where rugby seems to matter more than anything else.

I couldn't help thinking, though, that the journalist concerned had not spent too much time examining some of his own All Black forwards up close. They weren't exactly pin-up boys themselves. Anyway, I enjoyed that article so much that I think I still have it somewhere in our house.

Mitchell also had a go at us in the media, complaining about us slowing down the ball at the breakdown. My reaction to that was: 'Of course, your guys would never try it, would they, Mitch? But who taught us, exactly?'

The propaganda continued as we landed in Australia. Eddie Jones, as usual, was slagging us off, saying we played 'Premier League soccer style', working our way down the field from set play to set play before trying to score. Well, yes, Eddie, that's rugby basics for you, and that's what you have to do in the lashing wind and rain of Wellington. He said we were very pragmatic, as if that was somehow wrong. For us, it was a compliment. I think we'd have preferred to call it intelligent, winning rugby.

David Campese, England's greatest critic, chipped in, saying we never scored tries against top sides. The only guy in the entire country who seemed to think that we could play was Australia's captain George Gregan. He suggested that people who kept labelling us as a ten-man rugby side had perhaps not been watching over the past ten to twelve months. I'm glad to say that George was proved right a few days later and Campese very wrong.

The game against the Wallabies was in Melbourne, the scene of my concussion with the Lions. There was another echo of that game. Elton Flatley had been dropped, so Nathan Grey came in at fly-half. There was a bit of chat in the press about that 2001 Lions incident. Anyway, towards the end of the game, I had been benched and so had Nathan so I went over and shook his hand. As far as I was concerned, it had never been an issue.

I said the win over New Zealand was right up there. Well, in terms of pleasure, the Australia game may have been the best I ever played in for England. Winning the World Cup, of course, was something else. But this one, apart from culminating in England's first win in Australia at the eleventh attempt, was special because of the way we played.

Clive made two changes, replacing Leonard and Rowntree with Vickery and Woodman at prop. Fourteen of the fifteen guys who started the game would start the World Cup final against the same opponents a few months later.

The conditions this time were perfect for running rugby, so we ran. Having shown we could play tight, we now proved we could go wide as well. We were always in control, scoring three excellent tries. Greenwood got the first after five minutes, followed by Tindall on the half-hour. Perhaps the best, though, came when Cohen surged onto a short ball from Jonny and broke clear to put us 22–9 ahead with a quarter of an hour left. They got a consolation try right at the end. It was a pretty impressive run by Wendell Sailor, but that's all it was – a consolation. We had won 25–14.

There were other moments to savour, like Lewsey's unforgettable tackle on Matt Rogers. He lined him up and caught him perfectly in the chest, hitting him backwards and dumping him on his back. Not the sort of tackle you want to be on the wrong end of. Matt had to give up surfing for a while after that, apparently.

It might have been the perfect game, in fact, apart from one slip-up. Having run the ball all over the pitch, we changed tack at one stage, set up a maul near the halfway line and drove it right up to their try line. We seemed sure to score when the maul mysteriously collapsed. Completing that one would have been a perfect way to show how we could mix up our game. That was one of Backy's strengths, latching onto the back of mauls. We always accused him of doing it to keep up his try stats but he was an expert at it. He would get into an ideal position, with his low centre of gravity, and organise the guys around him perfectly.

It was only during the days immediately afterwards that we realised how tired we were. In retrospect, though, you have to agree that Clive got it just right on that tour. We stayed in Australia for a few more days, to go and check out our World Cup base in Perth. It wasn't that popular a decision. Most of us were pretty desperate to get home and enjoy what little time we had available before World Cup training began. Our fitness coach, Dave Reddin, always set the bar pretty high when it came to personal fitness but we all knew he would push it even higher this time. Still, it did give us the rare luxury of a few nights out together. It didn't happen that often. Even on evenings immediately after games we'd often split up. We always agreed to meet in this or that bar only for people to get lost or sidetracked. Sometimes people wanted to catch up with friends. After the Australia game, for instance, I met up with Peter Coryndon that night, my former school mate at Bishop Wordsworth School.

There was just still time, before we flew home, for Rowntree to disgrace himself in public. We had been invited along to a winery for a tasting. 'Could we taste the apricots?' we were asked. 'Could we smell the raspberries? Could we taste the...' Suddenly, Graham let rip spectacularly. 'Pick the grapes out of that,' he said with a self-satisfied grin.

15

A CLOSE-RUN THING

The 2003 World Cup was the highlight of my career but I came pretty close to missing it entirely.

At one stage during the tournament Clive was advised that I should be sent home because of injury. That would have been tough to take. Missing Saracens' cup final in 1998 had been bad enough. Missing the last stages of a World Cup would have been indescribable.

As it is, there was a happy ending for me this time. The memories of the Sydney final will stay with me forever. It's not that you think about it all that often. Life moves on. But every now and again, at an official dinner or function, say, somebody will mention something and you're right back there, at the Telstra Stadium on 22 November 2003.

I don't suppose I've ever experienced anything to match it. People often ask me what it feels like to win a World Cup. How can you start answering that? Ask anyone in the England team and each would highlight a different moment or a different emotion. For me, the most important thing of all was just being there.

We had switched to full World Cup mode after returning from Australia in June. We weren't due to reconvene until 21

July, but we were all given personal fitness programmes to follow during the break. For quite a few guys, it was a nervous time. The first hurdle was the announcement of a forty-three-man preliminary squad, which would be whittled down to thirty later. Mike Catt, though, wouldn't have been nervous at all, for the simple reason that he seemed to have no hope after struggling with injury for two seasons. Sure enough, he was left out of the initial selection. The door, though, was left slightly ajar. If he could prove his fitness, he might just still have a chance. So the World Cup would be a close-run thing for Catty as well.

For the next two and a half months, Pennyhill Park hotel in Surrey became our second home as we worked on becoming the fittest team at the World Cup. Usually it was a five-day week, with weekends off. Everything was done to make us comfortable. The Twickenham stadium gym under the West Stand was transported lock, stock and barrel into a marquee in the hotel grounds, where they had also upgraded the rugby pitch. We would start each morning with a fitness workout before breakfast, working our way down the lanes of gym machines. There would be another extended session before lunch, which might include skills work, although we did very little with the ball during the first month. Afterwards they packed us all off to bed, wearing recovery tights designed to improve your blood circulation (but not your self esteem – I was sharing with Backy at the time and he looked ridiculous in them, so I suppose I must have done as well). Taking those naps felt very strange at first but you got used to it. I had not slept in the afternoon since having glandular fever as an eighteen-year-old.

We certainly worked hard. Pre-season training is always tough, but I often missed part of it at Saracens after getting back late from a summer tour. It was good to be in an international environment and to be able to really go for it, pushed along by the guy next to you.

At some stage we were allowed a short break and Claire and I escaped to St Lucia. I carried on training, though, as best I could. They had a pitch-and-putt golf course which I used as my running track, as well as a sparsely equipped gym. I improvised by filling my ruck-sack with weights and lifting that.

Occasionally there would also be a day off from Pennyhill Park and I'd meet up with some of the Sarries boys. On one occasion an Aussie called Patrick Phibbs came along. He was one of several players brought in as cover during the World Cup. After I left Patrick asked: 'Hey, that guy who's going to the World Cup, what does he do? Is he the kitman?' Unsung Hero strikes again.

While we trained, New Zealand were busy confirming them-selves as World Cup favourites by winning the Tri Nations. They caused a stir by crushing the Wallabies 50–21 in Sydney, although the return match was much closer. Down Under, our World Cup credentials were being questioned. Yes, we had won thirteen matches in a row and were ranked world number one, but what about our age? We were a Dad's Army outfit, as New Zealand had been in 1991 and Australia in 1995. The argument went that guys like Leonard (35), Backy (34), Johnno (33), Rowntree (32), Lawrence (31), Dorian West (36) and – wait for it – Richard Hill (30) would not be able to cope with the heat of an Australian summer. We would probably have laughed at the idea, but we were too busy gasping for breath after another of Dave Reddin's sadistic work-outs.

Everybody, that is, except Jonny. He had always impressed us as a player but this was the first time we had spent such a long time training together and it was a real eye-opener. Everybody knows he is meticulous with his practice routines, but it was even more impressive when you saw it first hand. As for his fitness levels, they were just as mind-blowing, particularly in the running exercises. I thought I worked hard but Jonny pushed himself to the very limit. He was out on his own. There was one exercise where you had to run as far as you could in a minute, sit down for a short break, then repeat the exercise twice more. Jonny would be way off in the distance somewhere. Nobody else got near him.

Occasionally, there would be a welcome change from the routine. One of the most enjoyable was when we were addressed by a member of a British unsupported expedition to one of the Poles. We had done a really hard set of workouts that day, so most of us weren't too keen when the talk was scheduled for seven o'clock in the evening. He was fascinating, though, particularly when talking about the importance of teamwork in life-or-death situations. If anybody fell through the ice they had just over a minute to get them out, dry them off and get them into new clothes, otherwise it was curtains. He also explained how he went about selecting his teams, which made us all perk up and listen. The World Cup squad was about to be cut back to thirty at that stage.

It was a hot summer. On the hottest day of the year, it was decided we should train at midday in an attempt to reproduce Australian conditions (Nice idea. Pity it rained during the semi-final and final of the World Cup). When Reddin was pleased with us, or just feeling ever so slightly related to the human race, he'd magic up a box of Cornettos for us at the end of the final session of the week.

August arrived and with it our warm-up games. Clive was mixing up his line-ups, so as to take a look at everybody, and I did not get a game in the first two matches, when we beat Wales 43–9 at the Millennium Stadium, which was a great result, then lost 17–16 against France in Marseilles. Paul Grayson almost nicked that game with a late drop goal that went just wide. It was disappointing to see our run of fourteen successive wins come to an end, but we put things right in the return at Twickenham by winning 45–14. Lawrence was struggling with injury so I turned out with Cozza and Backy that day.

When the final squad was announced there were some tough calls to make, with Austin and Graham Rowntree among those to miss out. The training was scaled down, a farewell dinner held, and suddenly we were heading for Perth.

We could not have been much better prepared. Organisation was one of Clive's strong points. He created an environment where there could be no excuses. We had everything that we needed during the period: the best hotel, the best travel arrangements, the best everything. We even had newly designed shirts, made of state-of-the-art materials designed to disperse sweat and so tight-fitting that it made it hard for opponents to grab hold of them.

Clive also tried to plan for every eventuality. When we set off, our support team included a lawyer, a chef, a referee and a visual awareness coach. Clive might have begun his England career as a romantic, but now it was all about ensuring the basics were in place. Only then would he look for something which might add one per cent to our performance and which, in turn, might help to turn a match. If you needed anything, there was invariably someone on hand, ready to help.

If you wanted to check out an unfamiliar opponent, for instance, you went to our video man, Tony Biscombe, and he could put together a DVD for you. He would prepare general team DVDs, ones on particular units like the back row or particular positions, or even on specific phases of play. I used to watch all the team ones and I certainly learnt things from them, while the ones on the back row tended to confirm things I had picked up on the pitch. Today, having been out of the game for so long, I would definitely use Tony to brush up on things. Guys certainly picked up on important things because of those

DVDs. The line-out guys, for instance, would study clips to try to pick out calls or opponents' particular patterns of behaviour. Sometimes the position of a jumper's leg would give away whether he was going to move forward to jump or back.

Before leaving London, we were also addressed by security experts. Some of the stuff they came out with, like rooms being bugged, sounded a bit James Bond to me. But that didn't stop Clive having our rooms 'swept' with an anti-bugging device during the tournament. The security experts also did a bit of their surveillance on us, around the hotel or while training, just to prove how easy it was to pick up useful information.

I suppose it made sense, actually. Rugby is full of stories about teams trying to spy on each other and it's not all in people's imagination. One of the most amazing came out of the 1995 World Cup, when half the All Blacks squad fell ill shortly before the final against the hosts, South Africa. The New Zealand coach, Laurie Mains, believed that his players' food had been spiked. You also get all sorts of tales about teams losing a copy of their line-out calls and hotel staff or cab drivers passing them on to their opponents. During the 1999 World Cup, it was even rumoured the Australians left sets of false calls lying around as an attempted bluff. A few of us could also remember the breaking of the Lions line-out codes in 2001 – things like that mattered.

The last thing you want is people watching your training sessions. During the final stages of the World Cup our training ground had been shrouded by a wall of two-metre-high black plastic sheeting, following several suspicious incidents. Before the quarter-final against Wales, we were training at Brisbane Grammar School and a car was spotted parked on the hard shoulder of a flyover overlooking the practice pitch. Before the South Africa pool game, a helicopter started hovering over the pitch – it turned out it had been hired by the local media who were looking for pictures of Prince Harry, but it still meant they were in position to film us. There was another comedy moment, when a TV truck accompanied by a bunch of photographers pulled up nearby, so the England bus was driven over and plonked right in front of them to obscure the view. Every time the TV truck moved, so did our bus.

Our QC, Richard Smith, also earned his seat to Australia, by arguing our case after we ended up with sixteen players on the pitch against Western Samoa. Then there was Sherylle Calder, the visual awareness trainer. Some guys took a bit of convincing that they needed to learn how to see, even if her CV included stints with the All Blacks and Australia's world-beating cricketers. A former South African hockey international, she believed you could be trained to better appreciate what is going on around you. She argued that if you wanted to improve your passing, you practised it. So, since your vision is a big part of rugby, why not spend twenty minutes a day improving that skill as well?

I liked the idea. Ball-watching is a common problem, particularly among forwards who have their heads stuck in the bottom of rucks all the time. Attackers, too, sometimes focus so hard on the ball or their immediate opponent that they miss a gaping hole somewhere else in the defence. Wingers occasionally find themselves facing a prop and need to take in the situation quickly to exploit the mismatch. I like to think that I am pretty good at reading the game, but I felt there was a lot more I could learn.

First there were computer programmes, focusing on letters or shapes while wearing 3D glasses. Then it became more practical. Sherylle would hold up colour cards about twenty metres away as you went through a ball skills routine and you had to shout out the colour. I was injured by then, so I used to concentrate on one particular exercise where someone standing just behind me threw different-sized balls against a trampoline leant against a wall. I then had to try to catch them.

Clive's forward thinking did not take long to surface. Our British Airways flight was meant to be heading to Sydney but the plane made an unscheduled diversion, allowing us to get off at Perth. Clive, I presume, had a quiet word with the airline beforehand. The rest of the passengers must have been wondering what was going on as we trooped off.

We began with a few days acclimatising before the hard graft began. There was also a mayoral function to attend, where we found ourselves rubbing shoulders with our Pool C opponents – Georgia, Uruguay, Western Samoa and, of course, the South Africans. We circled each other warily around the canapés. The one exception, weirdly enough considering our last meeting with him, was Corne Krige, who seemed to be pretty friendly.

We all knew, though, that the England versus South Africa match was vital. Whoever lost faced a far tougher route to the final, with New Zealand their likely opponents in the quarters and Australia in the semis.

First up, though, were the Georgians.

On the face of it, that match on 12 October at the Subiaco Oval should not have been too dramatic. It almost turned out to be the most significant game of my career, though. We knew the Georgians would be up for a physical battle, so the priority was to come away with a win and no injuries. Oh well, you can't get everything right. For starters, Danny Grewcock somehow managed to break a toe in the warm-up after being trodden on by Ben Cohen. Then Daws went off at half time after tweaking a leg muscle. It was my turn twelve minutes later.

To be honest, I don't quite know when it happened. It felt like a bit of cramp in my hamstring. I hit a couple more rucks and then called on the physios. I went off as a precaution, sat there with my bag of ice watching the last half-hour of our 84–6 win and didn't think much more about it. Next morning, though, the leg was still sore so I was packed off for an MRI scan. As expected, it was nothing more than a minor tear, so insignificant that I was selected for the next game.

It was just a case of putting in a little extra work with the physios. Or so we thought. Little did I realise that I was to become their most regular visitor over the next five weeks. With the Springbok game a couple of days away, Daws and I were given fitness tests. I knew right away that my niggle had not cleared up and I pulled out.

There was no smokescreen involved. I had genuinely expected to play in the game – so much so that I've still got the shirt that I was due to wear, embroidered with the South Africa match details.

Even then, though, it wasn't really an issue. There was a lot more concern about our scrum-halves. Daws also failed his fitness test while Kyran's dodgy back was playing up.

Yet another problem was looming, going into that game. Will Greenwood's wife Caro was having complications with her labour. Will and Clive decided he should fly home straight after the match. It must have been a hugely traumatic time for Will and Caro. They had tragically lost their first child, Freddie, forty minutes after the birth. I had sensed that something was up with Will during the week. At one point he had come into the medical room, taken a phone call and rushed straight out. He'd seemed on edge but it was still a shock for all of us to find out he was leaving.

Will put in a hugely courageous performance that day – God knows how he kept things together – as did Kyran, who was still getting treatment on his back right up to kick-off and had to wear a support to get through the game. The match was level just before half time when Louis Koen slid a penalty wide. The ball landed up in Will's hands and – inexplicably but equally understandably, considering the circumstances – he forgot to touch the ball down. Instead of facing a 22 drop-out, South Africa suddenly found themselves with an attacking five-metre scrum. Kyran, though, harassed their No. 8 and we regained possession to clear the danger.

The turning point came midway through the second half. Two Jonny penalties had made it 12–6 when Lewis Moody charged down a kick and Will fly-hacked the ball over the line to score the only try of the game, prompting Backy to comment: 'I'm glad Will decided to touch down the ball that time.'

It had been a tense, stop-go affair but by the end we came through 25–6 for our fifth successive win against South Africa. One thing it had not been was the bloodbath Krige had seemed to promise, almost a year before.

Will headed to the airport with everyone's best wishes, the rest of the guys headed back to the hotel and I headed back to the physio table. I had just missed my first game through injury in five years and I had not enjoyed it. I am not a good watcher. It's fine before the kick-off, but then the nerves kick in almost as badly as if you were playing, only you can't do anything to affect the result. Those emotions got worse and worse as the tournament progressed.

Many of our supporters were probably already looking ahead to the quarter-finals after that result but we knew our next game, against Western Samoa in Melbourne, wouldn't be a walk in the park. They were without a lot of their best players, who had been forced to stay with their clubs, but one thing Samoans never do is punch below their weight.

I knew fairly early on in the build-up that I would not be playing. 'Take a bit more time out and get it right,' Clive told me. I felt almost ready but I continued with my 'hamstring runs', devised by the physios, while watching the other guys from afar. I was getting close to running at around 90–95 per cent of my usual speed when suddenly, stretching out one day, I felt another sharp pain. I eased down and the pain went. We were making good progress so Barney Kenny, the physio, decided to end the session there. That, though, is where all the niggly problems began. With hindsight, I'm pretty sure that it was at that exact moment that I suffered a second hamstring tear. I did not know it at the time – nobody did – but my World Cup hopes were hanging by a thread.

The game against Samoa, in the end, was almost tougher than the one against South Africa. It was certainly more controversial. We were pretty lucky to win 35–22. It took until the last fifteen minutes for us to take control. The start, indeed, was close to disastrous as the Samoans rattled up ten points in the first six minutes. They were shipping the ball about at speed, with their big runners offloading well. Soon their captain, Semo Sititi, had scored an awesome try after they broke out of defence. They stretched us from one side of the pitch to the other, zig-zagging up field and keeping the ball alive through around a dozen phases before Sititi crashed over on the left. At that stage, we just couldn't hang on to the ball. Finally, though, Backy managed to latch onto the back of a rolling maul and we struggled back to 16–13 down by the break.

Things did not get much better afterwards. We continued to look flat but somehow dredged up three tries to edge home. We had been leading by a single point with ten minutes left.

The controversy came when Mike Tindall went down with cramp. Reddin was told by the management to get Luger on immediately but Steve Walsh, the fourth official, told him to wait. They got into an argument and in the confusion we ended up with an extra man on the pitch for thirty seconds or so. Reddin and Walsh then had another row involving a water bottle down in the tunnel.

I don't think the incident affected the result but it did spark the first negative press. All sorts of rent-a-quotes came out of the woodwork and demanded that we should be docked points, sent home or shot at dawn. There was an inquiry and both Reddin and Walsh got short-term suspensions. I think we also got fined.

That was when Richard Smith did his bit. Back home, he was more used to dealing with murder cases. This time it was the case of the mystery of the extra body rather than of the missing one. He stayed up for most of the night to prepare the defence and helped defuse the whole thing. He was good to have around. I used to like chatting to him about interesting cases he had been involved in. He had brought stacks of folders along with him to work on. When he wasn't busy with that, he'd come to training and collect balls for you or act as your catcher during passing practice.

There was one charge we were clearly guilty of at that stage – that of playing badly. It was hard to put a finger on it but we looked slow and lethargic. Our next win, 111–13 against Uruguay, did not exactly tell us much. At least Will was back, with his wife's scare behind her. Shortly afterwards, though, Grewcock was packing his bags for good after breaking a bone in his hand. He's not the sort of guy to make a public fuss about it. He just shook a few hands – gently – and he was off. That, though, got me thinking that there was less and less reason to justify keeping me out there.

The worst thing about my situation was that nobody could explain exactly what was wrong with my leg. I began to doubt whether they knew, which did not help my confidence. I was having no problem working on my fitness on the gym bikes or in the pool but whenever I stretched out the leg while running I became aware that things were not right. I would have a good day but then a couple of bad ones. Hamstrings are notoriously tricky to sort out. Basically, I needed a breakthrough and it wasn't coming. To make matters worse, the press were sharing the same hotel and I was aware of being watched. Each week I seemed ready to play, but each week I missed the deadline or failed a fitness test.

There was no suggestion of an ultimatum from Clive – the only thing I received was reassurances – but I couldn't help wondering how many lifelines would be thrown my way. I was so worried that I told my parents that, by the time they got out to Australia to watch the final stages of the tournament, I might no longer be there. I had this vision of us crossing paths at Singapore airport.

As for Claire, she had school commitments and didn't want to come if I was going to be sent home. It was impossible, though, to give her any exact information on how I was progressing.

Things came to a head just before our quarter-final against Wales. I was told to undergo a second scan. I couldn't help thinking I already had one foot on the plane home. That feeling of dread seemed justified when they brought out the results. The tear had got worse.

With that, my dream seemed to be over. I got the strong impression that I was about to be told to pack my things. Indeed, I discovered later, after the World Cup, that exactly that recommendation was made to Clive. The medical opinion was that I wasn't recovering fast enough. I'm not the sort to give up, but I was close to it at that point. If I had been on my own, I might have broken down.

But Barney Kenny and Phil Pask, backed up by Richard Wegrzyk, the masseur, were having none of it. As I've already said, I've often been called 'Unsung Hero'. Well, those guys proved to be my unsung heroes. I reckon I spent more time with them during the World Cup than with my own team-mates. I would get up in the morning, check in with them and start my treatment. They were always positive. The longer my injury dragged on, the harder I found it to stay as upbeat. Walking around, you would pass one of the other players and they would ask you how you were. I always found it a fine balance – I didn't want to sound depressed or pessimistic, but I also didn't want to sound like I was having a good time. The medical guys, though, never lost faith. They explained to me that scans could lie. Yes, it was showing more tearing, but it could have happened some time ago and might therefore already be all but healed. They then went off and argued my case with the team doctor by telling him that my running was better than the clinical diagnosis suggested.

Was that true? I'm not sure. But one thing was sure. It had to become true. As we got back from the scan, Barney and I decided to go out and train there and then. I wanted to know one way or another, rather than hanging on for another week: would the hamstring stand up to a more rigorous workout, or it would go completely?

As we set out for the training pitch, the squad were beginning to head back the other way after finishing their session. Within an hour or so, I expected to know whether or not I had a chance of staying with them.

Barney and I go back a long way. He was the physio at Saracens when I was a fresh-faced student. He takes a while to get to know. He never looks you in the eye until he's happy in your company. Even back then, though, he would fit you in for treatment, whatever the time. There I was, a nobody from college, and he would tell me to come round to his home at Twickenham at around half past nine or ten in the evening and, despite having already put in a long day at work, he would treat me on his lounge floor. Once, he used a lump of ice the size of a tennis ball to break down some scar tissue after the operation on my groin. Not the sort of thing you forget in a hurry. Even now, as I struggle to save my career, Barney has been round to our house to offer encouragement and opinions. I'm not part of his remit anymore but he's still made the effort.

And all he has got in return is me winding him up royally. These guys work hard for their qualifications and their degrees. The year before the World Cup, though, Brunel University, my old college, awarded me an honorary Masters in recognition of my sporting achievements. It used to bug the physios that a bloke with my chequered academic history could end up with as many letters behind his name as they had. Later, the University of Hertfordshire also awarded me a Masters. Initially I had to decline. 'Dear Sir/Madam, thank you very much for your kind offer,' I wrote back. 'Unfortunately I will have to decline as on the date of graduation I hope to be playing in the World Cup final.' Following the World Cup win, the offer was renewed, only this time it was an honorary doctorate. I was with England when I received the letter so I walked up to the front of the team bus and said to the physios: 'Sorry guys, I'm not very good at reading, can you tell me what this says?'

They should be grateful. I mean, I did invite Barney to the ceremony when I received my doctorate (he declined – must have been busy that day). At least I don't demand to be called Dr Hill. Well, not all the time.

Anyway, Barney and I marched out onto the pitch at Brisbane Grammar School and we got to work. I remember the muscle was a bit painful during the warm-up but I just worked through it. I suppose it was an all-or-nothing gamble. I pushed up the work-rate, and Barney responded by cranking it up still further. By the end, he was pretty much working me flat out and I was lying on my back, gulping for air. Nearby there was a scaffolding tower, from where our training sessions were videoed for the management. I looked up, saw the camera pointing down at me and made an appropriate salute. But I couldn't hide my smile. I knew I had to wait to see if there would be a reaction but deep down I knew it was a breakthrough. I was going to make it. It was a huge moment.

Barney ambled over. 'Good effort, Hilda,' he muttered, and walked off without looking back.

Later, some of the guys asked me the same old question and this time, at last, I was able to say that I had just got through a really good session. I felt like phoning Claire up immediately but it was the middle of the night in England. In any case, I didn't want to tempt fate.

Bizarrely and as if by magic, the leg felt 100 per cent the next day. They held the daily management meeting and Barney reported that I seemed to have turned the corner. Shortly after the Wales game, I rejoined the squad training and was greeted with universal abuse. 'What are you doing here?' 'Who are you, who's the new kid?' 'Holiday's over, is it? Got bored of smoking cigars?' It was great to hear.

To this day, my dad thinks he played a key role in my recovery. When he got to Australia, egged on by Mum, he told me the injury was all in my head and that it was time to pull myself together. To be honest, he wasn't the only one. Everyone I spoke to was trying to boost my confidence and some did tell me to snap out of it. Claire was more subtle – she can judge my moods pretty accurately – but she also came out with something similar eventually. Positive thinking, of course, has a part to play when recovering from injury but I don't think I was paying much attention to what they said. I was in one of my in-one-ear-out-the-other moods by then. I still think I was handling things the best way I could. If anybody played a key role in helping me – sorry, Dad – I think it was the physios.

I felt better and better over the next couple of days and was so confident of my recovery that I even took my boots and gum shield along to the quarter-final game against Wales, just in case there was a last-minute injury and someone needed to be added to the bench. There was no way that the physios would have let that happen, but they allowed me to cling to the hope that it might. It also allowed me to feel part of the squad at last. If anything, their problem with me now was how to hold me back.

At half time, though, it looked like all our chances of playing in another World Cup game were fading fast. Wales, who we had crushed earlier in the year, were playing some credible stuff while we were struggling for fluency. Their winger, Shane Williams, inspired an early breakout try which was touched down by Stephen Jones. Then Colin Charvis was driven over and Wales were 10–3 up at the break.

Waiting for the restart, my mobile lit up. Back home, Sarries were about to play in the cup and I started getting texts from the guys: 'Fancy Penzance next weekend?' No disrespect to Penzance, but I had my eyes on other things.

Wales's great display was not a surprise. They had pushed New Zealand hard in their previous game. Clive and Andy Robinson, though, found the solution by bringing on Catty. Suddenly we regained our shape. Catty, one of the last names to be written down for the World Cup, simply took control of the game, taking the pressure off Jonny with his decision making and his kicking. Jonny relaxed visibly and started to find his kicking range. Jason Robinson set off on a dazzling run before putting Will over, one of our few moments of quality, and we eased ahead.

It was close right up to the end but, despite being outscored by three tries to one, we came through 28–17. If there was a plus point, it was our stubborn refusal to lose. You also have to take your chances and kick your penalties if sides continually infringe against you in an attempt to avoid conceding tries. We did that. The moods of the two teams at the end, though, told the story. We had won yet it was Wales who went round the stadium to acknowledge their fans, while our guys headed for the dressing room looking at the ground.

The Western Samoa match had suggested we were playing badly. This confirmed it. Clive called a clear-the-air meeting behind closed doors. It was not bad tempered, but it was pretty frank, from both sides. He said some guys were not performing and pointed the finger at Lawrence in particular. It was brutally honest stuff. There was some truth in it, although Clive was playing mind games to an extent. He always tried to wind Lawrence up to try to get the best out of him. I'm not sure Lawrence would agree that it worked – he is the sort of guy who would admit it himself if he felt he was playing badly – but on this occasion he may have been taken aback by what was said. It's certainly true that Lawrence was at his best in the last two games of the tournament.

Clive also argued during that meeting that Jonny was playing the best rugby of his life, which wasn't really true. Jonny was not at his best but Clive was trying to take the pressure off him and he knew what he was doing. Jonny needed to be wound down, not up.

Jonny is a good mate. We've spent a fair amount of time together over the years. I wouldn't say he's obsessive – I'm not sure he'd thank me for that. Meticulous, perhaps. Or obsessively meticulous. That is meant as a compliment – no one puts more into his game than he does. But I think the pressure did get to him during the early stages of the tournament. I'm not exactly laid-back myself, to be honest, although I don't let on when I get nervous. He certainly needed to relax. The World Cup was a stressful occasion for everybody, but it was twice as hard for Jonny. As our match winner, the spotlight was always firmly on him. At one stage I was talking to his dad Phil and he asked me about Jonny's state of mind – it wasn't a case of talking behind his back, but it was clear Jonny was becoming a bit tight.

His work ethic is such that it can be hard to persuade him to take a break, but we managed it on one occasion. I was still crocked at the time, so Dave Reddin hired a car when we were on the Gold Coast and some of us packed off in this convertible Suzuki jeep and headed off down south. In England, on our free Thursday afternoons during match weeks, it was pretty easy for us to get in a car and turn up in a place where no one expected you to be, whether it be a zoo or a tea shop, in Guildford, Reading or Windsor, but in Australia it was a lot harder. But we drove for about an hour and eventually found a long thin beach with barely anybody on it. While Richard Wegrzyk worked on my leg, the other guys kicked a football about. That was a good day.

The main point to come out of that meeting after the Wales match was that the guys felt they were being overworked in training. They were slightly jaded going into the previous games and it was agreed to taper back the workload. I couldn't exactly argue, but I had just got to the stage where I wanted to become more involved with team training and suddenly everybody was getting days off. So I had to remind myself of our line-out calls or new moves from paper, or by quizzing the other players.

I think *I'm a Celebrity, Get me out of Here!* must have been on television around that time, because there were a couple of moves called Jordan and Lord Brocket. A lot of set plays were named along topical lines. Our line-out calls tended to be a mix of letters or numbers, which is fine in theory, but can sometimes lead to problems when someone shouts them out with a gum shield in their mouth, 15 metres away from you and in a noisy stadium.

For me, it felt as if the World Cup was about to begin; England versus France in the semi-final in Sydney. It was a strange time for me during the build-up. I got almost Jonny Wilkinson-style coverage in the media at times. I think the press were trying to pinpoint a reason for England's lack of form. It was an easy option to say it must be because Richard Hill is missing. So they added two and two together and came up with five. I seemed to get more written about me when I wasn't playing than when I was, which doesn't make any sense. A lot of the stuff was over the top. Zinzan Brooke wrote at one stage that England would not win the World Cup without me, which seemed to miss the point that rugby is a fifteen-man game. He bracketed me in importance with Jonny and Johnno. In my mind, that would be doing the squad a disservice.

Quite a few journalists jumped onto the 'here's an easy story' bandwagon. A lot of the same writers thought that we would lose against France, so I rest my case. As far as I was concerned, England had not done too much wrong. It was just a matter of clicking back into rhythm.

The things I hoped to bring to the team were my high workrate, my tackling and my reading of the game. It's not just about getting the ball, it's about getting good, fast ball for your scrum-half. As a kid, I had a picture of Dean Richards on my wall. Part of his mystique was that he seemed to have an uncanny ability to be in the right place at the right time. For me, that's called reading the game.

When I started, I was a loose, ball-playing openside, so it's a bit ironic that many people seem to remember me now as the 'Silent Assassin', working secretly away in rucks and mauls. Defence, though, and work in the tight are big parts of the game. The first priority is completing an effective tackle, of course. Then you evaluate the best way of stealing the ball, or of at least slowing it down. Against Samoa, for instance, that had been a big problem – we were tackling but we couldn't seem to disrupt their off-loading of the ball.

Sometimes it's best to hit your opponent head on, sometimes it's best to come in from the side and then get up quickly so that you can contest the ball. In other situations it might mean tackling him in such a way that he falls facing your side. Ideally, you want to dislodge the ball. Certain people are very good at different techniques. Backy would be very good at bringing someone down and getting to his feet quickly, Dips was very good at flipping opponents over. I work hard to develop all the tackle skills.

Then there are the breakdowns. Some people may think that all you have to do is plough into a ruck, but there are plenty of options. The first thing to ascertain is who is the biggest threat – the tackler, the man coming in next or the guy coming in second? You also have to check how the ball is being presented.

Basically, I try to work out which problem needs correcting first. Should I contest the ball, either by trying to steal it or disrupting their possession, or should I remove someone from the breakdown area? If we're attacking, should I drive my team-mate with the ball through the hole, to change the focus of the ruck by a few yards? If we're defending, is it worth counter-rucking to make it harder for them to get the ball away? Sometimes it's best not to go in at all, and instead secure the fringes or even drop back and get ready to defend out wide. If the ball is already lost, or if your team-mates are winning it without you, there's always something better you could do elsewhere.

Shortly before the selection meeting for the semi-final I was taken aside at the Manly Pacific Hotel and told I would be playing. I was definitely more nervous than usual. The hamstring wasn't the problem. If it went, it went (although I was praying that if it had to go then it should be at the right time, not when I was trying to make a cover tackle). I just wanted to make sure that I didn't embarrass myself. My conditioning was OK. It was 16 November and I had played only a game and a half since June but my fitness base, built up at Pennyhill Park, was good and I had done enough in the gym to keep things ticking over. It was more a case of being up to speed mentally and knowing all the plays.

In the lead-up to the game, we trained in our waterproof gear to simulate the warmth of a sweltering Sydney evening. It didn't turn out that way but the weather played right into our hands. We had a game plan worked out but that changed on Sunday morning when we woke to heavy rain. Clearly, we were going to have to play tight, percentage rugby in pretty horrible conditions. France, who were looking like the team of the tournament, always have big, tough packs, but their instinct is to play with width and style. We felt we were pretty versatile. Rain would do just fine.

The game did not begin well for me. I had gone into it with more praise ringing in my ears. Serge Betsen, a member of France's highly impressive back row, said I was a key player who came 'from the shadows, from the darkness', which sounded good, even if I had no idea what it meant, while the former Springbok coach Nick Mallett compared me to the great All Black breakaway Ian Kirkpatrick. But I soon got brought down to earth by gifting France their first try.

A line-out went wrong, the ball landed in Betsen's hands without him even needing to jump and he galloped over the line. I can't even remember whose throw it was but I should have been closer to him. I got to Betsen as he went over and tried to dislodge the ball while getting my arm underneath him but without success. So much for my public reputation. For a horrible moment I wondered if that score might cost us the game, but I knew the best response was to forget about it and get straight back into the game. 'Sorry lads, my fault,' I said as we waited for the conversion, and left it at that.

From then on we pretty much controlled the game and went on to win 24–7. The wet certainly didn't suit their young fly-half Frederic Michalak. He had been one of the finds of the tournament but Backy and I managed to get to him a few times and his confidence was shot by the time he was substituted in the second half. Jonny, meanwhile, had an impeccable game, playing the percentages and kicking five penalties and three drop goals.

The French lost their discipline as they got increasingly frustrated. Two of their players ended up in the sin bin. Christophe Dominici must have been more miserable than anyone. Jason Robinson side-stepped him and Dominici shoved his leg out and tripped him up. His football tackle got him a yellow card and he was forced to leave the game having been injured. For me, though, things could not have gone much better, despite my Betsen blunder. I did OK for the rest of the game, before being taken off inside the final ten minutes.

Even better, I remembered Claire's birthday. By the time the team got back to the hotel it was around 11 p.m. so I didn't see too much of her, but I reckon it was a pretty memorable birthday all the same.

We were to play Australia in the final. We had watched on television as they beat New Zealand 22–10 the day before. The All Blacks had been the team to avoid, so it was a surprise. Australia, though, got an early interception try and then suffocated the All Blacks into making mistakes. The Kiwis, put under pressure, tried too hard as they became increasingly desperate. Like us before them, they would be branded as chokers by their national press as they headed home. You can use the stats to support the argument – since winning the trophy in 1987, the

All Blacks have lost in three semi-finals and one final – but, to me, it was composure they lacked, not heart or skill.

Australia's presence in the final ensured that we would be hit by a press onslaught for that final week. It started immediately, with a picture of us with our hands in the air as we celebrated the final whistle against France. 'Hands up if you think we're boring' ran the headline. As if anyone with any sense would have risked running the ball from all parts of the pitch in those wet conditions. It had been a day for playing for territory first, and only then looking to go wide. Clive's response, though, was always spot on. 'It doesn't matter how we win,' he used to say. 'We're not Torvill and Dean, we're not here to get marks out of ten.' Other articles said we were too old, we were cheats and Johnno was the grumpiest man in world rugby. There were even cut-out voodoo dolls of Jonny for Aussie fans to stick pins into. One newspaper called on all good Australians to make such a racket outside our hotel at night that we wouldn't be able to sleep.

Amid all the abuse, there was the occasional compliment. I'm not sure I was too aware of it at the time, but Eddie Jones, the Wallabies coach, handed me just about the biggest one I have ever received that week. I was the glue that held England together, he said. If he could poach one England player for the final, it would be me. Probably, though, all this was part of the greater propaganda campaign. Eddie was the master of the wind-up. By building me up, he was probably trying to make the fourteen other guys in the England team feel that he didn't rate them. I don't think any of us took any notice at all.

That final week felt a bit like being under siege. We were based in the Manly Pacific, on the beach front. Fans from both sides were soon congregating outside. They could see us clearly when we went into our eating area, which resembled a conservatory on the first floor. Talk about living in a goldfish bowl. They would chant and shout and try to get your attention. One woman, decked out in gold and green, parked her 4x4 right outside, opened the boot and fired up this huge sound system, blasting out Australian songs as she danced about the vehicle. 'What are you doing?' I thought. I couldn't help laughing – she actually helped me relax.

It was pretty hard to get out, even for a quiet walk. With the front of the hotel surrounded by barriers and cordons, the only escape route was through the back via the underground car park. But even then you were bound to be approached by a fan as soon as you went into a café or restaurant, so most of us stayed inside, fighting over the PlayStation to while away the time. On the face of things, people were still joking and laughing as they normally did in the team room, but I wouldn't say it was a fun week. There was something massive at the end of it and you never forgot it for more than a few minutes at a time.

The situation must have got to me because I didn't sleep very well all week and occasionally resorted to a sleeping tablet, something I only ever did before big matches. I also kipped a fair bit in the afternoons. England had thought of most things but I don't remember ever getting any advice on how to handle that sort of pressure. By then, I suppose we were used to dealing with it, each in our own way, though perhaps not on this scale. Something like the Grand Slam decider in Ireland would have helped. By then, anyway, a fair few friends and family members had arrived to offer a distraction. Not that it always worked that way. At one stage Backy and his wife took their daughter Olivia to the beach, only to be mobbed. He said it was like being a superstar walking through an airport. It gave you an idea of what we were heading into.

Monday and Tuesday had been recovery days before we got

back to training at the Brookvale Oval on Wednesday, surrounded by our wall of plastic sheeting and security guards.
Until then, the Australians had not even been mentioned. On
the Thursday, I went out for a meal with Claire, my parents and
my sister. The next day, on the eve of the match, Claire came
over to our hotel. She was aware of the tension as soon as she
arrived. Normally, she said, you would be greeted by all the
other players and back-up staff as you walked in, but this time
all she got was little nods of the head, raised eyebrows or half
smiles. Nobody was really talking.

We escaped out of the hotel and sat on the sea wall, then,
back in my room, we put on a DVD. We barely exchanged a
word. After a while Claire decided enough was enough and
asked if I minded if she left. She was on holiday, after all, while
I had a job to do. It was the right decision.

Claire says she was more nervous before the semi-final – she
couldn't bear the thought of me missing out at the final hurdle
– but it was the other way round for me. From about nine
o'clock on Friday evening, time seemed to stop. It just dragged.
Think of the longest day of your life and then double it. No,
treble it. That is what it felt like. I woke up at about eight
o'clock on the day – twelve hours to kick-off. We went off to do
a few line-outs at 11 a.m. but that only took up an hour. As
usual, I stole off for a massage, then plonked myself in front of
the TV and watched a video.

The last team meal was at around 4.30 p.m., just before we
set off. It wasn't too hard to get some food down – it can often
be worse when you have to eat at around 11.30 a.m. before a
3 p.m. start. By the time of our final team meeting we just
wanted to get on with it.

It was a long drive to the stadium, and we were taken down
some eerily quiet estate roads to get there. The only people you
saw were either heading to the venue, wearing their team's

colours and with their faces painted, or off to house parties to watch the game. As usual, I found myself locked into negative rather than positive thinking. 'Please don't muck up,' I kept saying to myself. 'This day is going to be remembered in English sporting history for a long time. Don't be the one who makes a mistake.'

Time suddenly started moving fast. Clive told us to leave nothing behind in the changing room. Johnno told us to look around at each other. We were a team. We had been together a long time and there was a bond. Several guys had gone through personal tragedies during that time, and those events had pulled us close together. We owed it to each other to win.

The first guy I would have looked at would have been Lawrence next to me, pulling those ridiculous faces of his and clapping his hands as he always does before games. 'Come on, come on!' he would say. Backy, the consummate professional, would be in a world of his own, frowning as though he was try-ing to solve some impossible puzzle.

Johnno – or Ferengi as we sometimes called him, after the race of *Star Trek* monsters – was snappier than usual, which was always a sign that he was ready to produce a monumental effort. He's good company and has a good sense of humour, Johnno. The public persona couldn't be further from the truth. Not until match time, anyway.

There was Ben Kay, the son of a Lord Justice and our line-out brain. Phil Vickery and Trevor Woodman were together, tied at the hip as usual. Close friends and proud Cornishmen, they went a long way back. They were similar as players, with much more pace and ball skills than your average prop. Vicks was two animals rolled into one – quiet off the pitch, a man of mayhem on it. Trevor, sadly, would be forced into premature retirement through back trouble. He should have had another World Cup in him.

Daws, given half the chance, would have been asleep. The guy's a dormouse. The day before a game you'd find him curled up asleep in the physio or massage rooms, often covered with a blanket that somebody had thrown on him. The more nervous he got, the more likely he was to drop off. Once awake, though, he is very chirpy. Put him together with Austin and there's a never-ending battle as they take the mick out of each other.

Jonny, stern-faced, would have been going through his routines and just itching to do a little extra kicking practice before the start. Mike Tindall, in contrast, would have managed a few smiles. He even smiles during games. He's a hardworking guy, strong and quicker than people realised. He plays an abrasive game – his face matches his play. Alongside him sat Will Greenwood, all arms and legs and at the centre of every conversation. He has a good set of hands and a good eye for a hole and had been instrumental in improving our back play. 'Shaggy', he was called, in honour of the character from *Scooby Do*, or sometimes 'Rodders', after the character in *Only Fools and Horses*.

Then there was Jason Robinson, a family man and a devout Christian, following a tough upbringing and his wild younger years. Ben Cohen, on the other wing, was pretty reserved. He lost his appetite for the game a year or so later but came back. His uncle, the 1966 World Cup winner, was watching in Sydney that day.

As for Josh Lewsey, well, he's an all-action guy. Give him a holiday and he would go and ride horses on a ranch in America rather than go anywhere near a beach. He punched way above his weight on the pitch, despite suffering from occasional back trouble. Sometimes, in restaurants, he would eat while kneeling on the floor because it was too uncomfortable for him to sit.

Suddenly it was time to go. As we headed out, Johnno turned round, opened his mouth and then realised there was nothing more to say. This was the moment we had been waiting for. Enough said. Just do it. We ran out onto the pitch and suddenly there was the Webb Ellis Trophy, on a stand in front of us. You could have touched it as you ran past. Then there were the national anthems (G, A, B, C). And then, with the evening drizzle falling, we were off at last.

Within no time we were a try down. Their fly-half Stephen Larkham kicked across field for Lote Tuqiri to leap up on the left wing and take the ball high above Jason Robinson and touch down. It was a tactic we had used quite a bit. It worked perfectly, pitting the biggest back on the field against the smallest. I was quite surprised that Australia never tried it again, having had that success with their very first attempt.

We dominated the rest of the half, though, to lead 14–5. It should have been more, as Ben Kay has been reminded more than once. With twenty-five minutes gone the Wallabies had knocked on in midfield, and I managed to get a toe to the ball and hack it through before re-gathering ten metres out. We spun it right via Lewsey and Daws before Ben, a couple of metres out, somehow spilled the pass. It was just one of those things; 99 times out of 100 he would have caught it and scored. After the game, as the leg-pulling began, Ben moaned: 'I'll probably feature in a pizza advert now.' I gather Pizza Hut – who filmed that advert with Tony Underwood and Mike Catt after they were trampled underfoot by Jonah Lomu during the 1995 World Cup – have been supplying him with free pizzas ever since.

Jonny, though, kicked us ahead with three penalties before we hit back hard just before the break with a great score. It wasn't pre-planned. Lawrence burst left off the back of a ruck and angled his run towards the left-hand touchline. He then reversed the ball inside to Jonny who, in turn, flung the ball outside again for Jason Robinson to squeeze in at the left corner before punching the ball away in delight.

The ball was pretty greasy but we were playing with width and moving it about. Perhaps we overdid it and didn't look after the ball enough. For whatever reason, we just couldn't get our game going again after the break. We were also getting penalised in the scrums, which was difficult to understand. We clearly had the stronger scrum but the Aussies worked it well and managed to get the ref on their side. Just before the final whistle Andre Watson awarded another penalty against us at a scrum and Elton Flatley coolly slotted the ball over forcing extra time at 14–14. I gather the ref Watson stood by his inter- pretations after the game. All I can say is that front row play is an alien world. I often have no idea why a scrum has collapsed. I'm not sure the front rows always do either. We seemed to be pushing them around pretty much at will but once you get a ref on your back the 50/50 decisions tend to go against you.

As the whistle went for full time, it dawned on me that we hadn't scored a single point in the second half. I honestly think that a lot of teams might have panicked. Instead, Johnno called us around in a huddle. Eddie Jones had come down to address his team, but when Clive arrived Johnno told him to leave everything to him and the players. 'Clive, no problems, we know what we are doing,' he said.

Clive was an organiser, a facilitator and an original thinker. One thing he wasn't, though, was a master motivator. I had a good relationship with him – he never dropped me, after all – but a few guys had had their problems with Clive over the years. In a way, by putting together a side full of key players and lead- ers – and where even the foot soldiers, like myself, were highly motivated – Clive had made himself redundant as a leader. We were very lucky over that period to have had a large number of players who had captained England, while others had captained their clubs. The key man in that situation, though, was Johnno alone. To his credit, Clive understood. It was an absolutely crucial moment in our rugby history. Clive, instead of trying to hog centre stage, turned around and let Johnno get on with it.

Johnno got the tone just right at that point. There were around 83,000 fans in that stadium, all in a state of hyper-excitement, yet that huddle was one of the coolest and calmest environments I've ever experienced during a match. 'We know what we have to do and we don't have to change much to win this,' he told us. It was just a matter of tightening up and concentrating on what we did well. Johnno knew we were going to win, you could just feel it. Only one guy wasn't listening. Jonny had slipped quietly away to practise his kicking.

The other masterstroke was for Clive and Andy to bring on Jason Leonard. Within no time Jason was chatting away politely to Watson, asking what problems he had with our scrummage and what needed sorting. From then on, the penalties against us dried up.

As for me, I found myself thinking back to that Saracens–Leicester play-off game that had gone into extra time earlier in the year. The likes of Johnno, Backy and Ben Kay had been part of their winning team that day. It had been even hotter then. 'I'm on the right side this time,' I thought. 'These blokes won't run out of gas.'

We continued to set the agenda as play got under way. Jonny put over a monster penalty in the first half of extra time and you could see their faces drop. If he could kick that, he could kick anything. Back they came with another last-gasp penalty, though, to level at 17–17. A period of sudden death, with victory going to the side scoring first, looked inevitable.

By then, I was off the pitch. Late in the second half of extra time Australia had gone blind at a scrum and Gregan put through a grubber for Tuqiri to chase. I managed to read George's intentions and get to the ball first, scrambling it into touch, but that was the end of me. My leg seized up with cramp. I went off and on bounded Lewis Moody.

Now Lewis may be crazy at times, but he did not put a foot wrong during his cameo appearance as the clock wound down. I think there were less than two minutes left but it was obvious, even to us on the sidelines, what we had to do. We kicked long, Lewis belted after the ball and Matt Rogers shanked his clearance into touch. Lewis then won the line-out at the back – of course I would have done exactly the same, salmon like, had I been there! Catty took the ball up and Daws then made a trademark snipe right through the middle of a ruck only to be pulled down at the edge of the 22. With him stuck at the bottom of a pile of bodies, Backy took over as scrum-half while Jonny dropped into the pocket, ready for one final drop goal attempt.

It would have been better, of course, to have Daws giving that pass but Backy was certainly no mug. Our back row had worked on our passing with former England No. 9 Nigel Melville earlier that summer, in anticipation of just this sort of situation. Instead, though, Backy passed short to Johnno who charged up and set up another ruck. Johnno was acting as a diversion as well as a second option, which meant the defence had to worry about him as much as about Jonny. The other advantage was that Johnno's run allowed Daws to get back into position. He put his hands to the ball – a move which made a few of the Australians false start – then, with less than thirty seconds of the game left, fired his pass out. The rest is history. Jonny, who had already missed three drop goals and was now on his weaker right foot, got out his pitching wedge and the ball spiralled upwards. Watson followed the ball right under the bar, almost as if he intended to catch it himself, and then raised his arm.

On the bench, the whole squad jumped up, then sat down just as quickly. There was time for one more play. We almost made a mess of things. Australia put up a Hail Mary, we caught it – actually, Trevor Woodman caught it, God knows why, he was meant to be lifting one of our locks – Will Greenwood almost got in the way of the pass from the ruck but dived to the floor just in time and Catty booted the ball into touch to end the game.

There was this huge initial euphoria. Everything was a blur. Then it was a case of finding where the family was sitting. Then came the presentation of the trophy. The picture of Johnno lifting the trophy will always stay with me. I remember making a few laps of honour around the pitch, soaking everything in, after Claire had joined me.

Then we were back in the changing rooms. Prince Harry turned up – he's a nice lad and has got some good banter – and so did Tessa Jowell, the Culture Secretary, although Lewis famously did not recognise her as she edged into one of the photographs and unceremoniously told her to get out of the shot. Australia's Prime Minister John Howard, also made an appearance – he'd seemed quite grumpy handing out the medals but was very gracious afterwards.

After some pictures with Backy and Lawrence, I walked around the ice baths – funny how nobody bothered to have one that day – and, still in my kit, sat down on a chair in the showers, drinking a quiet beer while trying to let it all sink in. Two weeks before, I had thought I was on my way home and now I was a World Cup winner. Jonny, the man of the moment, did the same by sneaking into the physio room for a few minutes on his own.

We all went out to a restaurant with our families afterwards, staying into the small hours before the party gradually broke up. I remember standing at the bar with Mark Regan. His medal was around his neck, inside his shirt, and mine was still in its box in my inside pocket. Every now and again he would nervously look inside his shirt and I would pat my jacket, just to check they were still there.

Claire was flying back in the early hours of the morning, so we walked back through Sydney, with dawn breaking over Darling Harbour, to her hotel. You couldn't get a cab for love nor money, not even if you were a World Cup winner. It was a weird, weird sensation. Everywhere there were fans, still wandering about or asleep in doorways. A few of them recognised me across the street but nobody bothered us. They just waved or said 'Richard, Hilly, well done', then walked on. They were in their own worlds, enjoying the moment.

Claire's mobile kept beeping with text messages from all her friends. Things like: 'Oh my God, it's great, it's fantastic, we're hammered in Fulham.' Like most of the players, I didn't get any texts. Our phones jammed up completely that night. The next day, they started coming through, each one repeated three or four times.

Claire says she smiled all the way back to England, even when she was asleep during the flight. When she returned to school, the kids greeted her with a huge banner: 'Welcome home Miss Pilling and Richard.'

It was light by the time I headed for bed. At the hotel I crossed paths with Steve Thompson. He was heading for the beach with his girlfriend, about to propose to her. Lawrence, Jason Leonard, Cozza and Paul Grayson partied well into the next day before being given a lift back in a police van.

Our sense of satisfaction was made complete by an apologetic editorial in the *Sydney Morning Herald* the next day: 'You were not too old (although we hoped you would be when the game went to extra time). You were not too slow. You scored as many tries as we did. You kicked no more penalty goals than we did. You ran the ball as much as we did. You entertained as much as we did. You did it with one of your own as coach. You are better singers than we are (and just quietly, "Swing Low, Sweet Chariot" is growing on us, as is Jonny without an "h".'

Later I got sent a few copies of English newspapers, their World Cup pull-outs packed full with pictures. Most of them used the same team picture as we celebrated after the final whistle. All you can see of me is my forehead and a tuft of my hair, sticking up from the back row.

It was only some time later that I learnt that Claire, having travelled 12,000 miles to watch the World Cup final, almost missed Jonny's match-winning score. She had been sitting alongside my sister for most of the game but suddenly, for the first time ever, I think, her nerves got the better of her. She went and hid in the ladies' toilet during extra time. There, amazingly, she met Ali Back – they've sat together for years at Twickenham, where wives and partners sit in the order of our shirt numbers. They chatted for a few minutes, and then persuaded each other to go out again. As Claire got to the top of the stairs at the back of the stand, Jonny dropped his goal. Two seconds later and she wouldn't have seen it.

16

A SAD WAY TO GO

24 April 2006. Today, this morning, I was advised to retire. The consultant just came out with it. It took him barely half an hour to come to his conclusion. He examined my knee, asked some questions and then said: 'I think you should think about your future from now on, not the past.'

It took me a few seconds to get over the shock, then, when he asked me what I thought, I said: 'You're the bluntest man I've met so far.'

'It's my job to be blunt,' he replied.

When I told Claire she burst into tears.

Fares had sent me to him for a second opinion following consultations with Saracens and England after my knee kept swelling up. April had begun well. I'd put in my best sessions to date but suddenly the fluid around my knee wouldn't disperse. You could poke a finger into the knee and see the fluid moving around, up and down and side to side. The joint had also become increasingly painful and kept me awake at nights.

So back I went to Fares yet again, only to discover that the fluid had been there for a while and was too thick to draw off with a syringe. There was no way round it – that meant more surgery. That's when it was suggested that a second opinion was required.

For a while, after the consultant's verdict, I thought that that was it. When an expert tells you something, you tend to listen. But it gradually dawned on me that there was absolutely no point in making a final decision before the surgery. We'd got this far against the odds, so why rush the final chapter? Fares agreed.

The best-case scenario would have been Fares discovering the cause of the aggravation inside the knee and dealing with it there and then. If, on the other hand, there was a serious infection in the knee which needed to be cut out, or if the bone surfaces had failed to recover, then that would definitely spell the end for me.

I went to a nearby pub with some friends and put away eight pints in two hours. I can't remember the last time I did something like that. Probably I'd have to go back to my student days. I don't train well after drinking, so I hardly do it nowadays. Mind you, I'm not going to be doing too much gym work for the next few weeks. It took me five minutes to walk to the pub and twenty minutes to get back.

I had to go back on crutches for a few days that week to help deal with the pain, which wasn't a great signal to give to Mark Sinderberry, the Sarries chief executive, who spotted me in the car park. I have no idea how all this will affect the offer of a new contract. Talk of a contract may be irrelevant anyway, if the surgery goes badly. All I want to know is where I stand. Until I know more, all my plans, like returning to the US for more rehab with Bill Knowles, aren't even worth thinking about. A happy ending looks further and further away.

At least Sarries look safe from relegation. Eddie Jones has helped Mike Ford produce a pretty amazing turnaround, with four wins in a row, including a 13–12 win over Wasps. Eddie will head back to Oz with some pretty good memories.

(* (* (*

I have to go right back to 2003 for my last good ones. There haven't been many since. For just a short while, we had everything – the World Cup, the Grand Slam and wins home and away against everybody. Our success even led to David Campese walking down Oxford Street in London, wearing a sandwich board painted with the words 'I admit the best team won the World Cup'. That was probably as big an achievement as winning the tournament itself.

But it was pretty obvious that we were coming to the end of a cycle. To be honest, our peak as a team probably came just a few months before the World Cup. It was character and grit which got us through during the tournament. Could we have won the Cup if it had been held a year later? Most people would say no and point to the team's rapid decline during 2003–04 as evidence of that. I'm not sure, though. I think the team began to fall apart because of people's mindsets, not because of age or their physical condition. A lot of the guys had set the 2003 World Cup as their ultimate goal and they'd never looked beyond that. For some, there didn't seem much point in carrying on after winning it. For others, it may have been tricky to readjust after fulfilling such a dream.

On the face of it, my life didn't take long to get back to normal, though. Seven days, to be exact. A week after the World Cup final I was lining up for Saracens against Rotherham. They were bottom of the league, we were one place above them, so it was a big game. It may sound odd, but I got very nervous beforehand, mainly because I thought people would be expecting so much from me, even though I could barely remember any of our calls.

To be honest, though, things didn't really get back to

normal for months. The World Cup celebrations carried on and on. First and foremost was the visit to Buckingham Palace and Downing Street after the victory parade through the centre of London on Monday 8 December.

I remember driving in with Kyran to meet up with the squad that morning and thinking: 'What are we letting ourselves in for? There's nobody there.' London was empty. We met up at the Intercontinental Hotel at the bottom of Park Lane and boarded two open-topped double-decker buses. Near Marble Arch we began to realise there were people up ahead, as the radio and TV had forecast, but none of us had any idea quite how big an event it would be. By the time we got to Regent Street on the way to Trafalgar Square, the crowds were huge, with people hanging off lamp posts and out of windows as the ticker-tape streamed down. I think 750,000 people turned up that day, which was mind-boggling. I sat at the back of the bus with Jonny, although he was forced to go to the front for a while to acknowledge the cheers (and the 'Jonny, I want to have your babies' placards), before sneaking back.

Meeting the Queen was fine, even if Claire forgot to call her 'Your Majesty'. Claire was kneeling down with Victoria Bracken (who gave birth to their son Charlie the next day), stroking one of the corgis – they were all over the place, in and out of your feet – when she suddenly noticed a pair of shiny black shoes in front of her and, looking up, saw the Queen smiling down at her. Mind you, it was such a relaxed atmosphere that lots of people completely forgot the etiquette we had been taught. Claire, who by then thought she had left it a bit late to curtsey, asked the Queen if she had watched the final. 'Oh yes!' she replied.

I was chatting with the head of the Palace's security beforehand and he said everything would be fine, so long as no one trod on one of the dogs (there was a yelp later, but I don't know who was responsible). We were organised in a horseshoe shape and introduced to the Queen, who spoke a few words to the lucky ones as she went down the line. She was never going to talk to me, though – I was standing next to Jonny.

Buckingham Palace was awesome, with huge staircases, massive paintings on the walls and gilt everywhere. The only bad bit of the day was that Clive had banned overcoats, so it was left to our grey suits, designed for the Australian summer, to protect us from a British winter's day. We almost froze to death on those buses.

Next up was a 'victory match' against the New Zealand Barbarians at Twickenham. Unfortunately, though, they didn't quite enter into the spirit of the occasion. In a way, they showed us what we were in for during the coming months. As world champions, everyone wanted a pop at us from that day on. By the end of the game, I had a badly fractured nose – it was spread halfway across my face and needed surgery – and a bunch of stitches around one of my eyes.

I have to say I wasn't too happy about my nose. Actually, let's be blunt, I was angry and fired off a few verbals at their lock, Troy Flavell, as I left the field. I haven't met him since and I'm not sure I would want to. Rugby's a hard game and that's fine. But there was absolutely no need for him to smack me in the face. Flavell, who ended up being banned for four weeks, had already had a go at a few other players. In my case, I saw his straight-arm coming but I couldn't protect myself. I had the ball in one hand and was handing off someone else with the other. It was a pretty cheap shot.

At the banquet afterwards, I had to shepherd Claire to the other side of the room from Flavell. She was seething. She kept trying to get hold of a programme to try and identify him. She wouldn't have made a scene – she knows that that would have been ridiculous – but she would have been quite happy to glare at him all evening.

That put me out of action for six weeks but the World Cup hangover continued. There seemed to be functions every week, as well as the *BBC Sports Personality of the Year* awards and the New Year's Honours List, where Clive became a Sir and most of us got MBEs. The Mayor of Salisbury put on a civic reception for me and the trophy was put on show in the Market Square. I even did an advert for Easyjet (my co-star, I think, was Windy the Snowman) and a few speaking engagements.

I remember breathing a huge sigh of relief when it all began to calm down. It wasn't as if Claire and my life had changed much really – I was back playing at Sarries and she was going blue, shouting from the stands every week – but there had been quite a bit more fuss to deal with off the pitch. Not that many of us had become household faces (except Johnno and Jonny, of course). When Kyran held one of his testimonial year events in Battersea to coincide with the first anniversary of our World Cup win, there were a few over-zealous security guards on duty and at one stage I was barred from going to have a chat to Jonny. So I ran around the other side of the table, shouting: 'Jonny, Jonny, do you remember me?' Jason Leonard was also stopped from sitting down at his table at one stage.

It was nice, though, that April, to get a bit of time off at last. I managed to get away for a couple of days, fly fishing with Don and Kev Sorrell. My mobile phone suddenly started ringing underneath my waders. I ignored it.

By then the break-up of the team had begun. Johnno had been the first to announce his retirement – I think he might have been happy to play in the Six Nations but he wouldn't commit himself to the summer tour, as Clive wanted – and a few others, like Kyran and Jason, soon followed.

The other thing that worked against us was injuries. We were cursed with them. There had been a bit of a mental come-down after the World Cup and it almost seemed as if there was a physical one as well. I don't know why there were so many injuries, it was a mystery. There wasn't any particular pattern. Look at Jonny, for instance. Over the next two years he had a nightmare run. First it would be one problem, beginning with his neck and shoulder, then another. It's strange to think that he and I haven't played in the same England side since the final.

Clive had talked about creating a dynasty rather than just one winning team, but it did not turn out that way. We had an aura at that stage – we'd won twenty-three of our last twenty-four games, after all – but that went up in a puff of smoke almost immediately. Things seemed to go wrong on all fronts all at once. For a start, we lost a captain in Johnno and a match-winner in Jonny. There was also the question of how quickly new faces should be brought in to regenerate the team. Clive later admitted he made mistakes in this area, like axing Backy too early. Looking back, we lost too many of our leaders in a short space of time.

The first challenge was to find a new captain. Quite a few names were thrown into the mix, including mine, which was a bit of a surprise. I hadn't led a side for any length of time since I was twelve. I had been given the role against the New Zealand Barbarians as a one-off, although that had gone all right. In the end, though, Clive went for Lawrence.

Secretly, I was relieved. By the time the decision was due I was still worrying over whether to accept the job if it came my way. I tried to sound disappointed when he told me that he had opted for Lawrence and I did the same with the press but, to be truthful, it took a weight off my shoulders. By nature I'm a foot soldier. You need foot soldiers, and that's what I do best.

For the first time in years, Lawrence and I went into the Six Nations without Backy after he was dropped. It was the end of an era, I suppose. I'm not quite sure how many times we had played together as a unit – it's more than forty, I've been told, but quite how many depends on whether you include the times when one of us came on as a replacement – but it never happened again after Sydney. I don't get too excited about world records and statistics but we certainly had had a good run together and it felt odd not having Backy around.

I returned to openside, Joe Worsley came in at blindside and we began well enough by winning 50–9 in Italy and 35–13 away to the Scots. The next game, though, was the start of the team's downfall. We hadn't lost at Twickenham for twenty-two matches, going back to 1999, but Ireland turned us over 19–13.

Our line-out went wrong that day and the Irish knocked us out of our rhythm early on. We missed certain players as calming influences and panicked a bit. Johnno, I think, was doing some TV commentary that day and must have found it hard to watch.

We beat Wales 31–21 next time out, without really convincing, then lost again, to France. On paper, the Paris scoreline of 24–21 didn't look too bad but we were always struggling. It was 21–3 at half time, with their scrum-half Dimitri Yachvili having an inspired game. We needed two late tries to avoid a major embarrassment. I remember thinking that it had taken only a couple of months and the teams' roles had been reversed. France had applauded us after we beat them in the Sydney semi-final, now we were clapping them as they went up to collect the Grand Slam.

I'm not one to discuss ad nauseam where or why it all went wrong. I think you can overdo it and I'd probably become a manic depressive if I thought about it too hard. Nor do I like looking for excuses. I suppose it is interesting, though, to see how little most of the World Cup-winning squad played for

England after Sydney. Johnno, Backy, Kyran and Jason Leonard never started an international again, while Jonny has yet to do so. Catty started two more matches – until, that is, he was picked again for the 2006 summer tour – while Will Greenwood managed five starts. Woodman started seven more matches before he retired, the same number as Iain Balshaw. I've played in eight. And as for Clive, well, he had resigned within nine months.

The press and the public may have found it hard to lower their expectations, but as a team I think we accepted what was happening – we tried as hard as ever and we kept on believing but we knew we weren't the same anymore.

That 2004 Six Nations was my worst ever, in terms of results. The tour to New Zealand and Australia which followed was even harder to bear. Probably for the first time, I wasn't sure about the wisdom of going. After what we had gone through, a long extended summer break wouldn't have done anybody any harm.

Things went wrong from the very start. We kicked off against the All Blacks in Dunedin, their giant winger Joe Rokocoko got hold of the ball and carved through six tackles as he ran the ball back 50 metres. That set the tone. We struggled in the line-outs as well, while they had beefed up their front five and produced some excellent counter-rucking when we failed to commit enough people at the breakdowns. They had some great runners as usual but they also did a lot of damage up front. Richie McCaw was at his best, stealing a lot of ball. Because of our line-out problems, I was used as a front-line jumper which did not help my play in the loose.

To make matters worse, we went into the game with a new defensive system, blitz rather than up-and-out. Blitz relies on everybody moving up absolutely together. If someone is out of line it becomes very obvious. We didn't get it quite right that day – at one stage New Zealand waltzed in for one of the easiest first-phase tries you will ever see. Basically, we got panned in the House of Pain. The only consolation – a pretty meagre one, admittedly – was that we limited the damage to 36–3 after being 30–3 down at the break.

The second Test in Auckland was all about self-respect as far as I was concerned, but things soon went badly wrong again and we lost 36–12. We were 6–0 up after about ten minutes when Simon Shaw got sent off for kneeing Keith Robinson in the back as he lay over the ball. Simon was later exonerated – Robinson said he hadn't felt a thing – but that red card made things doubly difficult for us.

If that felt bad, though, worse was to come. We began that game with five players who had started in the World Cup final against the Australians but I did not last the eighty minutes. I had twisted my ankle at Eden Park and it went again, completing a demoralising tour for me. The major difference between the sides was the way the Aussies took their chances. Things did not look too bad just after half time – we were 24–15 down after Lawrence and I had scored tries – but then the wheels fell off in a big way. The stats for that game, indeed, were incredible. Australia had about 45 per cent of the possession but by the final whistle they had buried us 51–15. It was their first win over us for five years.

I was pretty depressed that evening and just wanted to get home and fix my ankle. We had lost our last four games on the trot, and five matches out of six. We hadn't lost that many matches over the past three years put together. My team-mates obviously thought I needed cheering up. There I was in the bar, chatting to Mark Bartholomeusz, who had just joined Saracens, when the first of my crutches mysteriously disappeared. When it reappeared by my side, it was bent in the middle at a 45 degree angle. It snapped as I tried to straighten it out. Soon after, the second one went walkabout and came back in two pieces.

Still, I would have been even more depressed if I had known then what I know now – that, barring a miraculous change of luck over the coming months, that was probably the last game I will ever play for England. Considering everything, it will be a sad way to go.

We had barely got back home and started preparing for the new season when the next shock hit us.

First Lawrence called time on his England career then, in the same week, Clive called it a day. Lawrence complained about the structure of the game in England and the number of games we were playing, while Clive argued that he was not being allowed enough time with the players. Both those arguments have raged on for years without being solved.

About a month later my knee went for the first time.

There had never been even the merest hint of trouble before that day, 3 October 2004, as Saracens travelled to London Irish. The way it happened was rather embarrassing. It wasn't even in contact. I was chasing the ball down in their 22 when Catty gathered it, looked to go to my left, then side-stepped to the right. I changed direction but my knee didn't come with me. There was a pop, I hopped a couple of strides and then collapsed in a heap. By then Catty had disappeared, zipping up field to set up a score for Irish at the other end, while I was left lying there. There had been a sudden sharp pain and I went off immediately but the knee felt much better after I'd iced it. Andy Robinson, the new England coach, came into the changing room to check up on me. 'I'm fine, nothing to worry about, see you later tonight,' I said. I was put on crutches that day but was soon walking again. I thought it was just a twinge.

A scan, though, revealed the extent of the damage – a tear

to the anterior cruciate ligament. I still thought it would be a matter of weeks rather than months. It was only when I started getting phone calls from the England medics, reassuring me that they would be there to back me up after the surgery, that it dawned on me that it was perhaps more serious.

As I've said, that recovery was pretty straightforward. As with my second injury, the thing that held me back was not so much the ligament itself but the damage to the bone surfaces. There was a second visit to the operating table just before Christmas, to remove a bit of cartilage which had broken away, but that was a pretty routine affair. With complications, it might have taken nine months to recover but the target was always six – just in time for the end of the Saracens season and possibly the 2005 Lions tour to New Zealand.

The most enjoyable part of my first rehabilitation came during my visit to Bill in Vermont. I wasn't the first England player to go there. Charlie Hodgson and Austin had paved the way, after wrecking their knees just before the World Cup.

We went in February 2005. I say we because Barney Kenny, who was in charge of my rehab, came along with me for the first few days of my three-week stay. I was really pleased he was with me. Strange as it may seem, I was thirty-one years old and had never been away on my own. As a young guy, I would always have travelled as part of a rugby squad. Claire says I'm a nightmare on my own, without my team-mates around me. I'm not the only one like that, apparently. Most of the partners and wives of the players at Sarries joke that we're all hopeless outside the group.

On the day Barney left I had an empty feeling in my stomach. I put the TV on for company. The film *Home Alone 2* was on. 'If Macaulay Culkin can do it, so can I,' I told myself.

By the end of my stay there, though, I had really enjoyed it. I was in a pretty spectacular environment, in an apartment at the foot of a snow-covered mountain with a ski lift nearby (sadly, I had never skied before and I don't suppose I ever will now). I had to wait for a snow plough to clear the road before I attended my first session.

Bill was fantastic to work with as we strengthened and balanced my leg with gym and pool work. He had a good manner, on the one hand taking the mick – when you lost your balance in an exercise, he would say things like: 'Sorry, I must have left the window open' – and on the other he was inspirational. He'd talk about unleashing the athlete from within. He has many patients who are world class skiers and snowboarders, and the walls were covered with mementoes and letters of thanks. When I left, I gave him one of my England shirts. I wouldn't have made the 2005 Lions tour without him.

I did a fair amount of my rehab at the Killington Medical Centre alongside an injured American Football player, Dave Boston. He was a nice bloke and it was interesting to compare notes.

We came from different worlds. For a start, guys like him earn several million dollars a year. As a Miami Dolphins wide receiver, he was very quick and his fitness was based around short bursts of explosive acceleration. He had a massive upper body and a small set of pins. I've seen him on TV since. I think he got thrown the ball twice in a game; once he dropped it, once he made a couple of yards. He would do a sprint and then everything would stop for a commercial break. So Dave wasn't interested in doing the same workouts as me, which were based more on developing stamina and power. He needed much longer recovery times in between exercises. Whenever Bill tried to get him to do a couple of extra sets with me, Dave would say: 'Jet Blue, baby, Jet Blue.' Which was the name of a domestic US airline and meant that Dave would be on the next plane out of Vermont if he was forced to join in with one of my sessions.

At one stage, Dave watched a DVD of our World Cup semi-final against France. He made some standard comments about the lack of padding and helmets, then asked to see one particular passage of play again. He'd seen a perfect tackle, he said. 'That is exactly the same technique we are taught,' he said, pointing at the screen. No prizes for guessing who made the tackle – Jonny Wilkinson esquire.

When I went out to the States, Fares had told me that a six-month return was beginning to look unlikely. Bill did not tell me at the time, but he had decided I had no chance at all after making his initial assessment. When I got back at the start of March, though, I was running again and it was more a matter of holding me back so that I didn't rush the final stages of my recovery.

I returned in time to see Wales wrap up the Grand Slam. They were playing some pretty stylish stuff, with Tom Shanklin going particularly well and making Gavin Henson look very good beside him in the centre. For England, though, things were looking less rosy. We had lost three of our Six Nations games for our worst finish in years. There was quite a lot of talk at the time about England recruiting Andy Farrell from league to try to lead a revival. (Poor old Andy, after his toe and back problems, didn't get on the pitch until September 2006.)

My immediate goal, in March 2005, was to get back on the pitch myself. Saracens were battling for a place in Europe, while trying to convince Clive that I would be worth taking on the Lions tour, was another motivation. I never admitted it in public – apart from to Fares, that is – but being selected for the Lions had always been a big motivation.

It was pretty tight in the end but I made it.

At first, I was put in a group of players working their way back from various injuries. 'The Dead Man Walking Group', Kyran called us. On 4 April, about a month before the end of the season and just a week before Clive announced his Lions squad, I was declared fit to return. It wasn't exactly the big time – a second XV game down in Gloucester on a Monday evening – but it felt pretty big to me.

The initial idea had been to play for ten minutes, but that gradually got extended to twenty, then thirty, then the whole first half. I felt fine and could probably have gone on but I decided not to push my luck.

I didn't realise it, but I had quite a gallery watching my every move. Barney, the England physio, was there with a video camera while Claire was in the crowd, alongside my dad, Don Parsons and my team-mates Kev Sorrell and Glen Jackson. Claire was not meant to be coming, but at the last moment Kevin rang her up at her school and said he would be driving down to the West Country with Glenn in about forty-five minutes. Claire bombed home and got a lift with them. There they were, all sitting in a row, giving each other nervous little smiles before kick-off. Claire said she felt physically sick watching the game, although she cheered up a bit when I got up after making my first tackle. When I came off, Barney turned round and gave Claire a little thumbs-up and a nod of the head. She told me she would have killed me if I had gone out again for the second half.

On the Sunday of that same week, on the eve of the Lions announcement, I was picked as a replacement for a first team game against Wasps at Wycombe. What followed was bizarre. We were playing away but that was probably the best reception I ever got from a crowd. Every time I went to warm up they started to cheer. I didn't really know how to respond. I felt elated. I probably just smiled.

I was sitting on the bench next to Kev, who kept winding me up and trying to get me to smile. I was so nervous though – it was like making my Saracens debut all over again. Kevin and I both got the nod after half time. 'Oh my God,' I thought, as I stripped off my tracksuit. In the end, though, everything went fine. I took a few good hard knocks without any problem, forced a couple of turnovers and, to cap it all, Kevin and I both scored a try. We lost the game but won the second half. The best bit about it was that I felt justified being on the pitch.

The next day, rather than sit around and fret about the Lions announcement, I joined some of the Sarries lads on the golf course at Trent Park. I had been told to expect a text around midday, if I had been selected. The text did not come – oh well, no joy – so we teed off. I sprayed my drive way right and out of bounds. As I was searching for the ball, one of the guys phoned up a mate who read out the list of names from Teletext. He then caught me up in his buggy. 'You're going, Hilda. You're in the squad,' he said. I wasn't convinced until I saw it myself. My text message, for some reason, arrived at around six o'clock that evening. I would have been disappointed, having got that far, not to go, but I wouldn't have had a leg to stand on, so to speak. I had only played two halves of rugby in six months.

To be honest, Clive did have a little more to go on than that. I certainly wasn't ringing him up with the latest news but I did receive a call from him at one point, to ask how it was going. Throughout that period, I was working with Dave Reddin, the England and Lions fitness adviser, and with Barney, who passed on any developments to Phil Pask, who was also accompanying the Lions squad.

Perhaps the most amazing thing was that, having had that long a break, I was actually producing better fitness scores than I ever had before with England. It still seems unbelievable but it goes to show how valuable a break can be, rather than being knocked about on a rugby pitch every other day.

There were a few more scares before I finally got on that plane to New Zealand.

Making my first league start since the previous October, for instance, I got elbowed in the eye by Cozza as we beat league leaders Leicester 19–17 in front of almost 18,000 people. He got sent off, while I breathed a sigh of relief – I had collected another six stitches but no broken bones. There were no hard feelings, though. Martin and I met up in the corridor afterwards and he apologised. I later made a statement for his disciplinary hearing, saying something along the lines of I didn't feel it had been malicious.

Then, on the way to a Lions meeting in Cardiff, I got clipped by a car behind me on the motorway and ended up in a four-vehicle accident. Again, though, no harm done.

The season at Saracens ended on a high, as we won for the first time at Kingsholm, and then reached the Zurich Wildcard final, with a place in the Heineken Cup up for grabs. We beat Gloucester again that day, this time at Twickenham, to end the season in perfect style. Towards the end of the first half, though, I landed heavily on my knee and it quickly stiffened up. Kevin tried to persuade me to go off – 'Don't ruin it all now,' he kept saying – but I carried on. Afterwards I got a bit worried, jumped in a taxi and rushed up to see Fares at the Princess Grace. Fortunately, it was only bone bruising and I was passed fit by the insurers for the Lions tour.

Which, in effect, brings my story full circle.

That tour is one I would rather not dwell on too much. There was some criticism after the Lions about Clive relying too heavily on the England guys who had won the World Cup for him. One thing everyone would agree on was that luck didn't exactly go our way. There might have been a chance of Lawrence, Backy and me teaming up again after we were all selected for the tour. But Lawrence dislocated and broke his ankle in the twenty-first minute of the first game against Bay of Plenty and I managed two matches before making my exit. Until then, I felt I was going pretty well. Ironically, on the eve of the first Test I got hold of a video which showed me doing my first rehab with Bill Knowles. I remember sitting there, feeling good about how far I had come. Little did I realise what would happen next. But that's all history now. I watched the second Test – the All Blacks were awesome that day – and then headed home and towards hospital.

(★ (★ (★

Which is where I am today, waiting for a date for my latest knee arthroscopy. The outcome of that surgery could mean that I will have retired before the final event in my benefit year, the match between a Saracens XV and a Rest of the World XV at Vicarage Road on 21 May.

Daws, incidentally, announced this month that he will be retiring at the end of the season. Better news for Jonny, though – he's just got back on the pitch for Newcastle, for his sixth or seventh comeback since the World Cup. Hopefully he'll get an extended run at last and get his career back on track. Phil Vickery, meanwhile, has been signed up by Wasps after leaving his long-time club Gloucester. He's recovering from a third back operation. Gloucester weren't keen to gamble on his fitness but Wasps have offered him a contract. It would be nice to think that I could be in the same situation – without having to change clubs, of course – in a few weeks.

In the meantime, I'll look forward to that final benefit do of mine. We've got some pretty good names playing, like Lawrence and Carlos Spencer and Raphael Ibanez...and my old mate Don Parsons of Salisbury, of course.

EPILOGUE

19 August 2006. By my calculations, I've been injured for almost fourteen months, as well as for one and a half out of the last two years. That period has encompassed some of the worst times in my life. You hear talk of emotional roller-coasters, but my life seemed to have been careering in just one direction – downhill. People close to me say that I came close to losing the plot on occasions, and I suppose they're right. I've certainly had bouts of depression – not that I was always conscious of it at the time – and there have been periods when I have felt very isolated.

The important thing, though, is that I've got through it. The last few weeks have brought nothing but good news.

The Saracens physios probably had a vague timetable in mind for my comeback from the very start. I was never told, but I've got a rough idea of what they're aiming for now. Just under four months ago I was told to retire and here I am, six weeks away from a possible return in October.

In a way, it's a nerve-wracking time. I've been here before, after all, only for things to go wrong. This time there's a big difference. The knee feels better, the swelling's right down and there's no pain. I've yet to give up the antibiotics, but my latest blood test and white cell count couldn't have been much better. Best of all, I've put in three jogging and running sessions over the past week. I've got to put some muscle bulk back on my leg but that will come with hard work.

Things, indeed, have been so positive that I've allowed myself a look at this season's fixtures. I'm not aiming at a particular date but I just wanted to know what was around. Our A team games, on Monday nights, are beginning to go up on the clubhouse board as well. I'm trying not to get ahead of myself. I've got to continue concentrating on the process of getting fit again, rather than worrying about playing. Those sorts of thoughts are best kept in my head. But it's still great to feel upbeat at last. I've even got a player's diary for the upcoming season and it's gradually filling up with stuff: Saracens moves, calls, my thoughts on this and that. I didn't bother with one last season.

I was a lot less happy with life in the run-up to my operation on 1 May. That was one of the really bad times. I knew Bill had not been 100 per cent confident about things when he had come over from America to work with me, while my conversations with Fares weren't as positive as they had been either. Sending me to the consultant who advised me to retire may have been his way of giving me a shock or preparing me for the worst.

I certainly knew that it was a critical operation. Potentially, it was make or break. There was still something wrong in the knee and nobody knew what it was. There was a chance that I'd come out of the anaesthetic to be told it was time to call it a day. There was also the possibility that I might find that the ligament had been removed altogether because of some sort of damage or infection. I told myself that I was ready for that. People have played on without knee ligaments in the past and I was ready to follow suit if that was the only way forward. The full implications really hit home on the Saturday morning before the surgery and I woke up in tears. .

Beforehand, an issue had arisen over which of my insurance policies would pay out for my continuing treatment. That caused delays and got me fretting, but Fares and his medical team helped sort things out by giving up their Bank Holiday Monday especially for me to carry out the surgery.

By now, of course, I was a hospital veteran: another day, another operation, same old routine. I still know the route to the operating theatre off by heart (left out of my room, turn right, up to the nurses' station, right into the lifts, down to the basement, right, first left, anaesthetists' room at the end of the corridor).

Some people may have thought that I was mad, going under the knife yet again, but I'd talked it through with Fares. I've always listened to him. Anyway, the long-term effects of injuries to professional rugby players, when they've got to forty or fifty years of age, aren't really known. It's more obvious with retired footballers, but professional rugby's still in its infancy so we haven't got a clue. Without that information, you've just got to follow your instincts. And I wanted to give my comeback my best shot. Looking back, I don't know how much more bad news I could have taken at that stage, to be honest, but fortunately I haven't had to find out. When I came round after the operation, there was a simple message from Fares waiting for me.

'That is not a knee which needs to retire,' he said.

Not that I got carried away. He'd taken out some stitches, screws and bits of frayed or dead ligament but it was still not obvious what had caused the pain or swelling. There was no guarantee that it might not happen again. With that in mind, the decision was taken to forget all about comeback deadlines this time. Until my knee was 'dry' and clear of fluid build-up, we wouldn't push things. It gradually dawned on me that I wouldn't be ready for the new season after all.

At least I had my benefit match between a Saracens XV and a World XV to look forward to. I'd hoped at one stage to take part. However, Don, my old Salisbury team-mate and minder, made sure I'll never forget the game. We had some pretty big international names playing and drew 9,000 people to Vicarage Road. It might have been even more but the day clashed with Watford's Championship play-off final against Leeds at the Millennium Stadium. It also poured with rain. But it was still about 8,500 more people than Don had ever played in front of before.

He spent most of the game on the subs' bench but I was determined to get him on. The game wasn't exactly full-on smashing, but it was fairly serious and both sides made a good fist of it. With ten minutes to go I turned to Don but he was nowhere to be seen. He was on the toilet. Again. He'd been so wound up that day that he'd had to stop four times for breaks just while driving up from Salisbury. I think he went seven times in all, that day.

When he did finally make his entrance, he absolutely loved it. Playing blindside, he went down for his first scrum and immediately tackled Lawrence Dallaglio – admittedly without the ball, but you can't have everything – then brought down Rafael Ibanez, won a turnover and hauled down Justin Marshall. He'd barely been on the pitch for a couple of minutes and he'd already tackled three former Test captains from England, France and New Zealand. Don hasn't stopped smiling since. The only thing that seems to puzzle him is that no clubs or agents have got in touch.

It was a great day and since then things have just got better and better. It's been the longest run of consistent improvement I've had during my second rehabilitation. Before, there seemed to be weekly setbacks – my knee would lock, get sore on the medial side or suddenly get stiff. This time the recovery has been so much smoother that I've barely noticed the time go by.

There hasn't been any real defining moment. First the swelling had to come down, which took a while, but things just progressed from there.

It was a fairly quiet time at the club after the op. The 2005–06 season ended a week later. The only guys still left hanging around were either heading off on tours or were injured. Andy Farrell, after a bit of a relapse with his back, and I worked together, overseen by our new physio Andy Walker, who'd had previous experience bringing footballers back from anterior cruciate ligament injuries when he was with West Ham.

Not long afterwards I went on holiday with Claire to the Maldives, which also helped. Perhaps it was the change of environment, or just the break. I was set a light programme to follow which included a couple of swimming sessions. I'd sit by the pool in the early evening, hoping it would empty. I didn't want to frighten – or drown – any of the kids. My technique is not too shabby, but it's not the best and I can get a bit noisy when my heart rate gets up as I plough up and down.

By the middle of June Saracens had come back to life and I got another boost as the social side revived. It felt like I was really part of the club again. Perhaps some of the guys were secretly surprised that I had made it that far, still plodding along in the gym and around the pitch. The best part of it was that the conditioners and physios made a real effort to involve the injured players in training sessions whenever they could. I even found myself enjoying squad meetings for the first time in ages. The previous season, they'd seemed irrelevant. It wasn't that I wasn't interested, but I thought I could use my time better working on my knee, rather than listening to new moves or that I was never going to play out.

The walking wounded were also taken along this time when the squad headed back to Portugal for a week's training. On the final day they staged a mini triathlon. I wasn't back running then, but I took part in the cycling and swimming. I'd gone out on my own push bike at home just before the trip, to prepare myself psychologically – the only bike I'd been on recently was a stationary one, bolted to the gym floor. Anyway, it went fine. I'm not saying it proved anything, but I finished the ride in about sixth place out of thirty-odd, which was pretty pleasing. In fact, it must have got my competitive juices going. I was changing in and out of my shoes at the changeovers as fast as I could. While the others went off running along the beach, I was given a walk to do. I wanted to try and keep up with the rest of the guys for the final bike leg and apparently I got faster and faster, until I looked like one of those Olympic speed walkers.

As I said, there was no one single breakthrough in the rehab. The emotion of running for the first time after my first knee reconstruction was probably one of the highlights of my career but it wasn't like that, second time around. In fact, it ended up in a comical argument with the physios. I was doing an SAQ drill – speed, agility, quickness – stepping up and down ladders, with a rubber strap attached to my legs to stop me from stretching out too far, and I suddenly piped up: 'Hang on, let's be honest here…this is running!'

'No it isn't, it's not even jogging,' they said.

'Yes it is.'

'No it isn't.'

'Yes it…'

It sounded like a Monty Python sketch.

More than any one incident, though, I remember a change in attitudes. I suppose you realise you're really beginning to recover when you start seeing less of your surgeon – I haven't seen Fares for weeks at a time recently – but you also know you're on the mend when your team-mates stop looking concerned and start winding you up again. One pre-season session, for instance, involved us walking through moves between breakdowns on either side of the pitch. They slotted me in at scrum-half. First the guys took the mick out of my passing, then they let me struggle across the pitch to within a few metres of the new breakdown before pretending to lose patience, stepping into my position and whipping the ball away, leaving me to turn around and head straight back in the opposite direction. I tried to sneak into a jog to keep up but Andy Walker soon ran over.

'Don't run any faster!' he growled.

'I'm not,' I said. 'It's not even jogging.'

I went through a similar thing with Claire the other day, while we were playing a game of beach cricket with her nephews down in Devon. Every time I trotted after the ball I could feel the burn in the back of my neck before the inevitable: 'Should you be doing that?'

In a funny sort of way, my injuries have been just as tough on her. She's had to share my agony and all my lows but misses out on the highs. While I've enjoyed the recent improvements, she's just carried on worrying. Just like Fares, though, she's never given up on me. I can't describe how important that's been. They've never talked about me giving up or questioned what I was trying to do. They know I can't just switch off from rugby. I enjoy it. It's what I want to do.

At times I think some people out there have a romanticised view of things when it comes to retirement. They think players should go out at the top, retire after winning things like World Cups. That's not how I see it. Few people manage to write their own history. I was nowhere near retiring in 2003, it wasn't even a consideration, and I don't regret that despite what has happened since. Why would you want to cut short doing what you love by a year or two, just because it looks good on your CV? Ask most guys who have hung up their boots and they'll tell you there's no good time to go. When I started playing rugby, I turned out for Salisbury because I wanted to, not because I had any desire or inkling that I would make a living out of it. It was fun. That's still there.

So what of the future?

Well, I'm thirty-three now. No one has been at Saracens as long as me. Kevin Sorrell and Kris Chesney joined a couple of years after me, followed by Kyran. I may be one of the old-timers but I'd like to play on for a couple of years if I can. I don't have any particular age as a cut-off in my mind. I'll just see. Sarries have been really supportive, considering what I've gone through, and kept me on the pay roll. Most of my contract will be pay-and-play from now on and I'm happy with that. I need to prove myself again.

In my heart I feel sure I'll play again. Yes, I'm going to have to live with some pain and discomfort and, yes, I'll have to modify my training to suit what my knee can cope with. I don't think I'll be able to run every day, for instance. There's no fear, though, that's not a factor. My confidence in my knee is building up with the increase in training. You can't worry about past injuries, you just have to leave them behind.

It's difficult to say how good I'll be, compared to the player I was. I just don't know and there's no point in speculating. But one thing is for sure, I have no intention of embarrassing myself on a rugby pitch. That's not what I'm about.

Since starting to write this final chapter, I've just taken part in a series of four-minute runs at Saracens. You run as far as you can in the time available. I was way off the best distances, of course, but I managed and came tenth overall in the squad. It's another big step-up.

People probably think I'm not being completely honest when I talk about my ambitions. They may feel I'm trying to hide the fact that I'm desperate to get back into the white of England. That would be great to achieve, of course, and yes, every time a tour squad gets announced you can't help thinking: 'Could I be back there? Could I be ahead of those guys? Should I be included?'

The answer, though, is no, I shouldn't be included. There is no way Richard Hill should be anywhere near the England squad. I haven't played for the team for two years. I'm not even ready mentally to be back there, let alone physically. It's like talking about getting capped before your debut. Actually, it's worse than that, because I'm not even back on the pitch yet, so there's no form to draw on. Sure, I've had occasional chats with Andy Robinson now and then, but everything depends on how my knee stands up to the battering to come. England simply aren't on my agenda right now.

My immediate aim is the Saracens first XV and it's not going to be easy. We got some good back-rowers around. Taine Randell has left to work in the City but there's Paul Gustard, who's played England A, as has Ben Skirving. Dave Seymour went on the England Churchill Cup trip this year and Ben Russell is England Sevens. There's Kris, and Hugh Vyvyan, another England international and the club captain. And there's Andy Farrell, of course, as well as the young guys breaking through.

If someone offered me two good years with Saracens or a shorter, less successful stint with England, I'd choose Sarries. I'd be content with the fact that I got the chance to play rugby again.

Today, my head is high. If I can achieve what I want to on the pitch, and not be carried, then I'll be a happy man. There will be a huge pleasure in getting back and I'd like to think the guys at the club will be glad to see me back too.

If I had to give up tomorrow, well, I'd be disappointed but there would be no major regrets. I've had a great career and achieved far more than I ever imagined I could.

But I've no intention of quitting.

Not for a good while yet.

INDEX